AMERICANS'
SURVIVAL GUIDE
to
AUSTRALIA
and
AUSTRALIAN-AMERICAN
DICTIONARY
by
Rusty Geller

"Americans' Survival Guide to Australia and Australian-American Dictionary," by Rusty Geller ISBN 978-1-60264-074-0.

Library of Congress Control Number: 2007935500

Manufactured in the United States of America.

Dedication

To Sundance: one hell of a budgie.
She left us for the great billabong in the sky
just as I was finishing this book.
We'll miss her.

Acknowledgements

I moved to Australia from the U.S. when I was fifty. The transition looked deceptively simple. After all, I'd visited there a half-dozen times, I knew my way around, and the Aussies speak English—how hard could it be? I quickly found there's a big difference between being a tourist in a country and having to make a serious go of it. This book covers what I had to learn the first few years in order to survive.

Originally this was going to be a simple 500-word Australian-American dictionary. As things have a way of doing, it grew.

First I must apologize to my family and friends. In the name of research, I subverted many a social gathering into a cultural-linguistics lesson—with me as the pupil. I'd arrive with a list of a dozen Australianisms and emerge a few hours later with five times that many—the quantity seemed to increase in direct proportion to the amount of beer and wine consumed. I ended up with reams of information about Australian subjects I hadn't known existed. I soon realized that a mere list of Australianisms and their definitions wasn't going to be enough. I needed to write an introduction, which took a year and grew to almost 100,000 words. The dictionary alone would eventually top 1,500 entries.

I'd like to thank my Australian Brain Trust: John and Susie Wood; Chauncey, Fiona, Bruce, and Amanda Johnson; Adolpho and Claudia Zepeda; Gary and Trang Floyd; Mike, Marilyn, and Sian Davies; Jeremy and Jules Hurst. Also Peter Falk, Ian Sergeant, Spiro Mallis, Birgit Clark, Sue Ludemann Kristi Turner, Jack Seddon, Dr. Graham Thom, Ron Louis, Sandra Thornton, and Billy Hobbs. Thanks for putting up with the constant questions about things that must have seemed perfectly obvious to you.

A special thanks to my beleaguered family—Nanette, Emily, and Molly. They had to endure my constant questioning, not only of them, but of friends, acquaintances, and total strangers.

And then there are the people who read early versions of the manuscript, critiquing the grammar, spelling, punctuation, and content, but best of all, offering encouragement. Thank you, Bob and Margie Nock, Karen Treanor, Duke and Derek Rohlffs, Andy Scheer, Peter Anderson, and Woodsie.

Thanks to Mervyn Rothstein, our migration agent, and Steve Young, my LA mouthpiece. Thanks to Gary Anderson, who did the final edit. Thanks to my publisher, Bobby Bernshausen. Thank you Google and Yahoo, and you, too, Wikipedia.

And a very special thanks to the people of Australia for giving me such a ripe subject to write about and for allowing me to become a citizen of your country.

And finally, thanks to my dog, Lucky, who sat patiently at my feet every day waiting for me to finish writing. Now we can play…

Author's Note: In the text, Aussie words and terms are printed in *italics*. The Australian/American dictionary is in the back. If you're looking up a specific word or term, you might want to start with the dictionary. If you need more depth, check the Index or the Table of Contents to see if it's covered in the text section—or you can read the whole darn thing.

Table of Contents

AMERICANS' SURVIVAL GUIDE to AUSTRALIA
and
AUSTRALIAN-AMERICAN DICTIONARY

"Welcome to Australia. Everything you know is irrelevant."

Introduction

This book is intended as a reference guide for tourists, migrants, and business travellers to Australia. It covers the differences between American and Australian customs, culture, and language. When I refer to America, I mean the U.S. and Canada. Since North American culture and language is well known internationally, this book may also be helpful to visitors from other countries—and Aussies might even learn a thing or two.

It's a manual, a reference book, covering the basic and essential information this American author and his family had to learn during their first three years living in Australia. It will help you—for whatever the length of your stay—to avoid making the same embarrassing mistakes and asking the same dumb questions we did. Think of it as your cheat sheet.

I'd visited Australia a half dozen times before moving there, and I thought I knew the place. I soon discovered that being a tourist in a country, as opposed to actually having to make a life for yourself there, are two very different situations.

A tourist can enjoy things they like about a country and ignore the rest because they know they'll soon go home and leave it all behind. For these folks, this book should provide some background and help satisfy their curiosities.

For the business traveller, the information contained here will allow you to understand the people, culture, and customs, and help make your trip more successful. You can look like an old hand, even though it's your first time in the country.

For migrants or people on work contracts, this book should take the edge off your culture shock and make your transition easier and more graceful.

The first section contains information on the day-to-day things that you will encounter: driving, banking, eating out, shopping, and using a telephone. It will help you figure out what time it is in the next state, take measurements using the metric system, understand a bit about Australian sports, and get a feel for how the government and legal system works. It even takes a stab at explaining *Strine* (Australian English) and the Aussie mind-set.

The second section of this book is a dictionary of more than 1,500 Australian words, terms, and phrases, translated into North American English. It's probably the most complete list of Australianisms ever assembled.

Just because Americans and Australians speak a language based on English doesn't mean they use the same language. The big differences are obvious; it's the subtle differences that get you. To paraphrase Winston Churchill, we are "two peoples separated by a common language."

This book will help you navigate your way through Australian society. It will help you understand what's going on around you; things that might otherwise confuse you or would simply pass you by. It takes a critical look at Australia and does contain some opinion. All the facts as accurate as can be ascertained as of publication. Language and customs are constantly evolving. Meanings of words and phrases can vary by location and change with time.

Welcome to Australia. Keep your mind open as—like Alice—you step through the looking glass. Things are not as they seem...

"You're on your own, mate."

Australians are very independent people. They don't like to meddle in other people's business and they expect no one to meddle in theirs. This is part of the *Fair Go* attitude that is deeply ingrained in the Australian psyche: everyone deserves a chance, a "fair go". A fair go is an opportunity to succeed or fail on your own. It's yours; a gift from the Australian people. Good luck with it.

The down-side of this is, don't expect people to offer you help or advice—*you're on your own, mate*. If you do ask for help, people will generally be glad to assist—in a reserved way—but part of your problem as a new arrival is that you won't know which questions to ask, or even that there is a question. Keep this book handy. It's the Operator's Manual for Australia.

"Are you from Canada?"

When Aussies pick up on your "North American" accent, they will likely ask if you're from Canada, not if you're from the U.S. This is partly because they run into more Canadians than Americans, but mostly it's because they know Canadians are sensitive to being mistaken for Americans, while Americans don't care.

As for Americans: when asked that question, don't be offended, it's a great opportunity to strike up a conversation. Outside of tourist areas, Americans are a novelty.

Australian overview

The name *Australia* comes from the Latin term "Terra Australis" or "Southern Land". It's a continent surrounded by water, a giant island situated between Southeast Asia and Antarctica. The Pacific Ocean is on its east, the Southern Ocean is on its south, the Indian Ocean is on its west, the Timor Sea, the Arafura Sea, and the Torres Strait are on its north.

It's south of the equator, so all the seasons are reversed: winter is June, July, and August; summer is December, January, and February.

The country is almost the size of the continental United States, with the population of Southern California (as of 2007, Australia had 21 million people, while the U.S. had about 300 million). Population centers are along the east and west coasts, with three-quarters of the people living in the southeast corner. Forty percent of the population lives in Sydney and Melbourne, another twenty percent live in Brisbane, Adelaide, and Perth.

Being a large land mass the size of the U.S., the climate varies. The northern regions of Australia share the same relative latitude (same distance from the equator) as the southern Caribbean. The southern coast of Australia shares the same relative latitude as central California, while Tasmania (the island state off the southeast corner) is at the same relative latitude as Oregon or Massachusetts. Climates vary: the tropics are very humid and wet, with rain forests and mangrove swamps, the center of the continent is a dry desert, like Nevada on a bad day, the Australian "alps" (between Canberra and Melbourne), have 7,000-foot mountains that are snowed-in every winter. The central east coast, the southeast, and southwest corners are temperate, and that's where most of the people live.

The Australian continent is surrounded by water, which buffers and moderates the coastal climate. The exception is the northern coast, where tropical cyclones or *typhoons* (Australian hurricanes) periodically strike during the summer months of December through March. This is euphemistically called *The Wet*.

Australia consists of six states and one territory. They are, in clockwise order: Queensland (capital, Brisbane), New South Wales (capital, Sydney), Victoria (capital, Melbourne, [pronounced *Mel-bun*]), Tasmania (capital, Hobart), South Australia (capital, Adelaide), Western Australia (capital, Perth), and the Northern Territory (capital, Darwin). There's also the national capital, Canberra, located in the *ACT* (*Australian Capital Territory*), between Sydney and Melbourne.

Those are the facts. Here are the feelings: it's a small country in a big land. With scarcely the population of Southern California, Australia is really one community, spread out over a continent. If a murder occurs in Brisbane, you hear about it 3,000 miles away in Perth. A bad bus crash in Tasmania is common knowledge in Darwin, an election in New South Wales is covered in Western Australia. It's quaint yet modern, provincial and cosmopolitan, inbred and worldly: a microcosm of western life on a manageable level.

History

Australia is the oldest continent. I can walk out my back door and stand on rocks that were formed over 3 billion years ago. Australia separated from the other continents about 100 million years ago. Animals and plants evolved in isolation, which explains why they're so unique. Most of the land mammals are marsupials, most of the trees are eucalypts. Humans arrived about 40,000–60,000 years ago.

Australia was originally settled by nomadic people migrating from Southeast Asia over a land bridge created during the last major ice age. They came in several waves over tens of thousands of years and spread out over the land. The Australian continent was a wetter, greener place at that time. Besides the present day mix of marsupials, reptiles, and birds, there were *mega-fauna*: huge wombats the size of a hippopotamus, kangaroos ten feet tall and weighing 500 pounds, koalas the size of small bears; all of which were killed off by the early human settlers.

Europeans began exploring the region in the early 1600s; first the Dutch (Australia was originally called *New Holland*), then the French, and finally the British, most notably the great navigator, Captain James Cook. The English eventually claimed and settled the land at about the time of the American Revolution. This wasn't by coincidence, for when the British Empire lost most of its North American colonies (where they'd been exporting their outcasts for two centuries), they needed a new place of exile. Enter Australia: the English version of Devil's Island.

Why did England have such a substantial criminal problem? By the late eighteenth century, the Industrial Revolution was transforming British society from rural agrarian to urban. It brought prosperity, productivity, and employment for skilled laborers, but with it came poverty, unemployment, and crime. Britain had a surplus of criminals, many charged with petty crimes such as stealing food to feed their families. With jails overflowing, the Brits decided to ship these convicts off to a land so far away that most would never return. The system was antiseptically called *Transportation*. In reality, it was a convenient source of free labor to develop a tough, dangerous land on the far side of the Earth. This began an odd love-hate relationship between the Australian colony and the mother country. This relationship continues to this day.

The First Fleet, consisting of eleven ships and more than

750 convicts, landed in New South Wales in 1788 after a five-month sea voyage, and eventually established a colony at Port Jackson in Sydney Cove. While the east coast of Australia was a penal colony, South Australia (first settled in 1836), received no convicts and was always a free colony. Western Australia started as a free colony in 1829, but by 1850 requested convicts to fill a severe manpower shortage.

During the early years, small bands of aboriginals would occasionally raid a farm or attack a lone wagon on the road in an effort to retake their lands. Small skirmishes occurred, but these were local incidents treated as police actions and there was nothing like the U.S. Indian wars.

The British had had great triumphs in settling North America and expected the same in Australia, but where North America was forested and had plenty of rivers and rich soil, Australia had few rivers, the interior was mostly barren desert, and only the coastal areas were inhabitable. The Australian continent was eventually settled, but on a more modest scale. It was a hard land to pioneer, but the strong survived and the tradition of the Aussie *battler* was born: tough, tenacious, resourceful, and sometimes successful.

Agriculture drove the economy in the last half of the nineteenth and the first half of the twentieth centuries. It's said that Australia rode to prosperity on the sheep's back. Wool and wheat created wealth that enabled the cities to grow.

In the west, remote stations were established to raise sheep. Aboriginals wandered in out of curiosity and stayed for generations to do the bulk of the work. They were, in effect, slave labor, working for food, board, and old clothes. Some of these natives would run off and police would bring them back, often in neck chains.

The Australian culture evolved with English provincialism as a base, combining an inward reverence for the bush and an outward need to be accepted in the eyes of the world.

For years, being a descendant of convict stock was a stigma in Australian society, but recently it has become a point of pride, like Americans claiming lineage from the Revolutionary War. When convict *transportation* ended in 1868, many free immigrants—mostly British—came looking for opportunity.

Though isolated at the far end of the world, Australia prospered and bloomed.

On January 1, 1901, Australia was declared an independent nation, with the blessings of Queen Victoria and the government of Great Britain. Despite this, Australia to this day remains a constitutional monarchy with the Royal Family of England still officially the head of state [more on this in the section on **Government**]. The six Australian colonies became states and were federated, with the Northern Territory, into the *Commonwealth of Australia*. Unlike the U.S., there was no Revolutionary War, and no Civil War. There were also no competing countries on common borders, such as France (the Lousiana Territory), Spain (Mexico), and Britain (Canada). Violent rebellion at the birth of their nation and wars of territorial expansion are outside the Australian experience and explain why feelings of patriotism aren't as strong as they are in the U.S.

Tucked away on the far side of the world, Australia developed in quiet isolation through the first half of the twentieth century, evolving her own culture and language, the latter a colloquial version of English. She participated in the English wars against the Boers in South Africa (1899–1902) and against the Germans and Turks in World War I. Both were far-off adventures, performed under British command. At the start of World War II, she contributed troops to the British North African campaign against the Germans and helped bolster the defense of the British fortress of Singapore—and then came the Japanese war in the Pacific, which changed everything.

At the same time the Japanese attacked the United States at Pearl Harbor, they attacked Singapore, which the British had built at tremendous expense to protect their Southeast Asian Empire. It turned out the Brits had built the defenses to repulse a frontal sea attack by battleships and amphibious forces, and the Japanese had the cheek to stage a land attack from the rear on bicycles. When Singapore fell, the British Empire died with it, and Australia was left on her own. Against British wishes, Australia withdrew troops from North Africa and retrained them as jungle fighters, because by then the Japanese had invaded New Guinea, which was an Australian territory, a hundred miles off the north coast.

Meanwhile, the United States was being forced out of the Philippines by the Japanese and needed another base of operations in the South Pacific. Knowing a citadel was harder to defeat than an outpost, Australia welcomed the huge amount of men and material the Yanks sent. The Americans soon discovered that they had as much in common with Australia as they had with Great Britain. During the war years, the U.S. and Australia became close allies politically, socially, and economically—ties that remain strong to this day.

After WWII, improvements in communication and travel allowed Australia to emerge from isolation and to join the world community. Economically, things had also changed. Synthetics were replacing wool as the fiber of choice and the wool industry suffered a depression. About that same time, demand rose for minerals: iron ore, alumina, and precious metals, all of which Australia had in abundance. By the 1960s, Australia's ride to prosperity had shifted from the sheep's back to the ore train. New fortunes were made and Australia led the world in mining and mineral resource technology.

To the rest of the world, Australia merely changed from being a farm to being a quarry, with a few kangaroos and koalas thrown in for charm.

Fiber optic phone lines, the Internet, and satellite TV brought Australia closer to the rest of the world in a virtual sense, but physically it is still a far-off destination—an expensive fourteen-hour flight from the west coast of the U.S. to Sydney—and this has been a detriment to development. But the fact often missed is that being isolated from the rest of the world behind a circle of oceans can be an advantage, both in terms of safety and the need to develop self-reliance. Australia has had to develop her own industries and has been able to keep out disease, terrorism, and illegal immigration. The standard of living is among the highest in the world.

Australia's level of contribution to the world far outweighs her small population. Blessed with sunshine, clean air, abundant natural resources, an optimistic outlook, and distance from most of the world's problems, Australia can truly be called "The Lucky Country".

Indigenous Australians   As for the natives who'd lived on the island-continent for tens of thousands of years before the Europeans arrived, they got the shaft. Regarded as animals, they were hunted, starved, enslaved, killed off by disease, introduced to alcohol and drugs, and had their children taken from them by seemingly well-intentioned, but ultimately cruel and insensitive, welfare laws.

The nineteenth century white man's attitude was that the indigenous Australians would eventually die off or assimilate through a *breeding out the black* plan and cease to be a problem. Aboriginal Australians didn't have Australian citizenship until 1948, had no rights until 1960, couldn't vote until 1967 and weren't protected by anti-discrimination laws until 1975. This was in the land they'd occupied for over 40,000 years.

Like the indigenous American tribes who were stuck with the name "Indian" (commemorating Christopher Columbus' 10,000 mile navigation error), the indigenous Australians were saddled with being *Aborigine*. Aborigine is a Latin term meaning "from the beginning." There were between 300,000 and 500,000 indigenous Australians when English settlement began in 1788. They belonged to as many as 600 tribes, speaking hundreds of languages. Each has—or had—a rich spoken culture and ingenious survival techniques that allowed them to flourish in an environment that regularly killed Europeans who ventured beyond "civilization."

These hardy, tenacious, Aborigines were nearly defenseless as the lands and way of life they'd developed over thousands of generations were taken from them in just a few decades. Many died of European diseases for which they had no immunity. By 1900, 90 percent had been eliminated and the indigenous population had withered to less than 50,000. It truly looked as if they would cease to exist as a people, but the ones that managed to survive developed a resistance to European diseases and soon learned to demand their rights. A hundred years later, by 2001, the population had returned to about 450,000, but this is only about 2½ percent of the total population of Australia, so they have a very small voice.

Many Aborigines have assimilated and done well; many remain in an underclass. For the latter, they've had the wonders of the modern world dangled before their eyes, wonders that were—and to some extent continue to be—out of reach. Many are of mixed lineage and are impoverished, living on the fringe of society on urban welfare or in semi-independent communities out in the bush.

A vast number exist in third world conditions, despite millions of dollars and countless good intentions invested by the government and charities. There's a movement to celebrate them and their culture and inspire their independence. Some have thrived, keeping their arts and culture alive, but it's mostly a case of too little, too late. There's no going back to the old ways.

One bright spot was the 1992 Mabo federal court decision that established the idea of *native title* to some traditional lands. Another federal ruling in 2006 gave the Nyoongar people of Western Australia title to public lands in the Perth area. This allows the Nyoongar to "conserve and use the natural resources of the area, maintain and protect sites, hunt on the land and use it for traditional purposes", while not effecting individual landowners property rights. The ruling is being challenged by the state in federal court, not so much as to have it over-turned, but to more precisely clarify and define it. These fights are likely to go on for years

In the state of Western Australia in 2007, aboriginals made up only 3½ percent of the total population, while representing 42 percent of the adult and 80 percent of the juvenile prison populations.

This sad fact is compounded by a resentment among some white Australians who feel aboriginals are given too much welfare assistance. Others feel that welfare compromises their self-reliance. However, this is a subject for another book, and an American criticizing Australians about what should be done with their indigenous people is hypocrisy. Let's move on.

Immigration   The Australian government was no better than the rest of the world in the way it managed immigration. They'd always encouraged migration from the UK (United Kingdom: England, Scotland, and Northern Ireland). A *White*

Australia policy was instituted in the late nineteen century, mostly to keep Asians out. By the 1930s, the population of Australia—a country almost the size of the continental U.S.—was only about 7 million. When the Second World War began in the Pacific and the Australian mainland came under the threat of Japanese invasion, Australians realized they didn't have enough population to occupy their own country, let alone to defend it. After the war, facing the reality of crowded Asian nations to her north, Australia developed a *Populate or Perish* policy. Still maintaining her identity with Mother Europe, the government encouraged migration from that war-torn continent.

There was a time when citizens of the UK could migrate to Australia for ten pounds each (about US$50 in today's money), airfare included. Thousands took advantage of this—including entire families. They were called *Ten-Pound Poms* (Pom is a semi-derogatory term for someone from Britain—see **dictionary**).

Another wave of migration came from southern Europe, mainly Italy and Greece. At first there was friction between the Australians and these darker, non-English speaking European immigrants, but eventually everyone found their place. By the second generation, all had assimilated. It was an ideal place for refugees: work was plentiful, the opportunities were vast, and it was one of the safest countries in the world.

The *White Australia* policy began to change after WWII and was eliminated by law in 1973 (a modified "learn to speak English" policy took its place). Migration from China, Vietnam, Hong Kong, and the Philippines followed, and later from the Middle East and Africa.

In the 1990s, there was an influx of English-ancestry immigrants from Zimbabwe (the former English colony of Rhodesia) and post-apartheid South Africa. Australia is now a multi-cultural society. It has its growing pains, but generally things get worked out on their own.

Oddly enough, you meet few American residents. In fact, you're more likely to meet Canadians living in Australia than folks from the U.S. Most U.S. citizens living in Australia are either married to an Australian or are there on work contracts.

Given a choice, Americans tend to stay in America.

Modern Australia   When you consider that the country began as a colony of convicts enslaving an indigenous population, it's amazing to see the enlightened semi-socialist democracy she has developed into. Her modern cities are spires of glass and steel, standing alongside scenic rivers and bays, surrounded by bucolic suburbs. There's an abundance of parks, public sports facilities, walkways, bikeways, and patrolled beaches.

Innovation and invention are common. Arts are celebrated and public funds are set aside to nurture them. There's housing for the poor—not in ghettos, but in mainstream neighborhoods. Universal health care is available to all, as is public education, inexpensive universities, and career training. Government subsidies help the lower middle class afford a decent standard of living. There's a sincere effort to maintain the environment, as much as can be expected from a government of a large country with a small population that has to satisfy business interests, fund itself, and exist in what can be a hostile international community.

British and American influences

Because of its history, Australia is heavily influenced by its British heritage and culture. Prior to WWII, Australia was in isolation. Sea voyages were lengthy and transoceanic phone calls were expensive. During the war, thousands of American soldiers and sailors were stationed there, and the American influence began. One could say there's a melding, and in practicality, Australia looks American, sounds British, but is entirely of itself.

Australians do not want to be the 51st state, nor do they wish to be a puppet of the UK. They love to poke fun at the *Yanks* (Americans), the *Poms* (British) and the *Kiwis* (New Zealanders, whom they consider lesser siblings). Just as Americans have their own brand of English, so do the Aussies, along with their own culture, including sports, automobiles, foods, and media.

Australians get a large dose of American media, so they're aware of many American cultural references. On the other hand, when most Americans think of Australia, they imagine the stereotypes: kangaroos, koalas, Crocodile Dundee, and the late Steve Irwin. There's a lot more to Australia than that.

Most Australians would love to travel to the U.S., and many have. Most are dazzled by the diverse geography and the variety of regional cultures in America but are bewildered by the crowds and aggressive lifestyle. Many of Australia's best and brightest have moved to the U.S. because the larger American marketplace allows for greater personal achievement. Mel Gibson and Rupert Murdoch are prime examples.

As much as Aussies hate to admit it, Australia is still quite British.

As Barry Humphries, known to the world as his alter-ego, "Dame Edna," once said, "Whatever American affectations we may maintain here in Australia, we are really provincial English society."

What is the British attitude toward Australia? "Once a colony, always a colony" The Poms will always think of Australians as the "colonials." Aussies will reluctantly acknowledge this, and that's one reason they like Americans, because the Yanks kicked the Poms out long ago. On the other hand, the links with Great Britain are much deeper than just being the ancestral homeland for much of the population. It's more about being part of the British Empire, even though that Empire died in the 1940s.

Attitudes about Americans

Living outside the U.S. but constantly observing it gives one an international perspective. What strikes one is how inwardly fixated the American people are. They seem to ignore what's going on beyond their shores unless it intrudes directly and obviously—such as the 9-11 attack. Like Narcissus staring at herself in the mirrored pool, Americans see international realities as something out of focus, floating in the background of their own reflection.

Australians generally like Americans. They watch our movies and TV shows, listen to the music, and read the books, but they don't quite get why Americans work so hard and are so *over the top*: hyperactive, aggressive, and determined to boss the world around

Aussies are more relaxed. The prevailing attitude is "*she'll be right*" and the answer to any question is usually "*no worries.*" Personal freedom is the most important issue, and anything that compromises that is a hard sell.

The Australian identity

"The Australian identity was forged by the struggles of the pioneer settlers, by the dauntlessness of the often ill-fated explorers, and by the courage of the ANZAC soldiers who sacrificed their lives at Gallipoli."

(Inscription on the wall of the National Gallery of Australian Art, Melbourne.)

Culture

For a country with a small population, Australia has provided more than her share of world class contributions. Culture doesn't begin and end at the Sydney Opera House. Each of the capital cities and dozens of regional areas, have symphonies, opera and ballet companies, and jazz scenes. Australia has her own writers, actors, painters, and composers, many of whom have been exported, while others are known only at home.

Australian culture developed far from the influences of America and Europe. Australia has its own music, movies, TV and radio shows, along with its own musicians, actors, stars, and celebrities, so be prepared to "not get" many cultural references.

Some Australian music stars and groups you probably haven't heard of: Percy Grainger, Delta Goodrem, John Butler Trio, Eskimo Joe, The Waifs, James Morrison (the jazz musician, not the British blues-rock singer), Kate Ceberano, Jane Rutter, and Slim Dusty to list a few.

Some Australian writers: Tim Winton (*Dirt Music, Cloud Street, The Riders*), Thomas Keneally (*Shindler's Ark, The Chant of Jimmy Blacksmith*), Christina Stead (*The Man Who Loved Children*), Miles Franklin (*My Brilliant Career*), and Morris West (*The Shoes of the Fisherman*).

Sad fact is, once someone has made it big, they tend to go to the U.S. or the UK. Famous Aussie movie star exports: Nicole Kidman, Hugh Jackman, Heath Ledger, Mel Gibson, Cate Blanchett, Russell Crowe, Geoffery Rush, Naomi Watts, Paul Hogan, Toni Collette, Helen Reddy, Olivia Newton-John, Rolf Harris, and my favorites, Errol Flynn and Rod Taylor.

Here are a few movies to watch to get a feel for the culture: *The Castle*, *Muriel's Wedding*, *Strictly Ballroom*, *Rabbit-Proof Fence*, *Lantana*, *The Dish*, and *A Town Like Alice*.

Country music is popular, especially in rural areas. Australia has its own artists and industry. For some reason, most of the singers adopt an American southern accent for their songs.

Basic economics

The Australian dollar is written A$ or AUD, and is sometimes referred to as the *Aussie*. U.S. dollars are US$ or $US. Exchange rates fluctuate.

The value of the Australian dollar is related to, but not directly connected to, the American dollar, European Euro, and Japanese Yen. It seems to mirror the rise and fall of gold prices. At one point in 1974, the AUD was worth more than $1.43 to one U.S. dollar, but by 2001, it had dropped to barely 50 cents. It was a good time to visit Australia, since everything in the country was priced 50 percent off when you based your thinking in U.S. dollars. I bought a A$6,000 vintage motorcycle for US$3,000 and had enough left over to put it in a crate and fly it home in the belly of a Qantas jet. The *Aussie* has slowly risen since then. It was fairly stable 2004-6 at about 70–80 cents to the U.S. dollar, rising toward 90 cents in 2007. [More in the section on **money**.]

Interest rates are in a different cycle than in the U.S., reflecting Australia's different circumstances controlling inflation. In 2003, when the U.S. prime interest rate was 1 percent and you were lucky to get 1.5 percent on a passbook account in an American bank, Australians were getting 5 percent. In financial year 2005/6, the Aussie *share* (stock) market went up more than 20 percent while the U.S. experienced a short spurt and ended where it had begun. In

2007, as the U.S. stock market hit record highs, the Aussie dollar was also up—meaning U.S. dollars had lost value. The U.S. stock market boom was an illusion in actual international monetary value.

Australia is a small market. Importers seem to artificially fix prices high, since there's little competition. Plus, almost anything imported from North America and Europe will have the double whammy of customs duty and shipping costs. Many things are significantly more expensive. A pair of Levis can cost A$90. A Bosch cordless drill can be A$200. A Mercedes E380 can invoice at over A$100,000.

Conversely, Australia is in Asia, so there are lots of cheap imports. A pair of Chinese-made jeans at K-Mart cost A$20. A Chinese GMC cordless drill sells for A$50. A Malaysian Proton car goes for A$14,000. Of course, the old saying "you get what you pay for" applies, so keep your receipts.

Because of the cost, Aussies tend to make things last longer. There are many well cared-for older vehicles on the road. People tend to fix things rather than discard them. *DIY*, (do-it-yourself) is a national tradition. Things get re-used. A paperback book can cost A$20–25 new, but there are *book exchanges* (used book stores) where you can buy books at a third that price and then return them for a credit against the next purchase.

Lifestyle

Lifestyle is a term that's used a lot in Aussie advertising and in everyday language. It means "quality of life." At first I thought it was overused, but the more I see of how Australians live and what they value, the more I realize that it's appropriate.

Ordinary Aussies work thirty-eight hours a week, with four weeks *holiday* (vacation) per year. They enjoy a great deal of recreation: early morning walks with their dogs, afternoons at the beach, surfing, kite-sailing, boating, pony club, playing in netball leagues, or in weekend cricket games. Most activities end up around the *barbie*, a *stubby* of beer or a glass of wine in hand, enjoying the company of mates. Not a bad *lifestyle*.

"She'll be right" attitude

This is an interesting attitude and it seems to prevail across the culture, though less in the bigger cities of the east. Simply, it's the belief that everything will turn out OK. Australians are great optimists. *Truckies* assume their old crate will hold together, farmers assume the rain will come, pensioners assume their checks will arrive, drivers assume pedestrians will get out of the way. In other words, that things will turn out OK: *"she'll be right."*

Of course, in practicality, problems arise, whether on a huge project or a backyard task. Those involved will puzzle over the situation, then someone will say *"she'll be right,"* and everybody will nod in agreement, and move on. The rationale is not to make too much over something that might not be a problem. This is generally true, but obviously, if done too often, can be a formula for failure. Thank goodness Qantas doesn't share this attitude.

The *she'll be right* attitude is often criticized by outsiders as being too laid-back, while insiders say it eliminates unnecessary fuss. You can't buck it—so when you run into it, just do what you have to do, but do it quietly.

"Ned Kelly" attitude

It's been said that you can tell a well-balanced Australian by the chip on each shoulder. This was personified by Ned Kelly.

Ned Kelly was the Australian Everyman, the struggling noble underdog—in the Australian vernacular: the *battler*. Kelly was an Irish-Australian who became the iconic Jesse James/Robin Hood of Australia, glorifying the individual's battle against authority. In the 1880s, he achieved the dubious status as the most notorious *bush ranger* (outlaw) in Australian history. His family—discriminated against because they were Irish and poor—was hounded and abused by the local authorities until Ned, his brother, and some mates decided they'd had enough. They started robbing banks and killing police, but were eventually hunted down. The last epic gun battle saw Kelly wearing boiler-plate armor, including a full-head helmet, shooting it out against a small army of constables (the *traps*). The police shot his legs out from under him and he was eventually tried and hanged. The image of the gunman in the iron helmet is still seen on the back of cars, on T-shirts, and in sculptures throughout the country.

What makes Kelly significant is that—to the ordinary Australian—he was a hero, standing up and fighting for his rights against a cold and corrupt government. This attitude underlies an important mindset of most Australians: a distrust of authority and a thirst for independence from government interference. Aussies routinely disobey laws they disagree with, whether it's behind the wheel or behind a desk. *Rorting* (defrauding) the authorities can be sport. They hate politicians with a passion. They'll back their candidate, then as soon as he or she is in office, turn on them as being just another *pollie*. Perhaps this is why Australians work better independently or in small groups.

This feeds into the *never dob* attitude. To *dob* is to inform the authorities about someone, to tell on someone. Australians don't like to do this. It's partly the attitude of the *fair go* and partly the idea of "us against the powers of authority." In other words, no matter how bad a person is, turning them in to the police is worse. With a rural population, this could be workable, but with a modern urban social environment, it's a formula for anarchy.

This distrust for authority is deeply ingrained. For example, all moves for a National ID card (like a U.S. Social Security number) have been defeated. There are government Tax File Numbers and Medicare numbers, but neither of these is asked for outside of their specific uses. Every time the National ID card comes up, it's shouted down by public opinion, driven by the deeply ingrained distrust of authority.

Much of this disdain for authority can be traced back to the convict heritage, personified by old Ned Kelly, with his iron helmet and a chip on each shoulder.

Kids' freedom

The Ned Kelly attitude extends to the way kids are dealt with. When we first moved to Australia, we noticed that parents didn't control their kids as much as parents do in the U.S. We'd be in the audience at a school performance and a baby would start crying or someone's toddler would start talking loudly. We expected the parent to try to quiet the kid, and if that didn't work, take the child out of the room. We were surprised to see that the parents would do nothing, and nobody seemed to be bothered by this. We thought it odd at first, but noticed it happening again and again.

We eventually came around to realizing this might be cultural. It's as if restricting the kids' freedom was worse than having them interrupting the proceedings. It's common to be in a public place like a shopping center, school, waiting room, etc., and see and hear small children throwing tantrums or behaving badly, and the parents doing little or nothing to stop it. You get used to it, but you wonder if this indulgence leads to the sociopathic *hoon* behavior of young adults [see section on *hoons*].

Mateship

Mateship is a strong friendship between *blokes* (men). An Australian man has a wife and a mate, and rarely are the two the same person.

Day to day, the term *mate* ("*How ya goin', mate?*") is used loosely, just as an American male of a certain age might use "man" or "buddy" ("What's happenin', man?" or "How ya doin', buddy?").

But to be one's *Mate* is to be someone special.

Egalitarianism

Egalitarianism is a belief that all people are equal. This is an underlying attitude in Australia and the basis of the *fair go*. A white Australian might complain about the "aboriginal problem" or about the influx of migrants from the third world, but then include several of each as friends. This is because the Aussie tends to take each person on his or her own merits and character. It's said that it doesn't matter how much money a man makes, what counts is whether he's a good mate and can spin an entertaining yarn at a party.

This egalitarianism is most evident along the *foreshores*.

Australians love the water, and everybody wants to live next to it—be it a brook, river, bay, or the ocean. Now this might be a bit of a *shocker*, but with few exceptions, in an Australian city you cannot live <u>on</u> a beach, bay, or river.

You can live <u>across the street</u> from the water, but there will always be a road in front of you. There are a few exceptions: some very old *blocks* (lots) established before the zoning laws changed, manmade canals in waterside developments, and property far from a city—but in ninety-nine percent of Australian urbanized areas, you can't build directly next to the water.

Why? Water features are considered public property, and institutional egalitarianism mandates access for all. The government has eliminated the possibility of having a wall of rich people's houses blocking ordinary folks from the water, as has happened in California and Florida.

This makes for an odd juxtaposition. You can buy a million-dollar *block* along the coast, build your million-dollar dream house on it, and as you sit on your veranda watching the sunset, sipping your chardonnay and nibbling beluga, some poor *battler* without a pot to piss in can drive up in his rusted old Ford Falcon, park across the street blocking your view, stumble barefoot down to the beach, beer in hand, and enjoy the same sunset. That's egalitarianism.

Tall poppy syndrome

Australians tend to resent anyone who is successful. That person is considered a *tall poppy*: standing above the rest, needing to be cut down to size. This was stronger in previous generations, but is still subtly in practice. The problem with this attitude is obvious: if success and achievement are resented, how can there be progress? Luckily, not everyone accepts this, but it's a common trait to be aware of. You might not be aware it's going on, but it's there. Be careful of being perceived as too flashy, especially in business: tone it down, let your deeds speak for you.

Culture shock

Enough about them, what about you? How do you deal with all this? Is it enough to produce Culture Shock?

Culture shock is real. Tourists and business travellers won't be in the country long enough to get more than an inkling of it—and that will probably seem amusing—but for permanent migrants or those on long-term work contracts, the day-to-day differences from American culture can get on your nerves.

Sometimes a migrant will go into what amounts to a state of mourning, longing for the familiar world they left behind. Some people, especially older migrants, may never recover from this. These people either wither or return to their homeland. The answer to culture shock is to have a good support system, consisting of understanding people who can help you maintain your sense of humor.

There comes a time for every migrant when they deeply and emotionally realize they're not going home—that this is it. It finally sinks in that they're going to have to deal with the cultural differences. I'm not talking about complex concepts, but about day-to-day living.

This adaptation won't take place overnight. It's been called "The Thousand-Day Sentence," as that's about how long it takes—three years. It's not just the big differences; it's the small, subtle ones that sneak up and gnaw at you.

This culture shock will come to you one day after butting your head up against some Australian way of doing things, trying to accomplish something that would be so easy to do in America, yet is difficult in Australia because you don't understand the terms, don't know where to look, who to call, or what to ask for. Take heart. You're not alone. Others have suffered through the same frustration—my family and I, for example—that's what this book is really about.

Sometimes Australia feels surrealistic, as if you've landed in a science fiction movie—or maybe the Twilight Zone. The Bizarro World from the old Superman comics of my youth comes to mind: a parallel universe where everything is recognizable but backwards from what you'd expect.

The cities look quite similar to the U.S., with wide boulevards, neat suburbs, freeways and downtowns—but everyone is driving on the wrong side of the road! Many things have different names than in America, the Australian accent can be hard to understand, shops are closed at unexpected times, and businesses and government agencies seem to be run on a Monty Python management model. The longer you stay, the more differences you notice—and it starts to get to you.

Some examples:

You go into a restaurant and take a seat, and the waitress never comes—because you're supposed to know to go up to the counter to order your meal. You finally figure that part out and go the counter and wait in line to order a hamburger. The guy behind the counter asks you a question, but because of the accent and the different terms, you don't get what he's saying. Finally you realize he's asking you if you want *the lot*. You guess that means 'everything on it', and say yes. The burger arrives ten minutes later and it's huge. You lift off the top bun and see—besides the patty—there's lettuce, shredded carrots, a slab of bacon, a fried egg, and a thick, round slice of something red and juicy on top, but there's no cheese.

You ask the counterman what the red thing is and he looks at you like you're from another planet and says, "It's *beet root, mate*".

Beets! They put beets on a hamburger with *the lot*—but no cheese! Welcome to the Bizarro World.

Or you go to breakfast—which, for some reason, everyone refers to as *brekkie*—and ask for jelly for your toast. After a funny look from the counterman and after a delay of fifteen minutes, he delivers a bowl to your table—full of Jell-O. *Jelly* is Jell-O—you were supposed to know to ask for *jam*.

You get tickets to a play and see printed on them: "*Supper will be served after the performance*". You skip dinner, looking forward to a nice après theatre buffet, but after the play, all they serve is tea, instant coffee, and a few cookies (which, for some reason, they call *bickies*, apparently short for *biscuits*). You eat the *bickies* and have a cup of instant and realize you've learned something new: *supper* means refreshments or an evening snack.

You're asked to *tea* at someone's house at *half-six*. You figure out that means six-thirty—you're starting to get the hang of the place—so you think you'd better have dinner first so you won't be hungry, since all they're going to serve is tea. When you arrive, you discover they're serving a full meal. You've learned that *tea* means dinner—but don't get too smug with your new knowledge, since *tea* can also mean a coffee break, though these are usually referred to as *morning tea* or *afternoon tea.*

In the first year, these kinds of discoveries will happen to you a few dozen times a day. Hopefully, you'll have someone to share them with, because a good laugh is therapeutic. Nevertheless, it starts to get to you. One day you'll find yourself on the Internet, listening to a radio station from your old hometown, just to reassure yourself that it's still there and you haven't gone completely mad.

Sometimes you'll feel like you've awakened in a parallel universe, but you're the only person that knows about it. You look around, and everyone is going about their business as if everything was normal. It's not the Twilight Zone—it's culture shock.

Now, forget about all that. Leave what you knew behind; it no longer counts. Embrace the differences and make peace with them. Forget the cheese and take the beets. If you'd have asked, they would have held the beets and put cheese on your burger, no questions asked—it's Australia; anything goes. Learn to say what the Aussies say: *"No worries...she'll be right."*

Language differences

Australian English evolved in isolation long before the intercontinental telephone cable—and later, satellite and fiber-optics—made instant voice communication possible. In the mid-nineteenth century, it could take six months for a letter or magazine to make it from London to Sydney. The telegraph sped that up, but it was just dots and dashes. My guess is that when a new word or term arrived, the first people to use it—correctly or not—established standard Australian usage. Perhaps some of the unique language applications and interesting word pronunciations can be attributed to this.

Australianisms   The term *Australianism* is defined in

my old Thorndike-Barnhart dictionary as "an English word, phrase, or meaning peculiar to, or first employed in, Australia."

You can tell a lot about a people by how they treat their language. Australians are fun-loving, intelligent, sarcastic, flippant, irreverent, witty, and vindictive. Give an Australian a word, and in a minute he (or she) will have turned it into a plaything: breakfast becomes *brekky*, wishful thinking becomes *airy-fairy*, waving flies from in front of your face becomes *the Aussie salute*.

This is what the Australian government has to say about it on one of its official websites: "Australians use a lot of colloquial terms (slang). We also have a strong tendency to create a peculiarly Australian, diminutive word form during informal speech. This means that words are shortened and then a vowel is added to the end of the word—usually an 'i' or an 'o.' Although the diminutives would rarely be used in a formal written context, when diminutives are written, the 'i' is usually written as 'ie' or 'y.'"

Here's what the Aussies have done to the English language:

Some words are abbreviated with an *ie* or *y* added to the end, so a bricklayer becomes a *brickie*. An umbrella becomes a *brolly*.

Some words are abbreviated with an *o* on the end, so an ambulance driver becomes an *ambo*. A garbage truck driver is a *garbo*. I've heard the sound man on a movie crew referred to as the *soundo*.

Names get the same treatment, even in the media. Every Aussie knows Michael Jackson as simply *Jacko*, Arnold Schwarzenegger is *Arnie*, Paul Hogan is *Hoges* (rhymes with "rogues"). The name Barry becomes *Baz* or *Bazza*, Gary becomes *Gaz* or *Gazza*, Aaron becomes *Az* or *Azza*, Teresa becomes *Tez* or *Tezza*.

Some words are from Cockney rhyming slang: *Yank* rhymes with "tank", as in "septic tank". They grab the word "septic" and Australianize it to *seppo*, and an "American" becomes a *Seppo*. Another one: a "lie" is a *porky*. Why? *Pork pie* rhymes with *lie*, so—*porky*.

Some terms are from British English, like *back-to-front*, meaning backwards, or *anti-clockwise* for counter-clockwise.

Ta means thank you. *Cheers* also means thank you besides being a drinking salute. *Whilst* is often used instead of "while". A "jersey" is a *guernsey*. First names are *given* or *Christian* names, last names are *surnames*.

Some words come from other languages, like *abattoir* (slaughterhouse), or *abseil* (to rappel). The snack bar or ticket booth at a theater is a *kiosk*. Short-term day care is *creche*. They adopted several Yiddish words: *shickered* for drunk, *nosh* for snack, *kibbitiz* for chat, *motza* for money.

Some are just plain unique, like *arvo* for "afternoon", which becomes *sarvo* for "this afternoon". A promoter is a *spruiker*. To defraud is to *rort*. *Strides* are trousers.

Some words are from Aboriginal languages. A *yonnie* is a large rock. A *humpy* is a shack, from the Aboriginal word *yumpi*. A parakeet is a *budgie*, short for *budgerigar*. Many place names are Aboriginal, especially in Western Australia and the Northern Territory.

Sometimes a noun becomes a verb: to "work hard" is to *beaver*. To say "goodbye" to someone is to *farewell* them.

Sometimes a verb becomes a noun. To "wet" something becomes *give it a wet*. I've heard a "good question" described on TV news as *a good ask*. To try something, you *give it a go*. To decide against something is to *give it a miss*.

Some adjectives become verbs.

Clear weather is called *fine*, so to describe improving weather, you'd say, "The weather is *fining* up."

If a political situation is heating up, it's described as "*hotting up.*"

Some Australian words are subtly different. You think you know their meaning, but you soon come to realize you were dead wrong. For example:

In Australia, your *partner* is your *mate*, and your *mate* is your *partner*. In the U.S., one's *partner* is a person with whom one shares a project, be it a business, a trip, a boat, etc. In Australia, one's *partner* is their spouse—married or not, gay or straight. In America, you'd call that person your "mate", but in Australia, your *mate* is your best friend: the tried and true buddy you'd do anything for and who'd do anything for you.

In Australia, this can get sticky if a man introduces you

another man and says, "This is my *partner*." Without understanding this distinction, you might think they were business partners instead of a couple and might say something unnecessarily embarrassing.

Here's another example: *Pot plants*. As you drive around an Australian suburb, you'll occasionally see a sign proclaiming: "*Pot plants for sale*". This is completely innocent, for it means potted plants, not marijuana.

The lesson from this: <u>assume nothing</u>. Don't let the apparent similarity lull you into a false state of confidence. You're not in Kansas (or Manitoba) anymore. When in doubt, smile and say nothing, then look it up in this book. If it's not listed here, ask a friendly soul.

Everyday Aussie words

"*G'day*" means "good day," and is the basic greeting: hello, good bye.

"*Cheers*" means "yes", "thank you", or "good bye".

"*No worries*" means "OK."

"*Onya*" or "*good onya*" means "well done", or "good job".

"*How ya goin?*" means "How are you doing?"

"*G'day, how ya goin?*" is used reflexively, without forethought, expressing greeting.

Words with opposite meanings   Here are some examples:

Mooted: In America, something which is "moot" is a statement which is doubtful or self-cancelling. In Australia, to *moot* something is to propose or suggest it. "He *mooted* the idea before the executive board" means he put it up for comment.

Tabled: In America, to "table" something, is to put it on hold (to not deal with it at this time). In Australia, to *table* something is to put it up for discussion: to "put it on the *table*" and discuss it.

Punt: In America, to *punt* is to give up or get rid of something, while in Australia to *punt* is to try something or gamble on it. In Australia, a "gambler" is a *punter*. Also, a paying customer, such as a tourist, is a *punter*.

Mickey Mouse: In the U.S., something described as "Mickey Mouse" means it's bad. In Australia, it's usually used describing something that's good, though it can also be used describing something bad. This is an instance where you have to consider the context.

Spirit of salts is a seemingly innocuous term. One might think it meant smelling salts or something you'd put in your bath water. It actually means hydrochloric acid, the nasty kind that burns.

Blue or **bluey** is what an Aussie might call a person with red hair. This is beyond opposite meaning; this is pure contrariness.

Words not to use Certain words that are innocuous in North America are improper if not offensive in Australia. Some examples:

Fanny: In America, this usually means one's rear-end. In Australia, it refers to the female genitalia. Call a "fanny pack" a *bum-bag*.

Root: This can mean the part of the tree that grows in the ground or it can be a coarse way to describe the sex act. Don't ask a girl if she "*roots*" for her favorite team. She might like them, but not that much. You don't "root" for your team, you *barrack* for it.

Map of Tasmania (Map of Tassie): Refers to the fact that Tasmania is shaped like a woman's pubic region.

Stuffed: This isn't a bad word; it just means something that is screwed up, as in "I *stuffed* up" or "My car broke down and is *stuffed*."

Literal-ness Australian English has developed in a simple "say what you mean" way. A logger is a *timber getter*. A car accident is a *smash*. An auto body shop is *smash repairs*. The anchorperson on a TV news show is the *newsreader*. High school graduates are called *school leavers*, or just *leavers*. When a shop owner takes inventory it's called *stock take*. Payroll withholding taxes are called *Pay As You Go*, or just *PAYG*.

Language usage is based on British English. There are many differences from American English. In Australia:

One lives *in* a street, not on it.

Something doesn't occur during a weekend, but *on* or *at* the weekend.

Time is similar, but 6:30 is written *6.30*, and can be pronounced *half-six.*

A TV show doesn't start at 6:00, but *from* 6.00.

"A week from Thursday" is often spoken "*Thursday week.*"

One doesn't go "*to a hospital*", but "*to hospital,*" as if being in a hospital is a condition, not a location.

A woman *falls* pregnant.

One doesn't watch cricket; one watches *the* cricket.

Retrospective means retroactive, as in "the new law was *retrospectively* applied."

"*Not to be taken*" means the substance is poisonous; it shouldn't be taken <u>internally</u>.

One doesn't take a test; one *sits* a test.

One doesn't "call" someone on the phone; one *rings* them.

A "run" in a lady's stocking is a *ladder.*

The number "zero" is pronounced *nil* or *naught.*

The letter H is pronounced "*hay-tch*".

The letter Z is "*zed*".

There are a preponderance of British names. You meet more Graemes and Trevors than Bobs and Jims. Many *surnames* (last names) are hyphenates: Worley-Jones, Smyth-Hayter, which adds to the Monty Python feel of the place.

Plurals   The British system is used. A company or a team isn't considered a single entity, but as a group of individuals. A newspaper article might say: "Telstra *are* hiring" instead of "<u>is</u> hiring" or "NASA *have* launched a space shuttle" instead of "<u>has</u> launched." When the Australian cricket team won the World Cup in 2007, the ABC described them in this way: "Australia *are* the best." I recently hear this one on a radio ad: "Myer *are* having a huge end of year *stock take* sale."

Spelling differences   Blame the Brits again: jail can be spelled *gaol*, pajamas are *pyjamas*, tires are *tyres*, maneuver is *manoeuvre*, program is *programme*, airplane is *aeroplane*, dispatch is *despatch*, plow is *plough*, draft is *draught.*

Words than end in "-er" are often spelled "-*re*": center is spelled *centre*, theater is spelled *theatre*, fiber is *fibre.*

Words that end in "-or" are spelled "-*our*": humor becomes *humour*, color becomes *colour*, odor becomes *odour*; though the *Labor* political party is intentionally spelled American style:–*or*.

The ending "ed" can become "*t*". Burned is *burnt*, spoiled is *spoilt*, learned is *learnt*. Even "spelled" isn't spared, it's spelled *spelt*.

Some words ending in two L's in American usage get one L in Australian: enroll becomes *enrol*. Installment becomes *instalment*. Willful becomes *wilful*.

The letter S sometimes replaces the letter Z, as "criticize" becomes *criticise*, "cozy" becomes *cosy*.

C's can replace the letter S: "defense" becomes *defence,* but *defensive* is still spelled with an "S" and not a "C".

Hard C's can replace the letter K: "skeptic" is spelled *sceptic*.

Medical terms are spelled more in the Latin style: gynecologist is *gynaecologist*, orthopedist is *orthopaedist*. If you're looking up "estrogen" in an Australian reference book, don't look under E; look under O. It's spelled *oestrogen*.

"Ass" is *arse*, but pronounced "*ahss*", since the R is silent.

A recently observed bumper sticker read: "Unless you're a *haemorrhoid*, stay off my *arse!*"

Double & triple letters & numbers   When an Australian says a number that has the same repeating digit or letter, they'll say it as *double* or *triple*. For example: "tree" is verbally spelled "*T-R-double-E*". The number seventy-seven is spoken "*double-seven*", 999 is "*triple-nine*". Four repeating numbers are spoken double-double: 8888 is pronounced "*double-eight, double-eight*".

This gets confusing when someone is rapidly firing off numbers and spellings. Since the speaker says the *double* or *triple* <u>before</u> they say the number or letter, you have to wait to hear what it's double or triple of, then quickly write down the multiple numbers or letters. By the time you've done that, the speaker is halfway through the next sentence. If it's critical, read it back to them. People will be patient with you; Americans are novelties.

Punctuation

A period (**.**) is called a *full stop*.

Quotation marks are called *speech marks*, *inverted commas,* or *sixty-sixes and ninety-nines*.

Parentheses are called *brackets*.

Semi-colons are used in place of commas more than in America.

Pronunciation Differences   Accent differences aside, the most common differences are British-isms.

Aluminum is *aluminium*, with an additional letter "I". This comes from the British who discovered the metal in the first place (so they should be able to call it whatever they want). Originally they pronounced it the way Americans do. A few years later, British scientists decided to change the spelling and pronunciation to rhyme with the other metals, such as calcium, sodium, etc. The U.S. followed, but by the 1890s drifted back to the original pronunciation. Australians pronounce it as the Brits do: *aluminium*

Another interesting pronunciation difference is the name for a person who plays a saxophone. In the U.S., he or she is a saxophonist, in Australia they are a *sax-ah-fanist.*

Debut is pronounced *day-boo.*

Margarine is pronounced *mah-ja-reen.*

Nikon is pronounced *nick-on.*

Adidas is pronounced *ah-di-dahs*, with the emphasis on the first syllable.

Nike is pronounced *niik*, rhyming with "bike".

Fracas is pronounced *frah-kah.*

Debussy is pronounced *De-boo-see.*

Houston is pronounced *Hooston.*

January is pronounced: *Jan-yu-ry.*

February is pronounced *Feb-yu-ry.*

Rottweiler is pronounced *Rot-wheeler.*

Melbourne is pronounced *Melbun.*

Cairns is pronounced *Kans.*

Schedule is pronounced *shed-yule.*

Derby (as in a horse race) is pronounced *darby.*

Tuesday is pronounced *chews-day.*

Consumer is pronounced *kon-shu-mer.*

Kilometres is pronounced *kill-oh-meters.*

Methane is pronounced *mee-thane.*

Houghton (the winery) is pronounced *Horton.*

Nougat is pronounced *new-gah.*

Khaki is pronounced *kar-kay*, with emphasis on the first syllable.

Curiously, pronunciation within words can be inconsistent. The Australian Broadcasting Authority (the *ABA*) is sometimes pronounced *ah-bee-ay*. It's subtle; you have to listen for it.

Accent   The Australian accent varies with region and the background of the speaker. The basic variation sounds like cockney spoken with a lazy lip and pinched cheeks. Some accents are so heavy that, when laced with local words and a few beers, one might as well be listening to another language entirely. Some sound British, which is condescendingly attributed to "breeding" and expensive private schools.

Generally the vowels O and A tend to pick up an "i "on the end ("day" becomes *die*). E*'s* are spoken with tight lips ("where" becomes "*weir*", "ten" becomes "*tin*"). I *'s*, when they occur in the middle of a word, can be pronounced as a double E ("gig" is pronounced "*geeg*"). The combination "ei," as in "weight" or "eight," broadens out to become "*eye-t*". In some rural regions, "no" becomes *noi*.

This can lead to some interesting moments of misunderstanding. For example, a few years ago, a story ran on the ABC (Australian Broadcasting) about the American secretary of state meeting with the Israeli prime minister. In Australia, the word "meet" is pronounced "*mate*", so it sounded like the *newsreader* said, "Condoleezza Rice will be "*mating*" with Arial Sharon in Jerusalem." An unlikely couple, but they were both single and probably had a lot in common.

R's are dropped at the end of most words: dollar becomes "*dollah*", rooster becomes "*roostah*". However, just as in physics, where energy is never lost, in Australian, R*'s* are never lost. Instead, the dropped R*'s* turn up at the end of words ending in A. China becomes "*Choin-er*", Australia is pronounced "*Straylier*", and idea becomes "*ai-deer*".

I once had a lively discussion about this with an Aussie mate of mine who ended up chiding me, "You Americans roll your R's."

I disagreed, "Italians roll their R's; American's just pronounce them."

When the letter A occurs at the beginning of a word, it's pronounced as in "Al Bundy". So the City of Albany, Western Australia isn't "All-bany", like the capital of New York, but "*Al-bunny*". However, this is inconsistent, as the ABC is often pronounced "*Ah-bee-see*."

S is pronounced like a Z, so the name "Les", sounds like "Lez".

To an American, New Zealanders won't sound much different than Australians, but it's very obvious to an Australian, and they love to point out the differences. When an Aussie starts making fun of a Kiwi accent, you'll wonder what the heck they're talking about. It's mutual, because in New Zealand they love to make fun of Aussies.

It's all a matter of perception. In Australia, Australians aren't speaking with an Australian accent; rather, you're hearing with an American one.

Verbal Communication   Nevertheless, Australians will sound different to you, and you'll sound different to Australians. When you go into a shop and ask for something with your North American accent, you'll probably be asked to repeat yourself. There are three basic reasons for this:

First, the clerk was caught off-guard by your unusual accent and hasn't actually paid attention to what you were saying. Second, because your pronunciation of the words differs, they might not have understood everything you said. Third, you probably used the wrong term for the object you were asking for.

Australians call things by different names: *petrol* means gasoline, *flywire* means window screen, a *whipper-snipper* is a weed-wacker or string trimmer, *the lot* means "everything", as in "*a hamburger with the lot*." Relax; don't take it personally. Think of it as a challenging word game: it's better than Scrabble because it's portable and it never ends.

One other reason why Aussies ask you to repeat yourself: sometimes they just want to hear more of that "charming American accent." A North American accent will definitely be noticed, and you can use this to your advantage if you speak with calm confidence and use locally understandable terms.

Pronunciation becomes critical when taking information

verbally, especially over the phone. When in doubt, have the speaker spell the key words for you. For example: "Hay Street" spoken with an Australian accent can sound like "*High Street*". I once drove around the same block for ten minutes looking for High Street, passing Hay Street each revolution until I figured that one out. The city of MacKay is pronounced "*Mah-kigh*". "Tony" can be pronounced "*Toiny*" or even "*Tiny*".

When I first *shifted* (moved) to Australia, I kept hearing radio ads for some store called "*Maya*". I was wondering why there would be a Mexican shop in Perth large enough to buy all that airtime. Eventually, I figured out it was the national department store chain *Myer*, which in Australia is pronounced "*My-a*".

Once I was telling a car buff friend about an old classic Holden Premier automobile my father-in-law was selling. I pronounced it "*Pree-mere*", with the emphasis on the first syllable. He didn't seem know what I was talking about. Finally after three tries he got it. "Oh, you mean a *Pra-meer*," he said, with the emphasis on the second syllable.

The lesson is, people are used to hearing familiar words spoken a certain way, and to be understood you not only have to learn the words, but also how to pronounce them.

Pronunciation of foreign words   Aussies seem to do OK with French words, like *abattoir* (pronounced *ab-a-twa*) for slaughterhouse or *abseil* (*ab-sale*) for rappel, but Spanish seems to throw them.

When the Red Rooster fast food chain came up with a spicy Mexican chicken dish, they spelled it *pollo* (Spanish pronunciation: *poy-yo*), but the Aussies insisted on pronouncing it *polo*, like the game on horseback.

It wasn't just a fast food restaurant that was tripped up; so was the Prime Minister, John Howard. When American executive Sol Trujillo (pronounced "True-hee-yo"), took over the privatization of Telstra (the Australian phone monopoly), Mr. Howard introduced him to the country on live national television as "Sol *True-jello*."

Times & dates   Hours and minutes are written slightly differently: 12:30 becomes *12.30*, and is pronounced "*half-twelve*".

"A week from Saturday" becomes "*Saturday week.*"

A *fortnight* is two weeks.

Dates are where things really get confusing. In Australia, the day comes first, then the month, then the year. So 9-11 is *11-9.* This can really foul up bills, invoices, and *cheques* (checks), especially when the day is the twelfth or less. If in doubt, write the abbreviation of the month's name instead of the number.

Speaking the dates is similar, and to an American it may sound awkward: October twenty-first is pronounced "*Twenty-one October*", or "*October twenty-one*", "March second" is pronounced "*Two March*", or "*March two*". Notice that Australians rarely use the ordinals "th" or "ist" on the end of the dates: February tenth is *ten February* or simply *ten Feb.*

Music terms   There are different names for the notes:

A *semibreve* is a whole note.

A *minim* is a half note.

A *crotchet* (pronounced *crotch-et*) is a quarter note.

A *quaver* is an eighth note.

A *semiquaver* is a sixteenth note.

Slang   So much of everyday language is slang that it becomes hard to differentiate from proper Australian English. You could argue that in Australia there is no such thing as proper Australian English; it's all slang. Radio, TV, and print use slang as everyday words. I've heard news commentators call a false statement a *porky* (rhyming slang: pork pie rhymes with lie, hence *porky*). A *newsreader* (anchor person) might talk about a thunderstorm *sarvo* (this afternoon). The St. Vincent De Paul charity refer to themselves as *Vinnie's* and the signs on the Salvation Army's stores read *The Salvos.* Sorting the slang out is a constant source of confusion and amusement. The dictionary in the back of this book has a few examples (about 1,500).

Holidays

With tradition stemming from British settlement, don't expect the Fourth of July to get more than a passing glance in Australia. Halloween is barely mentioned, and Thanksgiving is irrelevant (November is late spring, hardly the time for a harvest festival).

Christmas is a big summer event, like the Fourth of July, but with presents. Almost everybody goes on *holiday* (vacation) from mid-December until mid-January, so don't plan on getting any serious business done during that period. It's sometimes known as the *Silly Season*.

It can be a difficult time for those of us who grew up in the Northern Hemisphere. Shopping for *Crissy pressies* (Christmas presents) and seeing Santas in shorts and flip-flops in the middle of summer just seems wrong. Admiring snowman displays as you swelter in the summer heat, and hearing Christmas carols about "Jack Frost nipping at your nose" when it's actually sweat that's dripping off it probably won't inspire you with the usual holiday spirit. You're more likely to get invited to a beach party or outdoor barbecue on Christmas Eve than a midnight mass. It truly feels more Fourth of July than Christmas.

Crissy traditions are a family *tea* on Christmas Eve or Christmas Day, with the whole family sitting around a big table to celebrate. Next to each setting will be a double-ended party-popper. Your neighbor pulls one end while you pull the other, and when it pops apart, the person that ends up holding the largest piece gets the contents: a cheap toy, a joke on a piece of paper, and a crepe paper crown, which you're obliged to put on your head (looks great in a restaurant; at least everybody is wearing one).

If you're visiting Australia for a short stay during *Crissy*, it'll be interesting and fun, but if you're going to be living there a while, you'll learn to suffer through December. Take heart. Australians also dream of a white Christmas, and in the dark days of winter there are *Christmas in July* parties.

Boxing Day is the day after Christmas. No doubt you've seen it on the calendar and wondered what it meant. It has nothing to do with the pugilistic sport. It's British, going back to the class system, when servants served the wealthy on Christmas Day and were given the following day off, along with Christmas leftovers in a box. In practice it's an extension of the Christmas holiday.

New Year's Eve and New Year's Day are big, a great

time to go to the beach, have a barbecue, and drink.

Australia Day, January 26, is much like the Fourth of July, celebrating the beginning of British settlement in 1788, with picnics and parties and *sky shows* (fireworks) in major cities. Beware, sometimes these public celebrations get out of hand. If you're on the street that night and hear a group of rowdy drunks yelling "*Aussie, Aussie, Aussie! Oi, Oi, Oi!*", get out of the way.

The Queen's Birthday is celebrated at various times throughout the year, depending on which state you're in. When The Queen ascends to that great throne in the sky and her son or grandson takes over, it'll be the *King's Birthday*. It's sometime in June in all states except Western Australia (where it's in September and coincides with the *Royal Show*, giving workers a day off to attend the biggest agricultural show and country fair in that state). None of the dates actually correspond to when the current monarch was born. It was originally proclaimed by King Edward the VII and is a celebration of the reigning British monarch. It wasn't Edward VII's birthday, either. His was in northern winter, but he wished it was in summer, and since he was king, he could do whatever he wanted, so he proclaimed his birthday to be in June. Of course, in Australia June is in the winter, but no worries, the only thing to know is that it's celebrated with a *long weekend* (three-day weekend), so the exact dates change to hook up with a weekend, and if you're in Western Australia, it'll be a different day than if you're in the *Eastern States*.

Good Friday, Easter, and Easter Monday combine for a four-day *long weekend.* School term breaks usually occur around then. It's a good time to go out of town on a holiday. Don't plan on getting much business done around Easter.

Labour Day is a long weekend (varies by state) and celebrates the coming of the eight-hour workday. Currently, the workweek is thirty-eight hours.

ANZAC Day is April 25. *ANZAC* stands for *Australia and New Zealand Army Corps*. It's probably the most important holiday in Australia, commemorating the 1915 invasion of the heavily-defended Gallipoli Peninsula on the Mediterranean coast of Turkey during the First World War. Australian and

New Zealand soldiers performed gallantly, but were defeated by the dug-in Turks during this ill-planned campaign led by British senior officers. The ANZACs lost more than 10,000 men (the Brits lost 22,000, the French lost 27,000, and the Turks lost 57,000). It wasn't the first or the last time the *Poms* considered their Australian offspring as expendable.

ANZAC Day now celebrates all the soldiers, sailors, airmen, and women who have served in the Australian armed forces in the Boer War, World Wars I and II, Korea, and Vietnam (yes, they were there, too), along with Malaysia, Indonesia, the Gulf War, East Timor, Afghanistan, Iraq I and II, and as part of UN peacekeeping forces. On ANZAC Day there are parades in all the capital cities and a nationally televised sunrise ceremony at the War Memorial in Canberra.

There are also ceremonies in small towns. Every Australian town has a war memorial, usually a stone obelisk in a town square, engraved with the names of fallen locals.

Melbourne Cup Day is the first Tuesday in November, when the most important horse race of the year occurs. It's the equivalent of Super Bowl Sunday. If you can't make it to the race in Melbourne, you can watch it on the *telly* with just about everyone else in the country. People generally take a long lunch and often don't return for work that *arvo* (afternoon). Parties and luncheons at *function centres* (banquet halls), taverns, and restaurants are de rigueur. Women traditionally dress up and wear fancy hats. Don't plan on getting much business done that afternoon.

Sorry Day is the official holiday to remember and apologise to the Aboriginal people for what the white Europeans did to them. A minor holiday more of a protest than a celebration. No time is take off from work.

Other holidays vary by state throughout the year. During *long weekends*, the general attitude is that people don't know what the holiday stands for, nor do they care, but they do their best to enjoy it.

Birthdays are celebrated similar to those in North America, with a party, cake, and candles, and the singing of the same "Happy Birthday" song. Birthday *pressies* (presents) are usually opened as the guests arrive with them.

Money

The Australian currency was originally the *pound*, but changed to the dollar in 1966. Like the U.S., there are 100 cents to the dollar.

In mid-2007, one Australian dollar was worth about 85 U.S. cents. In 1974, it was as high as $1.43, and in 2001, it was as low as 50 cents. For international money trading and in dealing with the exchange rate, Australian dollars are written A$ or AUD. Prices within the country will just have the "$," as all prices are in Australian dollars unless otherwise noted.

U.S. dollars are US$ or $US. Conversion rates are also commonly quoted in euros and yen. A great website for monetary exchange rates is **www.x-rates.com** [also see section on **tourist money exchanging** below.]

Currency   Bills are different colors, depending upon denomination. They also vary slightly in size, increasing with the value of the bill. They're made of polypropylene polymer plastic, are water-proof and un-tearable.

Denominations are: $5, $10, $20, $50, $100.

Coins are 5-cent, 10-cent, 20-cent, 50-cent, 1-dollar and 2-dollar. The 50-cent piece isn't round, but 12-sided. The $2 coin is about 1/3 smaller than the $1 dollar coin (this is opposite in New Zealand, so beware). The one and two-dollar coins are gold in color and are called *gold coins* (but they're not actually made of gold) to differentiate them from the lesser denominations. *Gold coins* are commonly requested for charitable and volunteer donations.

There is no 1-cent denomination coin. Cash transactions that come to less than 5-cents are rounded up or down to the closest 5-cents. Credit card and *cheque* (check) transactions use exact cents.

A ten percent sales tax, called *GST* for *Goods and Services Tax* is <u>included</u> in the price of anything you buy. There's no GST on food from grocery stores or on some medical expenses.

Tourist money exchanging   The best way to get the most for your money is to use your American credit cards, since the exchange rate will be close to market rate that day.

The best way to get cash in Australia is to use ATMs, but

check with your American bank to see which Australian bank has the best deal for you fee-wise. You can bring traveller's cheques and exchange them for local currency, but you'll be subject to the whim of bank check-cashing fees plus the exchange rate.

It's a good idea to have a few hundred dollars in Aussie currency when you arrive in the country, but the exchange rates at airport kiosks are ridiculous. You can order Australian cash through your American bank before you come over. Another way is to get a cash advance on your credit card, but watch the fees; interest is usually charged from day one.

Banking

The major banks are ANZ (pronounced *A-N-Zed*), Westpac, National, and Commonwealth. They're known as the *Big Four*. There are also smaller banks and credit unions. Most banks seem to follow a Monty Python approach to business and bureaucracy, so come armed with patience. If you don't like the answer you get, ask someone else (in Australia, an organization is truly a group of individuals). Just when you think everybody there is hopeless, someone will come through for you.

An exception is Benidgo Bank. The Bendigo Community Banks are franchises and are the fastest-growing banks in the country. They were started in response to people's unhappiness with the cavalier treatment that the Big Four dish out to little people (and even not-so-little people). Bendigo banks plow their profits back into the community, as well as paying modest dividends to their shareholders. They keep charges as low as possible and are responsive to their clientele because the clientele owns the bank. That's why some Bendigo Community Banks are even open on Saturdays (unheard of for the Big Four).

The equivalent of a U.S. Certificate of Deposit (CD) is called a *Term Deposit (TD)*. Checks are spelled *cheques*. Fees are charged on most transactions.

In Australia, there's no insurance on savings equivalent to the U.S. FSLIC or FDIC, but under the Banking Act of 1959, depositors in an *Authorised Deposit-taking Institution (ADI)* have to maintain assets to back their deposits (be it land, gold, cattle, etc.) and in the event that the bank goes belly up, the depositors are to be repaid first—before the bank's creditors. What does this mean to you? If the bank fails, you won't be paid out directly, but will have to wait in line and hope there's enough to go around. Bottom line: all money deposited is on faith in that institution, so it seems prudent to go with one of the big ones and learn to put up with the frustration. Besides, they usually have more ATMs.

Identification   To open a bank account, to apply for a driver's license, or to enter into other bureaucratic situations, you'll need ID. Identification has been formalized into a *100 Points System*, i.e. you'll be required to produce *100 points of identification*. Your passport is worth 70 points, a driver's license is 40 points, a credit card or a Medicare card is 25 points, and a video store rental card (I'm not making this up) is 25 points. Utility bills are 20 points.

Black ink   In the U.S., one signs important documents in blue ink so it's easy to tell an original from a photocopy. In Australia, one signs everything important in black ink.

Keeping your old American bank accounts   If you're moving to Australia but will still have dealings in America, you might want to hang onto both an American bank account and credit card to make transactions easier. To do this, you might also have to set up a post office box in America [for more information, see the section on **postal matters**].

Credit cards work the same as in North America, but do yourself a favor; sign the back of all your credit cards before you try to use them in Australia. Clerks check the signatures closely. When you use a card in a shop, the clerk will run the card through the scanner and then place the credit card upside down on the counter with the signature facing them. After you sign the slip, they'll compare signatures to make sure they match, so don't grab your card too soon or the clerk will ask for it back. This is all standard, they're not doing it just because you're a foreigner. Sign your cards.

Credit cards can be used to purchase on credit or *EFTPOS* (*electronic funds transfer at point of sale*), a debit card linked to either a cheque or savings account. When the sales clerk asks you "which account?" just answer "credit," "savings," or "checking." If it's an American card, it will probably just work on "credit".

ATMs are abundantly available outside banks, in shopping *centres*, in supermarkets, and in some *servos* (service stations). They work the same as in America. You can access an American account at an ATM in Australia, but before leaving North America, check to see if your bank has an arrangement with one of the Australian banks to give you a break on fees. Be aware that cash advances charge interest from day one.

Cheques are less common than in the U.S. In fact, many people don't have *cheque* accounts at all. Oddly, people will take a check with less scrutiny than a credit card. Credit cards, used either as credit or to debit (*EFTPOS*) from savings, are more common. Cheques are written the same as in the U.S. Some have "not negotiable" written vertically across the center, which means they can only be deposited, not cashed. Deposit slips are sometimes in the back of the chequebook and sometimes in a separate book.

Bank Cheques are the same as a cashiers check. It's what you use when you need a certified check to buy a car or lease an apartment. You get them at your bank for a small fee.

Internet banking is popular, with discounts on fees for transactions done online. It's called *B-pay*, and it's the easiest way to pay bills. You can also pay your bills by credit card on line.

Electronic transfers, directly paying from one person's account to another, are common. You'll need the person's name, bank branch name, *BSB* number (usually six digits), and account number (usually six digits). Many businesses pay employees and contractors by this method.

Phone banking using your credit card is common, with automated systems for paying bills and transferring funds.

Paying bills by mail is so twentieth century. It can be done, but don't expect return envelopes like you got with your bills in the U.S. Australians don't waste as much paper. Telstra, the Australian phone monopoly, uses reusable envelopes, where you flip a flap and use the same envelope the bill came in for the return payment.

Wiring funds is the best way for long-term residents to get large sums of money from the U.S. or Canada to Australia. You'll need an Australian bank account to receive wired money. You'll give the sending institution your name, account name, *Swift Code*, *BSB* number, and account number. Before you make a move, check with the banks on both ends.

If you're migrating and don't already have your own Australian bank account, you can wire money to a friend or relative in Australia. If it's a large amount, they can open an account in their name and list it *In Trust* to your name. However, beware: they may have to show it on their taxes. Don't do this if the money will be in their account at the end of the tax year, June 30th.

Of course, exchange rates constantly fluctuate and you'll want to time your move to your best advantage. A weak Aussie dollar and a strong U.S. dollar means you can buy more Aussie dollars for the same amount of U.S. dollars. When you start the transaction, you'll have to specify an amount in Australian dollars, and when it goes through, the proper amount of U.S. dollars will be deducted from the sending account. There will be fees, and the exchange rate will probably be slightly higher than the posted rate because the banks on both ends will take a cut. Time your move carefully; you can make a bit of pocket change if you catch the cycle—but you can also get burned.

FYI   The Big Four Australian banks have been showing record profits year after year. They've been getting away with charging customers for every little thing they do, and for things they don't. There are a wide range of accounts available, so take the time to shop around before opening one. Once you have an account, double check your statement.

Investing

Stocks are called *shares*, the stock market is the *share market* (also called the *Bourse*). Shares are traded through brokers and online brokerages (such as banks, etc.), just as in the U.S.

The Australian Shares Exchange is the *ASX*. All publicly traded companies are registered with *ASICS* (the Australian Securities and Investments Commission) equivalent to the U.S.

Securities and Exchange Commission. All securities traded online with the ASX are cleared and settled through *CHESS* (Clearing House Electronic Sub-register System), which is owned by *ASTC*, the Australian Stock Exchange Settlement and Transfer Corporation, which is owned by the ASX. Details are on **www.investasutralia.gov.au**.

Franking   The *Franking System* refers to the taxation of dividends. *Franking credits* or *imputation credits* are issued on dividends. Companies pay taxes on profits before they pay dividends, so it would be unfair to charge tax on the dividends, since tax has already been paid on them. Double taxation is avoided by allowing the investor a tax credit for the tax already paid by the companies. In this case, shares are called *fully franked*. This applies only to Australian companies and investors who are Australian citizens or legal residents.

What does all this mean? When you have *franked shares,* you get a discount on the dividend income on your taxes.

Entering the country

Visas   Unless you're a citizen of Australia or New Zealand, or have Australian permanent residency status, you'll need a visa to enter Australia.

If you're a tourist, an electronic tourist visa can be obtained through the airline you're travelling with or through any travel agent in the U.S. It takes seconds and the charge is nominal. They're good for one year, with multiple entries, but only for three-month stays.

For seniors, there's a four-year visa, if certain medical, financial, and background criteria can be met. This isn't meant as a precursor to migration, but as a way for older persons to spend leisure time in Australia.

In the case of work travel, the company you're working for should help you obtain a work visa.

If you're migrating, the process is lengthy, involving many documents, letters, and phone calls over several months or years in order to get a *permanent residency visa* [see **migration** below.]

When you arrive in Australia, you'll find that it's not a third world country. There will be no machine gun-toting soldiers waiting for you in customs. In many ways, it's more civilized than the United States, so there will be no machine gun-toting soldiers waiting for you in customs. Instead, there will be a nicely dressed immigration agent sitting behind a counter who will check your documents. If all is in order, the agent will direct you to another room where a friendly customs agent may wish to look in your bags.

Quarantine   There are strict quarantine laws. Australia is surrounded by a wide moat called the ocean, which has made it easier to keep out lots of unwanted diseases and pests, like rabies, bird flu, and mad cow disease. Some things you'd never think of are prohibited: honey (due to hive diseases), fruit, and most seeds.

Do be aware of the small beagle dogs strolling through the terminal with the uniformed customs agents. These dogs have amazing powers of scent and if there's anything in your bag that shouldn't be there, a dog will smell it and quietly sit down next to you and wait to be rewarded with a doggy treat by the agent. After rewarding the dog, the agent will ask to look in your bag. Don't be foolish; heed the quarantine notices and comply. You will be caught, the dogs love their treats.

Migration   There are several schemes to gain residency in Australia, and the details are far too involved and boring to go into in this book. A few years ago there were consulates in major American cities, and you started the process through them. Now most are closed and it's all done online. Skilled workers are in demand, successful immigration is possible, and for the right people, very likely. The Department of Immigration and Multicultural Affairs (DIMA) is the place to make contact. Their website is **www.immi.gov.au**. For best results, use a registered migration agent.

Shipping your household goods to Australia   If you're migrating, and you've been accepted, you'll have to send your stuff there. If you can fit it in a few suitcases you're home free. If it's a few additional boxes, just send them by sea through the mail, though this may take a month or so. Shipping by air can be very expensive [see section on **Postal System-Shipping**].

The most efficient way to ship an entire household is in

your own sea container. There are many firms that specialize in this. They'll send an agent to your home to estimate costs based on how large a container you'll need and how much time will it will take to pack it, and will give you a bid. <u>Get recent referrals</u>—some of these companies are good, some are bad, some are very bad.

Once you've chosen a shipper, they'll contract to have an appropriate-sized sea container trucked to your home, and contract out for a local moving company to pack your goods into boxes, inventoried, and loaded into the container.

Having professional movers pack your stuff is mandatory for post-9-11 security reasons and insurance coverage, although this can be a joke.

In 2003, we got estimates from several Los Angeles-based shippers. We chose the one who's salesman convinced us they were the best because they did everything with their own trained, professional staff. This turned out to be not the case. Imagine our surprise when on moving day a crew of non-English speaking illegal aliens arrived to pack our household. By then it was too late to do anything about it, the new owners were taking over the house the next day, our plane tickets were booked, the salesman wouldn't return our phone calls. The packers mixed up the items, mislabelled the boxes, botched the shipping manifest and left our goods overnight in the unlocked sea container on a trailer in front of our house. The packers even intentionally buried our kids' battery-powered karaoke machine, blaring a Mexican radio station in the bottom of the load. As the container was towed away toward LA Harbor, we could hear mariachi music, and imagined it playing deep in the bowels of the ship until it got out of range on the Pacific, then hissing static for a week until the batteries died. On the receiving end the manifest was so incomprehensible it had to be completely rewritten to pass Australian customs (almost everything was marked "miscellaneous"). It took us months to sort things out during the unpacking. Amazingly, almost everything survived intact, except for the glassware they packed with our axes and shovels. Learn from our mistake, get recent references.

When shipping in a sea container, weight is usually not the

limiting issue; it's one of bulk, so hang onto those exercise weights and get rid of that stinky old couch. I even shipped a motorcycle over in our container, with its own proper paperwork [see **importing a vehicle from America**]. It turned out our shipper was in the vehicle-exporting business, households were a side-line.

The filled container is trucked to the closest major seaport and loaded onto a ship. The sea leg takes three to five weeks from the U.S. west coast, a few weeks longer from the east coast. Transit time also depends on which coast of Australia it's going to. From Los Angeles to Sydney the container will likely travel on the same ship. Shipments to Perth will change boats in Singapore. You'll be able to track the container's progress on shipboard via the Internet, using the container number (painted on the end of the container). Write it down before the truck leaves your house.

The shipper will contract with a local *removals* (moving) company on the Australian end. The container will be trucked to a warehouse and unloaded, and all the goods put into quarantine for customs inspection. Don't ship any kind of raw wood, plants or guns. Once inspection has been completed and administrative fees paid, it will be delivered to your new home.

Generally, migrants can bring in their personal goods and work tools duty-free if they've owned them for one year or more. If it's less than a year old and you declare it, you'll have to pay ten-percent *GST* (*Goods and Services Tax*) on it. Migrants can bring in one vehicle per adult duty-free as long as that vehicle has been in that person's name for at least one year [see **importing a vehicle from America**].

Citizenship   First you become a *permanent resident*, then you begin the citizenship process. Before the laws changed in 2007, a permanent resident could apply for citizenship after two years; now it's four years. You're not asked to take special classes, though some proficiency in English is helpful. At the time of publication, more changes are being debated. A test in "Australian culture and values" and an ability to speak English may be required.

Seasons

Being below the equator in the Southern Hemisphere, the seasons are reversed. Also, in Australia, the seasons don't begin on the solstices or the equinoxes as in America (usually around the 21st of March, June, September, and December), but on the first day of that month. So winter begins 1 June, spring begins 1 September, summer begins 1 December, and autumn begins 1 March. Notice I said "autumn", not "fall". The term "fall" isn't used interchangeably with "autumn". My guess is that it's because leaves don't fall seasonably from eucalyptus trees.

I once went through all four seasons in three weeks: leaving the U.S. in Northern Hemisphere late spring, arriving in Australia in Southern Hemisphere late autumn, where it soon changed to winter, then returning to the U.S., where it had changed to Northern Hemisphere summer.

Time difference

Sydney (on Australian standard time) is one hour behind Manila; Perth (on Australian standard time) is the same time as Singapore. Australia is twelve to fifteen hours ahead of the U.S., depending on local time zones. It's ahead because it's across the International Date Line, which lies in mid-Pacific, near Fiji.

Sunday afternoon in Los Angeles is Monday morning in Sydney. Before we moved to Australia, my mother-in-law would call us during her Monday morning commute in Perth and catch us Sunday afternoon in LA.

Because not all Australian states have daylight savings time, and because not all U.S. states have daylight savings times, a chart would be large, unwieldy, and confusing. For detailed listings, there are several websites: **www.timeanddate.com/worldclock,** **www.timezoneconverter.com**, or **www.worldtimezone.com**.

Time zones   Sydney and Melbourne are two hours ahead of Perth and one-half hour ahead of Adelaide and Darwin. (Yes, there are half-hour time zones.)

During *Australian Standard Time*, late April to late October (exact dates vary from state to state):

When it's 12 noon in Sydney, it's:
12 noon in Melbourne, Canberra, Hobart, and Brisbane,
11:30 a.m. in Adelaide and Darwin,
10:00 a.m. in Perth.
During *Australian daylight savings time*, October to April (exact dates vary from state to state; see below):
When it's 12 noon in Sydney, it's:
12 noon in Melbourne, Canberra, and Hobart,
11:30 a.m. in Adelaide,
11:00 a.m. in Brisbane,
10:30 a.m. in Darwin,
10:00 a.m. in Perth.
Obviously, this gets confusing. It's possible for it to simultaneously be eight-ten in Darwin and twenty minutes to nine in Brisbane.

Daylight savings time changes at the beginning of April and October for Tasmania, the end of April and October for New South Wales, Victoria, South Australia, and the ACT (Australian Capital Territory). In 2006, Western Australia entered a three-year trial period for daylight savings time. WA changes at the end of March and October.

Queensland and the Northern Territory don't have daylight savings time. The joke in these states is that they don't want the curtains to fade or to confuse the cows about when to give milk.

In practicality, daylight savings time is a mixed blessing. It's easier for business people in Perth to call Sydney and Melbourne, but if you want to get up early to walk the dog, jog, or do some chores before work, it's still dark at 6:00 a.m., and if you're trying to take advantage of the evening sunlight, it gets dark so late in summer that it's hard to get dinner on the table before nine. Since all the states change on different dates, there's a month on either end when you don't know what time it is anywhere else.

Shopping

There's a different attitude in the Australian "service sector." Aussies generally don't like to feel subservient to anyone. This is cultural, perhaps resentment stemming from the convict days, and seems to apply to quite a few salespeople.

It's common to approach the counter at a store and have the clerk completely ignore you while he or she finishes some other task they've begun. They won't look up to acknowledge you; they'll just let you stand there and wait until they've finished. Then they'll turn to you and proceed as if you'd just appeared. If a salesperson does acknowledge you, they'll usually say something like *"won't be a sec"* and go about their business, ignoring you until they're ready to help you. After this happens a few times, you come to realize how true it is: it won't be a *"sec."* It'll be a lot longer.

Other times you'll find two or three clerks waiting on one customer. They know you're there, but rarely will one break away to help you or to even acknowledge you with a *"won't be a sec."* Americans find this rude, but Australians are used to it, and they don't expect anything different. This isn't true for all stores and for all salespeople. Some are just as attendant and provide as good service as in any store in North America, but it's common enough to mention. In the service sector, eye-contact avoidance is an art. You learn to wait.

On the other hand, salespeople don't seem to be as aggressive as in the U.S. They aren't as driven to make a sale. If they don't have what you're asking for, instead of trying to talk you into buying something they do have, they'll often direct you to another competing shop that might have what you want.

There are two major supermarket chains: Coles and Woolworth's (*Woolie's*). The smaller market chains have been gradually bought up by these two giants, who are called the *Duopoly*.

Woolworth's is the largest food retailer, with 700 grocery stores nationwide. Besides supermarkets, *Woolie's* owns the two major electronics chains, *Dick Smith* and *Tandy* (Aussie Radio Shack), plus two liquor store chains and *Big W* (a chain much like Target in the U.S.).

Coles is the largest all-around retailer, with 1900 stores in Australia and New Zealand. Besides supermarkets, Coles owns Target (which is more upscale than its U.S. counterpart), Kmart, Office Works (the largest stationary chain), a pharmacy chain, and three liquor store chains. Coles recently spun off the prestigious Myers department stores (sixty stores nationwide). Coles was recently purchased by Wesfarmers, which owns the huge Bunnings home-improvement store chain (based on Home Depot).

Shopping terms   In Australia a *shopping centre* is what Americans would call a mall, while a *mall* is a shopping street that is closed to car traffic. A shopping centre can also be called a *shoppingtown*.

One doesn't go to the store, one goes to the *shops*.

Supermarkets are often in the center of indoor shopping centres, so you can't enter directly into the store, but instead must walk past several other shops to get into the supermarket. This can seem inconvenient to Americans, who are used to parking in front of the market and going directly inside.

Supermarkets tend to be scaled-down about 1/3 smaller than in North America; this includes the aisles, which are narrower and more easily congested when the store is busy. Shopping carts are called *trolleys*, and one pushes them on the left side of the aisle, the same as when driving a car on the road.

In some states *restricted shopping hours* apply, and major supermarkets must close daily by 6:00 p.m., except on *shopping nights,* and close all day Sunday [see next section on **shopping hours**].

Fruit and veg markets offer better produce than most grocery stores.

A *chemist* is a pharmacy. Many non-prescription drugs are kept behind the counter and must be requested, even though you don't need a prescription for them. The clerk will question you to make sure you know what you're planning on taking. Conversely, some drugs that need prescriptions in the U.S. don't require them in Australia. Many drugs, like Tylenol and Advil, go by different names [see section on **health care, medical terms**.]

Convenience chains like 7-Eleven are rare, but there are corner groceries that are open a little later and on weekends. If you need to grab something quick or after-hours, try a *petrol station* (gas station), most of which have a convenience store inside. Petrol stations usually open early and close late. *Newsagents* have a more complete stock of newspapers, magazines, stationary, lottery tickets, and phone cards, but they're usually only open business hours, 9:00 a.m. to 6:00 p.m.

Beer, wine, and hard liquor is available only at *bottle shops*. Woolworth's often has a bottle shop next to their supermarkets. Taverns and pubs have bottle shops for after-hour and weekend sales.

In many cities there are *markets*, not to be confused with supermarkets or grocery stores. These *markets* are more like a bazaar: a large enclosed area with separate stalls selling various products: meat, fresh fish, produce, luggage, clothes, toys, DVDs, CDs, etc. Often these are only open Thursdays, Fridays, and weekends and are located in old warehouses, military depots, and former train stations. You can get some great deals there, and a lot of junk. Farmers or community markets are often held weekends in town centres, parks, and on streets closed for the day. It's how a lot of people stock up on their fruit and *veg* for the week.

Garage sales are usually held on Sunday mornings (church-going isn't big in Australia, so there's little conflict). Many garage sales are advertised in the Sunday paper or in local classified papers, while some people just put up a handwritten sign taped to a cardboard box on the closest street corner.

Shopping hours

Shopping hours are restricted by law and vary from state to state. Some states have no shopping hour restrictions: Victoria, ACT (Canberra), Northern Territory, and in Western Australia, above the 26th parallel (north of Carnarvon).

New South Wales, Queensland, South Australia, Tasmania, and Western Australia (below the 26th parallel) have restricted hours. In those restricted states, large retail businesses are allowed to be open only during normal working hours: 8:00 a.m. to 6:00 p.m. Monday through Friday, 8:00 a.m. to 5:00 p.m. Saturdays, and closed on Sunday. Smaller businesses are exempt (except for some *bottle shops*), but generally follow suit. Some small neighborhood markets and delis take advantage of the situation and stay open late and on Sundays.

In Western Australia, shops are open 8:30–6:00 Monday through Friday and until 9:00 p.m. on Thursday (which is called *late night shopping*). In Melbourne, Adelaide, Brisbane, Hobart, and Darwin, the shops keep those same hours, and are also open Friday nights. This means by law, in New South Wales, Queensland, South Australia, Tasmania, and Western Australia (below the 26th parallel), the large supermarkets must close every evening at 6:00 (except on *shopping nights*), Saturdays by 5:00 and must be closed all day Sunday. If you're used to being able to shop in a huge supermarket from 8:00 a.m. to midnight, seven days a week, as in a typical American city, this can be trying, especially when it's Sunday afternoon and you realize there's nothing in the house to make for dinner.

Why, you ask? How can a country be so egalitarian on property issues and personal freedom, yet so draconian about when shops can do business? There are several rationalizations given for restricting shopping hours. The most commonly mentioned is the need to give retail workers time off with their families. Another is to give small businesses an advantage by allowing them to be open when the larger stores are closed— though many don't take advantage of this. A third theory is that if large businesses were allowed to stay open anytime, small businesses would have to follow, and while large retailers can easily assign late shifts and Sundays to employees, small business owners would have to put in the hours themselves. The fear is that small businesses wouldn't be able to compete and would fail.

There are lots of inconsistencies: only large businesses are restricted, but what constitutes a large business? In Western Australia, the law says it's fifteen employees, while in Tasmania, it's 250. Many smaller businesses choose to close early anyhow, even though they could stay open late. Many are open half-day or not at all on Saturdays. This means shopping can be difficult or impossible if you have a 9-to-5 job.

The big hardware stores like Bunnings (patterned after Home Depot) are open daily until 9:00 p.m. and Saturday and Sunday until 7:00. Why can the largest hardware store chain be open when the largest supermarkets can't?

Car dealers are open 8:00 a.m. to 5:00 p.m. Monday through Friday, until 9:00 p.m. on Wednesday night in Western Australia, and Thursday night in South Australia; and all day Saturday except in WA, where they're open only half-day. All major car dealerships are closed on Sundays. This was inconceivable to me, coming from Southern California where car salesmen are just slightly less aggressive than hungry sharks. Imagine my reaction three days after my arrival in Perth when I walked onto a Toyota lot at 12:30 on a Saturday afternoon and was curtly informed that they were closing. When I told the salesman I wanted to buy two cars with cash, he wasn't the least bit impressed. He told me to come back on Monday and closed the door in my face.

In Western Australia, a popular household appliance chain, Harvey Norman, decided to break the law and open some of its stores on Sunday, hoping to inspire a mass revolt of other retailers. It fizzled and Harvey Norman found themselves alone, facing hundreds of thousands of dollars in fines.

The federal government's National Competition Council (NCC) has been pressuring states to allow unrestricted trading hours. Western Australia has held fast, instead insisting on holding a referendum in 2005 on *weekend trading*. After a heady "Vote No" campaign, funded by an association of small businesses opposed to extended hours, the bill was defeated. ("No" votes always seem to win in Australia.) The feds then held back A$134 million in WA's own tax money in 2005 as punishment. WA is enjoying such a boom in mining and oil production that it chose to ignore the fed's fine.

So, what does this mean to you? If you're new in town, check out the local shopping hours. And if you're in a bind, you can buy a pie at the local deli, a litre of milk at a petrol station, or a six-pack at the corner tavern.

Public toilets

Don't ask for the men's room, ladies room, rest room, or powder room; ask for the *male* or *female toilet*. Sounds crude, but it's what they call it. Other euphemisms for the toilet are: *the loo*, *the gents*, *the ladies*, *the bog,* and *the dunny*.

Ensuite means your hotel room or accommodation will

have a toilet and bathroom.

Not all restaurants will have a toilet. Don't be surprised if, when you ask for one, you're directed down the block to the public park or library.

Paper towels are not generously supplied in public toilets. Electric hand dryers are usually provided; otherwise do what the Aussies do, air dry them or wipe your hands on your pants. Likewise, toilet seat covers are not normally found, in fact the only place I've seen them is in the toilets in the Sydney airport.

Eating out

If you want to eat well and inexpensively, go to Melbourne. In the rest of Australia, take what you can get. This might seem like an exaggeration, but it can be hard to find good food and service at a reasonable price.

With no illegal migrants working as cheap kitchen help—the adult minimum wage is about A$15/hour—and no custom of tipping waiters and waitresses, inexpensive sit-down-and-be-served restaurants don't exist in Australia. The only exception seems to be Chinese restaurants, which are usually family-run and seem to have an abundance of just-off-the-boat relatives.

There are no mid-priced restaurants like Denny's, Marie Callender's, or Coco's. There will be no frowzy waitress calling you "hon" and suggesting the meatloaf. Instead of mid-priced restaurants, there are places that serve counter meals [more below].

There are some exceptions. Nero's is a chain of mid-priced American-style pizza restaurants where a waitperson actually comes to your table and takes an order. The service isn't bad. The difference is in the menu. For example, the lasagne comes with a big side of *chips* (French fries) piled on the same plate. I'm not Italian, but lasagne and fries don't go together.

On the bright side, there are many restaurants that provide *al fresco dining*: outside tables on a veranda or in a partial enclosure.

Just like shopping hours, dining-out hours can be restricted. Restaurants in some states can't serve drinks late nights or on Sundays unless they serve that patron a full meal. Hotels (taverns) that rent rooms are often exempt, as are certain tourist districts, like Perth's *CBD* (Central Business District) or the Western Australian port of Fremantle. This restriction results in partiers being concentrated into the open districts, which become overcrowded and occasionally turn violent. In such cities, many people do much of their entertaining at home.

There are private clubs, like lawn bowling clubs, yacht clubs, and surf life saving clubs that have their own bars and restaurants.

Why all this puritanical restriction? The fear is that if evening and weekend drinking is liberalized across an entire city, then chaos and debauchery will descend upon Australia. This was disproved in Melbourne, where just such a liberalization occurred. Melbourne now enjoys a vibrant nightlife with no apparent ill effects. Some areas of Brisbane, Cairns, and Sydney have also opened up.

So, if dining and music are what you're after, go to Melbourne; otherwise, take what you can get. Australian restaurants fall into three basic categories: fast food, the mid-priced counter meal, and the more expensive and usually slow, waited-on meal found in nicer restaurants.

Fast food works just like in North America. You wait in line, order, pay, take your food, then sit and eat or take it away. This could be a McDonalds, KFC, a fish and chips shop, a pub, a *bakery* or a *lunch bar* (also known as a *milk bar*). It's basic fast food: *take away* (take-out) or *dine-in*.

Counter meals are served at medium-priced restaurants and taverns. It doesn't mean you sit at the counter on a stool to eat. It means you order at the counter, are given a numbered placard to place on your table, and when it's ready, a wait-person delivers it. Don't be surprised if you have to order your drinks at a different counter. The only non-fast food American restaurant in Australia is Sizzler, which, of course, serves just such counter meals. Although the menu is almost the same as in the U.S., Australian Sizzler isn't cheap.

Nicer restaurants   With a few exceptions, just about the only time you'll be waited on for a meal in Australia will be in a nicer restaurant. Nicer restaurants have good service, though generally not quite the level of attention you're used to in North America. Dining is more leisurely and more expensive.

But first, before you can get a table at anything other than a fast food place, you have to make a *booking.*

Bookings are reservations, essential for places serving medium-priced counter meals and nicer restaurants.

You can walk into an absolutely empty restaurant at 5:00 p.m. and the hostess will look down her nose at you and say in her most haughty tone, "Do you have a *booking?*"

You look around—the place is empty—you look back at her and she's very seriously waiting for your reply. It's like a scene from a Monty Python movie. You keep waiting for the laugh, but it doesn't come. She's dead serious.

The reason is that by 7:00 p.m. the place will be full and the restaurant management can't count on you leaving by then. This is partially because of the lack of speed of the wait-staff, but mostly it's because patrons have no obligation to leave once they're done eating. They'll linger at the table and drink and chat. Generally, if you've booked a table, it's yours for the evening.

So don't be surprised if you go into an empty restaurant and can't get a table. Make a booking.

Tipping　　*No tipping is expected,* and in fact if you tip, you'll be looked at like you were from Planet Elsewhere, so don't bother. The tip is already in the price.

Service　　The downside to no tipping is: don't expect the service to be quick or for the waitperson to be interested in whether your meal was prepared to your liking or if you need anything else. Avoiding eye contact in the service sector is institutional.

Since there's no tipping, there's no incentive for a wait-person to turn over their tables several times during a shift. They get paid the same if they serve four meals or forty. They're happy to let you sit there as long as you like—it's less work for them. At a sit-down-and-get-waited-on restaurant, fast service is something you can't count on, so if you're in a hurry, go to a place that serves counter meals.

The bill　　When it comes time to pay your bill and the waitperson is nowhere to be seen or is avoiding eye contact, *no* *worries*, just go to *reception* (the front counter) and tell the host or hostess you want to pay—but don't expect to see an itemized bill. You'll just get a total. Look on the bright side; you don't have to figure out the tip.

BYO   Some restaurants are *licensed*, which means they can serve alcohol. In these you can't bring in your own liquor, and can't leave with an open bottle. Those that aren't licensed will allow you to bring your own (*BYO*). You'll see patrons arrive carrying a cooler bag with the night's refreshments. The waitperson will sometimes offer to put your drinks in the refrigerator. Some places will charge you a corking fee, others won't

If you haven't brought your own, and find the restaurant doesn't serve alcohol, ask the waitperson where the closest bottle shop is. Chances are one's nearby, and you can walk there and buy what you want before the food arrives.

The menu   Nicer restaurants serve several courses. An *entree'* is an appetizer, also called *starters*. The *main* is the main course. Salads often come without dressing. Instant coffee is still served in some restaurants and places of business.

Fast food chains   You can have lunch at a McDonald's in New York, get on a plane and fly halfway around the world to Sydney, go to an identical McDonald's, and have the same lunch that looks and tastes exactly the same. About the only difference is that McDonald's isn't nicknamed "Mickey-D's", it's *Macca's* (pronounced *Macker's*).

The other major American-style chains are Hungry Jack's, which is the same as Burger King (was the name changed in deference to the Royal Family?), Domino's Pizza, Subway, Baskin Robbins, and KFC. There are a few Taco Bells in the east, but they aren't going over that well. Mexican as fast food doesn't grab the Aussie tastebuds [more below].

The Aussie chains are Red Rooster, Chicken Treat, Nando's (spicy chicken), the Kebab Company (kebabs aren't meat on a skewer; they're wraps), Chooks (Aussie for chicken), Jesters (meat pies), and others.

Don't be surprised when you're asked to pay twenty cents extra for a packet of *tomato sauce* (ketchup). Paper goods aren't handed out like in the U.S. You usually don't get disposable paper placemats, coasters, and promotional handbills. Extra *serviettes* (napkins) aren't routinely given out unless you ask. At fast food chains, they're in the standard countertop dispenser.

There are lots of independent places that serve pizza, fish and chips, kebabs, noodles, curry, etc., and then there are lunch bars.

Lunch bars are independently-owned counter meal shops, often called a *deli* or a *milk bar*, that make a burger, a sandwich, or fish and chips to order. They have pre-made sandwiches and *rolls* (submarine sandwiches), *pies* (single serving meat pies filled with various combinations of meats and vegetables and eaten by hand like a sandwich), *pasties* (a pastry filled with diced meat, potatoes, and onions), and *sausage rolls* (a pastry-wrapped sausage). The drinks are in the 'fridge—grab one before you go up to the counter. Try a Coffee Chill or a Strong Coffee, you'll like it. Lunch bars are usually in working areas and industrial parks.

Bakeries have more than just bread and sweet pastries. They also bake fresh meat pies, and there's usually a fridge full of *cool drinks* (sodas and juices). You can grab a *pie and a can* and eat outside.

Ethnic food   There are Greek, Italian, Indian, Malaysian, Indonesian, Vietnamese, and Chinese restaurants, there are Japanese noodle restaurants and sushi bars, and much, much more.

Mexican food in Australia isn't fast food, but is served at pricier specialty restaurants. What's served often bears little resemblance to Mexican food from the U.S., because there's never any Mexicans working at these places. For a laugh, try teaching the waiters how to pronounce the items on their menu. Refried beans, tortillas, taco seasonings and salsas are readily available in supermarkets, so you can make it yourself. Try making fajitas with kangaroo meat, it's pretty good.

Coffee bars   It wasn't that long ago in Australia that if you asked for a coffee in a restaurant they'd bring you a cup of hot water and a packet of instant. Now most lunch bars have espresso makers, as do most restaurants and cafés. There are several chains, like Starbucks (east coast), Muzz Buzz (west coast) Gloria Jeans, and Dome (nationwide).

Try a *flat-white* (espresso in frothy milk), a *short black* (espresso), *a long black* (watered-down espresso), or a cappuccino. A *skinny flat-white* is one with non-fat (*skim*) milk. A *long mac* is a macchiato: a double shot of very strong espresso with a little bit of milk, served "up" in a glass. A *short mac* is a single shot in a demitasse cup. If you don't like coffee, try a chai latte. Aussies have traditionally been tea drinkers, though coffee is gaining in popularity.

When you order a basic *cuppa*, you will be asked how you like it. If you want it with milk and one teaspoon of sugar, ask for *white with one*, two sugars is *white with two, etc.* . Milk only is *white*. Black is *black*.

A **sausage sizzle** is a simple social gathering, similar to a weenie roast or a hot dog cookout, using Aussie sausages instead of hot dogs. It's also the typical community fundraiser found in a park or outside a shopping centre or hardware store on a weekend.

The *snags* (sausages) are cooked on a griddle BBQ and served on a *roll* (bun) with *tomato sauce* (pronounced *toe-mah-toe*), which is like ketchup. Grilled onions are optional. Don't ask for chilli; it'll just confuse them. At best, you'd get sweet chilli from India.

Cheap alternatives   If you're travelling or new in town, ask if there's an open night at the local lawn bowling or surf life saving club. The food and drink are cheap and abundant. You might need to make a *booking*.

Eating in

If you had to come up with a traditional Australian diet you'd list meat and potatoes, and fish and chips. My father-in-law is a *dinki-di*, *true-blue* Aussie and that's what he'd eat for lunch and dinner very day if possible. For *brekkie* he'd have buttered toast spread with vegemite, washed down with a cup of tea. If he was living large he might add a baked tomato, a few pieces of bacon and an egg or two. He had so much mutton during WWII he can't look at the stuff, not even lamb. But that's his generation; with globalization, immigration and international travel, everything is on the menu

Breakfast is *brekkie*, lunch is *lunch*, dinner is *tea*, and a late snack is *supper*. A *smoko* is a smoke break, but it can also be a coffee or tea break. *Morning tea* or *afternoon tea* is a coffee (or tea) break with a snack. If you get invited to someone's house for *tea* at 6:00 p.m., expect dinner. If you go to a concert and it says *"supper will be served,"* that means tea, coffee (usually instant), and cakes after the show.

If you're invited to someone's home for dinner or *tea* and are told to *bring a plate,* that means to bring a dish of food to share, like a potluck.

The barbecue is called a *barbie*. It's usually half-grill and half-griddle (older ones may be all griddle). Some may also have a deep iron pan. On the griddle you can cook fish, *prawns* (shrimp), sausages, eggs (in aluminum rings), potatoes, onions, tomatoes, etc.; everything else goes on the grill. Most barbies are gas-fired.

Many public parks provide gas-fired barbecues. If you're travelling, you can grab some fresh fish or meat at a fish market or butcher's, some tomatoes at a produce store, and have a cheap, hearty meal in the park. BBQ the tomatoes by slicing them in half and sprinkling some cheese and spices on top, then put them on the griddle next to the meat.

A *mixed grill* is sausages, steaks, and chops (pork or lamb).

Lamb is common, fish is great. Fish, *chook* (chicken), meat, vegetables, and fruit are labelled as to country of origin.

A *serve* is a serving, as in "one *serve* of rice."

Mushy peas are over cooked peas served mushy.

Try some Vegemite, a dark-brown paste. Spread it lightly over margarine (pronounced *mah-jah-reen*") on toast; it tastes like a bouillon cube. Don't be put off by it, even though it looks like wheel bearing grease.

Nutela is a sweet spread made from hazelnuts that can be used like peanut butter (though it looks just like Vegemite).

Jell-O is called *jelly*, and jelly is called *jam*.

Milo is a hot-chocolate-like drink that comes in a jar—like coffee—and can be served hot or cold. There are several brands of pre-made coffee- and chocolate-flavored milk drinks that come in small milk cartons, marketed in different regions under different names such as: Choc Chill, Coffee Chill, Strong

Coffee, Iced Coffee, etc.

Cordial (pronounced *kor-dee-el*) is a sweet Kool-Aid-like drink that comes in a liquid concentrate—don't try to drink it straight. You add a little bit to water to taste. It comes in different flavors and colors. It's a favourite with kids.

Sweets and savouries are terms used to describe types of breakfasts or snacks. *Savoury* snacks are salty things, like *crisps* (potato chips) and *chips* (French fries). *Sweets* are ice cream and cakes.

Aussies like a *savoury* brekkie: bacon or sausage and eggs, baked tomato, cooked mushrooms, and buttered toast with Vegemite. Americans like a *sweet* brekky: sugared cereal, doughnuts, and fruit.

Supermarkets

Supermarkets look much the same as in North America, that is, when they're open [see **shopping hours**]. Shopping at the market will look familiar, though the stores are on a slightly smaller scale.

A shopping cart is called a *trolley*. To an American, a trolley is a cute little train that goes "toot-toot," but in Australia, it's anything on wheels that one pushes, such as a shopping cart, a hand truck, or an equipment dolly.

As you push your *trolley* down the supermarket aisle, keep to the left, just as if you were driving on the road.

Some items and products are called by different names.

Aussie food terms

American	Australian
7-Up	Lemonade
Arugula lettuce	Rocket
Bell peppers	Capsicum
Bologna	Polony, devon
Bun	Roll
Candy	Lollies
Cantaloupe	Rockmelon
Fine-grain sugar	Caster sugar

American	Australian
Cheddar Cheese	Tasty cheese
Chicken	Chook
Cold pancakes (pre-made)	Pikelets
Cookies	Biscuits, bickies
Corned beef	Silversides
Custard	Pudding sauce
Frosted Flakes	Frosties
Ground meat (any kind)	Mince
Gum	Chewies
Hors d'oeuvres	Nibblies
Jelly	Jam
Jell-O	Jelly
Ketchup	Tomato sauce
Lobster	Crays/crayfish
Meat pie	Pie
New York steak	Porterhouse
Oatmeal (or any hot cereal)	Porridge
Papaya	Pawpaw
Peanut butter	Peanut paste
Popsicle	Paddlepop
Porterhouse steak	T-bone steak
Potato chips	Crisps
Raisins	Sultanas
Rice Krispies	Rice Bubbles
Romaine lettuce	Cos
Scallions	Spring onions
Shrimp	Prawns
Sodas	Cool drinks, soft drinks
Sweet roll	Sticky bun
Tangerines	Mandarins

Meat   Cuts of meat differ. For example, an American porterhouse is called a *T-bone* in Australia. An Aussie porterhouse is just the steak, with no bone or fillet (fillet is pronounced *fil-lett* with a hard T). *Mince* is ground meat of any kind (beef, poultry, or lamb). Hamburger is pre-formed patties of ground beef.

Chicken is abundant and lamb is cheap. *Crays* (lobsters) are local, as well as some fish and *prawns,* but a lot is coming from Asia. If it's imported, it will be labelled.

One thing unique to the Aussie supermarket meat section is kangaroo. 'Roo steaks are lean and healthy, and it'll put a little spring in your step. Try it barbecued with teriyaki sauce.

Misc.   Australian BBQ sauces are pretty bland and there are no hickory-smoked varieties. I've found that a good place to buy real American-style BBQ sauce is at a kosher meat market, often located near an Orthodox Jewish temple. It's also a good place to get sour pickles (called *cucumbers in brine*).

Aussie mayonnaise is sweet and runny. For American-style, try one listed *with whole egg.*

There are two kinds of mustard: *hot English* and *mild American.* Watch out for the former; it'll clear your sinuses. The latter is what Americans are used to.

Marshmallows look the same, but Australian ones are sweeter, though my kids tell me that they taste the same after roasting over a fire.

Camping

Caravan parks are private campgrounds. Every town has one. You can park your *caravan* (travel trailer) or motorhome, sleep in your van, pitch your tent, or sleep on the ground. Most also have *chalets* (cabins) to rent and sell provisions in a small store, along with *pies, cool drinks,* and ice cream. There's often a pool and a central cooking or barbecue area. It's the cheapest way to stay in a place with creature comforts like *ablutions* (toilets and showers). These are found in the *ablution block.*

There are books in most states listing *Free Camping Spots.* When travelling, you can also stay next to highways at rest stops or turn-outs. Police policy is they'd rather have someone pull over and sleep in their car than drive tired and risk an accident [see section on **motorhomes** and **camp trailers**].

Public transportation

Capital cities have commuter train systems, buses, and taxis. Smaller cities have just buses and taxis. Melbourne has an extensive system of trams that run on surface streets like a bus system.

In taxis or shuttle vans, it's common for a passenger to sit in the front seat (egalitarianism). Even the prime minister sits in the front seat of his chauffeur-driven Holden Statesman.

Buses   There are inter-city bus systems. For interstate or long distance ground travel, check **www.busaustralia.com**. A tour bus is called a *coach*.

Trains   As for long distance train service: The *Ghan* is a two-day trip from Adelaide to Darwin through the "Red Centre," stopping in Alice Springs, where you can take a side trip to *Uluru* (Ayers Rock). The *Indian Pacific* runs from Sydney through Broken Hill and Adelaide, to Perth—a three-day journey—you can put your car aboard and have it with you at the other end. The *Overland* runs from Melbourne to Adelaide, the *Sunlander* runs from Brisbane to Cairns, the *Sprit of the Outback* runs from Brisbane through Rockhampton to Longreach, and the *Westlander* goes from Brisbane to Charleville. There are several other vintage and tourist trains throughout the country.

Flying   Australia is so large that flying is the most common long-distance transport. Qantas, Virgin Blue, and Jet Star are the major domestic carriers. There are regional carriers, like Skywest, Airnorth, and Qantas Link. International carriers are United, Singapore, JAL, Emirates, Air China, Thai, Air Canada, American (shared flights with Qantas), Garuda, EVA, Scandinavian, Delta, Gulf, Cathay Pacific, Alitalia, and Air New Zealand. Charter air services are available; check the Yellow Pages or tourist bureaus.

Air commuting is common, with regional airports handling flights to mines and remote towns. "Fly-in, fly-out" work schedules service distant mine sites. Miners fly out to the mine site for two-week shifts, then fly home for a week off. On Monday mornings, the domestic terminals are full of skilled laborers in work clothes carrying tool bags, flying out to *site*.

Driving

Driving on the left side of the road   Australians drive on the opposite side of the road from America and Continental Europe. Get it out of your head that it's the <u>wrong</u> side of the road, it's just the other side of the road. It was an arbitrary choice made over a hundred years ago by people long since dead, so deal with it.

Driving on the left isn't that big a problem once you get used to it. You just have to follow a few basic principles, the most important of which is *keep to the left*. Every time you get behind the wheel of a car in the first few months, repeat these words: *Keep To The Left*. Repeat it several times if you wish— and continuously, if necessary—while you drive.

Another way to remember it is like Bert Munro says in 'The World's Fastest Indian': "Keep the steering wheel side of the car toward the center of the road."

Favoring one side of the road over the other doesn't end when you get out of your car. Australians also walk on the left side of the *footpath* (sidewalk) and push their shopping *trolleys* (carts) on the left side of the supermarket aisles.

First steps   Your first attempt to drive will probably be in a *hire* (rental) car. Request one with an automatic transmission. Don't try shifting with your left hand the first time out.

If you do end up with a stick shift, the pattern is the same, <u>not</u> a mirror image. First gear is still in the upper left, second gear is below that, etc. The pattern will be on the shifter knob. The foot pedal arrangement is also the same, <u>not</u> a mirror image.

Once in the car, just sit for a few minutes and become acquainted with where things are located. You're now sitting in what should be the passenger side of the vehicle, but instead there's a steering wheel and a panel of instruments in front of you. Everything inside you says "this is wrong". If you have an American passenger, by now they'll be freaking out, because they're sitting on the side of a car that should have a steering wheel but doesn't, and they'll feel absolutely naked.

Note the speedometer—it goes up to 220! Relax; it's in kilometres per hour. Don't worry about kilometres, you won't have to convert them to miles, all the speed limit signs are also in kilometres per hour. Just keep the speedometer needle under the number that the signs indicate and you'll do fine.

Speed limits in Australia are generally lower than those in North America.

Normal posted speeds (approximate):

40 kph....25mph	80kph.....50mph
50kph.....30mph	90kph.....55mph
60kph.....35mph	100kph....60mph
70kph.....45mph	110kph....65mph

[More on speed limits later in this section.]

Meanwhile, back in the car...

Note the location of the *turn indicator* (turn signal). It's the stalk sticking out of the <u>right</u> side of the steering wheel. The one on the left is the *windscreen* (windshield) wipers. You can always tell the recently arrived North American or European driver when, as they start a turn at an intersection, the windscreen wipers suddenly turn on. They've instinctively flipped the left-hand stalk, which in North America would be the turn indicators, but in Australia are the wipers. To save face in this situation, pull back on the wiper stalk to activate the squirters, thereby fooling anyone watching into thinking you intended to wash the windscreen. Then you can quickly flip on the turn indicator (the right stalk) and continue your turn without anybody catching on. As you complete your turn, <u>check to see if you ended up on the left side of the road.</u> If not, take corrective action.

The secret to learning to drive on the left is to concentrate while remaining relaxed. Anticipate.

Take along a navigator   When you're starting out, it takes two Americans to drive in Australia: one steers the car, the other points out that they're on the wrong side of the road.

Get a good map   In most cities, there are books of maps, (UBD, StreetSmarts, etc.). The AAA has some reciprocal arrangements with the RAC (Royal Auto Club) in some states, both for maps and roadside services. *Hire cars* (rental cars) in major cities are available with GPS mapping for an extra fee.

Have your navigator study the maps as if negotiating

through a minefield. If you're alone, chart your trip ahead of time on a piece of paper, with the street names in large writing and the direction of each turn clearly marked. Allow extra time, because you <u>will</u> get lost. This is normal, so don't take it personally.

Australians are good about putting up street signs <u>before</u> intersections, but they're really bad at putting signs at cross-streets that are visible to those already driving on that street. This makes it hard to be sure that you ended up on the right road. The attitude seems to be: if you're already on the road, why do you need a sign? This is compounded by the fact that in some cities the street names change every few kilometres.

Pedestrians   Don't worry too much about pedestrians unless you are one; then worry.

Even though pedestrians legally have the right of way in most situations, <u>drivers will not slow down or stop for them unless they think they're about to hit them.</u> Australian pedestrians expect nothing different. They patiently stand on the *kerb* and wait until there are no cars or they dash madly across the street, dodging bumpers. If you're crossing a street on foot in an Australian city, don't assume that drivers will stop for you.

When crossing the street on foot, first look to the right. The first line of cars will be coming from the right—unless you're on a one-way street. At intersections without traffic lights, be extra careful, as many don't have stop signs. There might be no sign at all or a *Give Way* (yield) sign, and drivers will roll through, assuming no one will cross in front of them (the *she'll be right* attitude).

In some areas there are marked crosswalks: sometimes lines, sometimes a brick section across the roadway, sometimes a raised brick section; most will have a pedestrian crossing sign. Here pedestrians are grudgingly given the right of way. Pedestrians also have the legal right of way crossing at all intersections, whether or not there are marked cross walks, but this fact is ignored by most drivers, including the police. Jaywalking is common, because legal crossings can be far apart.

When you're driving and see pedestrians waiting to cross

the road, proceed carefully, but unless they're in a marked crosswalk or actually step out in front of you, don't disrupt the flow of traffic by stopping for them: it will only confuse them and further endanger them. If you stop your car to let a pedestrian cross the road, they'll usually just stand on the *kerb* and stare at you, expecting some kind of trick, because drivers being nice to pedestrians is outside of their experience. While you wait for them to cross, they'll refuse to move and traffic will back up behind you.

If you do stop and find yourself in this situation, take a moment to notice that—despite the line of cars building up behind you—nobody will honk their horn.

Horn honking and the "attitude of tolerance"
Australians have an attitude of tolerance, which probably comes from their inbred sense of individualism (aka: the *fair go*). That's why you rarely hear horns honking in Australian cities, they might as well not even put them on the cars. Why? It's not just auto-etiquette; it goes deeper than that. Honking your horn means that you're intruding into someone else's life; you're making an overt judgement about them and are trying to force your will upon them. This just isn't done. An Australian has to be really pissed off to honk his horn.

Australians will allow you the freedom to err to the point of failure. Perhaps it's because they're curious to see if you're acting on a good idea that hadn't occurred to them, but more likely it's because they feel it's none of their damn business if you want to screw up. It goes back their ethos of personal freedom, egalitarianism, Ned Kelly fighting the powers of authority, etc.

As a people, Australians are tolerant to a fault, and you can dress outlandishly and do the most outrageous things, and all anybody will do is nod and say, "*Roit*" (right). However, once you've failed or you're having trouble, they'll quickly volunteer to help you. On more than one occasion, I've gotten my Land Cruiser *bogged* (stuck) in the sand while launching a trailer-boat on a deserted beach, and total strangers have appeared from nowhere with 4WDs and pulled me out (thank you, whoever you were). Fact is, Aussies aren't indifferent; rather they're terrifically indulgent and they expect the same in return.

Road rage   The tolerant attitude has its limits. Every once in a while, you hear about some incident of road rage, where two motorists *lose the plot* (go crazy) and beat on each other. Road rage is a pitfall of all modern societies, and Australia is no different. If you feel yourself *losing the plot* or anger some guy who loses his plot, do yourself a favor; stay in the car.

Keep left!   All drivers are supposed to stay to the left in the slow lane on multi-lane *carriageways* (roadways) unless passing slower cars. If you're a foreign driver, you'll probably find yourself driving at the speed limit or slower. You'll be passed frequently, because some drivers seem to be hell-bent on speeding, despite high fuel costs and sneaky portable speed cameras. They'll probably pass closely, coming right up on your bumper, then whip around you and cut in front of you, as if teaching you a lesson for driving so slow. However, oddly enough, while the bastard is cutting you off, he'll courteously use his turn indicators.

Left turns   Woody Allen once observed that the one cultural advantage Los Angeles had over New York was that in California it was legal to make a right turn on a red light. That changed when New York modernized their driving laws, and Woody lost a good one-liner. When it comes to turns, Australians aren't so culturally advantaged. In Australia, the inside turn, kerb lane to kerb lane, is a <u>left</u> turn. It's <u>illegal to turn left on a red light in Australia.</u> Just wait, mate.

Give Way   Australian *Give Way* intersections are common. They work the same as a <u>Yield</u> sign in America. *Give Way* signs indicate an intersection where you <u>can</u> make a rolling left turn on a red light. Just look to the right, toward the direction of oncoming traffic, and proceed when safe.

Filter lanes   These are the transition lanes, entering or leaving a roadway.

Right turns   This is the equivalent of making a left turn in North America. Making a right turn in traffic, from one divided road to another, can be awkward and difficult at first, since your coordination and instincts say everything you're doing is wrong. Relax. As you wait to make your turn, keep looking at where you want to end up. It's like throwing a baseball, you just keep looking at the catcher's mitt. When the light turns green and it's safe to move, keep your eye on the target until you finish the turn. It gets easier with practice.

Australia has eliminated many right turns with *roundies* (round-a-bouts).

Round-a-bouts   The *rounda-a-bout*, or *roundie* is common in Australian cities, as it is in some cities on the east coast of the U.S. In Australia, one gives way to cars already in the intersection, which will be coming from your right. When it's clear, you enter the roundie turning to the left, clockwise. You merge into the roundie, and when you come to the street where you want to exit, turn on your left turn indicator and turn left onto that street. Anytime you exit a roundie you use your left turn signal to indicate your intention.

Beware of two-lane roundies, where you can enter on the inside lane, then have to merge to the outside lane to exit. It's really hard to change lanes in a roundie, especially if it's busy, so be in the left lane if possible, though sometimes you'll be forced to exit as that lane will be routed into a side street. If you miss your street, there's no harm in going completely around the roundie to get back to it. Your kids will love it.

Roundies are also great if you have to make a U-turn. You can use the next roundie to reverse direction and go back the way you came.

Because of roundies and *Give Way* intersections, you can drive across substantial parts of Australian cities without ever having to stop.

Hook turns   These are particular only to Melbourne, on streets where there are *trams* that run on tracks. The trams (streetcars) go down the center lanes in each direction. Waiting to make a right turn from this lane would block the trams. Instead, you pull into the far left lane and turn on your right turn indicator. Then, when the light turns red against you, you make the right turn across all the lanes of traffic. Watch out for trams; they're really big and heavy and they don't stop easily.

Backing up   You look over your left shoulder to back up. Even if you've managed to flop left and right sensibilities going forward, backing up into traffic is an entirely different challenge. If you don't take care and plan the move, chances are that you'll end up on the wrong side of the road. Beware in reverse; it's a whole new ball game. Take the time to plan out your move.

One-way streets   These can be another trap. When a North American has to turn right from a one-way street onto a two-way street, the normal instinct is to hug the *kerb*. This, of course, puts you on the wrong side of the road heading directly into oncoming traffic. Don't do this. This usually occurs after you've been driving on the left for about two weeks and have been lulled into a false sense of confidence. You weren't paying attention, your mind wandered, and you forgot to aim at where you wanted to end up.

What to do if you end up on the wrong side of the road   Now you're on the wrong side of the road, facing a lot of cars coming at you, you're sure everyone in the entire world is staring at you, and you think you're about to die.

Your navigator, who is supposed to be on your side, shouts in panic: "You're going the wrong way!"

This compounds things, since your one ally has now deserted you. About then, your body decides it's a "fight or flight" situation and dumps a load of adrenaline into your bloodstream. What do you do? Don't Panic. Stop immediately. Don't try to turn the car around, you'll get broad-sided.

I guarantee, the oncoming drivers will also stop. They don't want to get killed, either. Look behind you and carefully back out of the situation the way you came. Once you're out of the intersection, have a good laugh and continue. It goes without saying after that you'll pay more attention—for another two weeks until it happens again.

Driving in the bush   Another trap is when you're driving in the outback and haven't seen a car for hours. One suddenly appears over the horizon coming toward you, and you can't remember which side of the road you're supposed to be on. Just remember the mantra: "*keep left*".

A tip: If you're on a single-lane *sealed* (paved) road and another car is barrelling along at you in the center of the road and it doesn't seem like he's going to get over to let you by, Don't Panic. At the last moment, he's going to swing over to his left and put his outside two wheels in the dirt as he passes you, so be ready to do the same.

If you do venture into the *back of beyond* (middle of nowhere), be prepared. The Australian bush can be brutal on people and equipment. Don't wander off if you aren't truly prepared with maps, tools, food, and most important: lots of water. Tell someone where you're going and when you plan to return. 4WDs can get stuck, so it's best to go in a group of vehicles with at least one person who knows what he or she is doing. Training courses are available through 4WD shops.

Important Note: Dozens of tourists get lost every year in the bush (for some reason, most seem to be either German or Scandinavian). Most survive, but some do die. If you do get *bogged* (stuck) or break down or run out of fuel far from help: stay with your vehicle; don't walk off for help. They always find the vehicle first. Please believe me, **stay with the car.**

Road trains   These are really long trucks, sometimes triple trailer rigs more than thirty metres (100 feet) long. Be careful when passing them. It takes a long time to get around them and the *hire* car you're driving probably isn't the fastest thing you've ever been in.

If you're on a dirt road in the *back of beyond* and see a plume of red dust approaching and a big truck in front kicking it up, Don't Panic; just get off the road and roll up your windows until the dust storm passes. When you do this, be careful not to drive into soft dirt and get *bogged*.

Parking   Parallel parking on the left side of the street with a right-hand drive car takes a little getting used to. Practice on a quiet street.

Parking spaces are called *bays*. *No Standing* means no parking. Signs that say *1P* mean you can park for one hour, *2P* means two hours, *¼ P* means fifteen minutes. If it says *ticket required*, look for a ticket machine—usually a silver-colored box on a nearby pole—and purchase a ticket for the amount of time you require. Keep a handful of coins in the car for parking. Some machines take credit cards, but may default to the maximum charge. If in doubt, pay for more time than you need: five minutes late could mean a $50 fine, and just because you're driving a *hire* car doesn't mean the ticket won't get charged to you. The hire car company knows who had that car and they'll just put it on your credit card.

Remember to leave the ticket face up on your dash. Take your valuables with you; what you can't carry, lock in the *boot* (trunk).

On narrow streets, Australians will routinely park on the *verge* (the grassy lawn next to the road). It seems strange to park on someone's front yard, but you'll get used to it. Give the bloke a break, try to avoid the sprinkler heads.

Speed limits   The basic speed limit in *built-up areas* is 50 kph. If you're driving in a residential neighborhood or commercial district, that's the speed limit, unless otherwise posted. Speed limits are generally posted 50 kph (30 mph) in residential areas, 60 kph (35 mph) in business districts, 70–80 kph (40–50 mph) on parkways, 90–100 kph (55–60 mph) on highways and freeways. Outside of cities you'll see 110 kph (65 mph), and in the Northern Territory, as high as 130. The Northern Territory introduced speed limits for the first time in 2007.

School zones are 40 kph during school drop-off and pick-up hours, which are posted. Crossing guards wear long white smocks, white cricket hats, carry dual orange flags, and usually work in pairs. They look like refugees from a Monty Python movie. Be nice to them; they're volunteers.

Speeding tickets   With an attitude coming from the convict heritage, disregard for the law and those that try to enforce it is both tradition and sport. Police aren't supposed to pursue speeders at more than 20 kph over the speed limit for fear of goading them into a high speed chase, during which the poor speeder might get hurt (actually, it's supposed to protect innocent bystanders, but, unfortunately, it lets the bad guys get away). In order to compensate for this, portable speeding cameras, sometimes called *Multanovas*, are common. There are also fixed cameras at intersections to catch drivers running red lights. Police also use hand held radar and laser speed guns. Radar and laser detectors for your car are illegal in all Australian states except Western Australia.

Fines vary from state to state. In Western Australia, as long as you're less than 10 kilometres an hour (6 mph) over the speed limit, a photo-ticket will cost you $75. It's a major source of state income, hence the *truckie's* (trucker's) term: *flash-for-cash*.

The speed cameras can take pictures at a fast rate, so just because the car in front of you is speeding doesn't mean he'll get the ticket instead of you. If you're speeding behind him, you'll both get popped.

Since the speed cameras shoot a picture of the front of the car, they also get a photo of your face, so think twice about your excuses. Don't think you can get away with it just because you're driving a hire car and will be out of the country the next week. The rental company knows you had that car and they'll bill your credit card.

Speeding cameras have been known to make mistakes, but it's hard to prove. Inaccuracies can result from cars changing lanes toward the camera at the moment the photo was snapped, other vehicles speeding nearby, or the camera being miscalibrated. Some drivers have fought and won, but you have to take the time to go to court.

The only exception to speeding is for motorcycles. Motorcycles have no front license plate—by law, so they won't slice up pedestrians in a crash—and most motorcyclists wear full-coverage helmets which obscure their faces, so speeding cameras have no effect on them. However, time is running out, as there's a move to allow photographs from behind. The owner of the bike will then be responsible, because there will be no way to prove who was driving.

Demerit points   There is a *demerit points* system, which varies state by state. These are the demerit points for Western Australia.

If you're caught speeding by a policeman or a speeding camera while going less than 9 kph (about 6 mph) above the limit, you receive no *demerit point*s, but you'll be fined $75. Going 10–19 kph over the limit, you get two demerit points plus a $150 fine, and it goes up from there. Using a *mobile* (cellular) phone while driving is three demerit points plus a fine. Drivers not wearing seat belts, allowing someone under sixteen years of age to do so, or allowing someone to ride in the open back of a pickup (or *ute*) are four points each, plus a

$500 fine. Running a stop sign or a red light can mean three points. You can get one point for driving with any part of your body "protruding" from the vehicle. If you accumulate twelve points, your license will be suspended for three months. Points expire after three years.

On holiday weekends, *double demerit* points are issued. These periods can extend for several days after a holiday— Christmas/New Year's extends until the following weekend. It's possible to have an immaculate record and get one speeding ticket for going 40 kph (25 mph) over the limit on a holiday weekend and—with double demerits—receive enough points to have your license suspended for three months. If you're driving recklessly, they can impound your vehicle.

Of course, if you're a tourist, you won't have to worry about points, though if you're way over the limit and get pulled over by a cop, they might just take your license and car for a souvenir.

Police have laser and radar and will nail you before they see you. I've come over a hill going scarcely ten kph over the speed limit just to see a police car approaching the other way with its red lights already on, pulling me over—they had me before they saw me. Police will also set up hand-held police radar check points at known trouble spots.

Intersections where an abnormal amount of accidents have occurred are called *black spots*. Once designated, they're subject to special funding, used to fix the roadway, to improve the sight-lines, to install traffic lights and as an excuse for hand-held police radar checks.

L and P plates   In case you're wondering what the *L* and *P* placards on the front and back of some cars mean, the *L* is for *Learner Driver*, the *P* is for *Provisional* or *Probationary Driver* (depending on the state).

Minimum age to get a learner's permit in most states is 16 (16½ in Queensland). In some states, learners must drive a certain amount of hours with a tutor before taking the test, and if they pass and they're over the minimum age (varies with each state), they move up to a *P* plate.

Newly licensed drivers must display the *P* plate on their car for two years. Unfortunately, many *P* plate drivers tend to think the *P* stands for *Permitted to do Anything* or *Privileged Arsehole* (asshole). Usually, if you hear squealing tires or see someone *hooning* (driving unsafely, erratically, or too fast), they'll be sporting a *P* plate. Be wary of vehicles displaying *P* plates.

Hoons   A *hoon* is a hooligan,—usually a young male— who sees himself as being above or outside the law. He believes he has a right to get away with doing anything he wants to, as long as he doesn't get caught. *Hoons* seem to feel this behavior is perfectly justified. After all, Ned Kelly did it, and he died a hero. It's kind of a throw-back to Mad Max.

The authorities have given this activity the antiseptically clinical, politically correct name of *anti-social behaviour*. When they're on, *hoons* drive drunk and street race. They've elevated tire burn-outs to an art.

Hoons seem to have a uniform: wraparound sunglasses and a bad haircut, and drive a customized car with threatening stickers on the back window, wide tires, loud exhaust, and a mega stereo. Often they'll be sporting a *P* plate. Sometimes they're in stolen cars.

There are *anti-hoon* laws. Someone caught *hooning* (driving recklessly) will have his or her car impounded and be liable for fines and lots of demerit points. Hoons who have lost their licenses will often continue to drive—recklessly. You're always reading in the papers about some hoons getting in a nasty accident while *drink driving* (drunk driving) on a suspended license. This is an ongoing problem.

Peculiarities of Australian cars   Some of the safety features standard on American cars are absent on Australian cars. For example, in the U.S., the ignition key locks the steering wheel and transmission and won't let the driver remove the key without the transmission being in "Park". In some Australian cars, the steering wheel locks, but the transmission doesn't. Many Australian cars with automatics will allow you to turn off the engine and take the key out of the ignition with the car still in "Drive". With a Holden Commodore, if you accidentally do this and don't set the parking brake, it can roll away on you. Be careful.

In the U.S., a car with a manual transmission won't start

unless the clutch is depressed. With a few exceptions, this is not the case in Australia. <u>Beware,</u> if you hit the starter key with the manual transmission shifter in gear and the clutch pedal out, <u>the car will lurch and could hit someone in front of or behind you.</u>

Aussies also have a strange way of differentiating car models. Besides going by the year it was built, they also go by the model designation. When I needed parts for my Holden, it didn't do any good to tell the counterman it was a '99 Commodore with a 3.8 litre V6. I'd have to say it was a Commodore *VT*. Likewise, my '97 Nissan Patrol was a *GQ*. This is because models run for several years, and they change models in the middle of the year. Aussie motorheads seem to know all the model designations. If you work on your car, you might be asked for the model designation when you go for parts.

Maintenance-free batteries are not the rule, many batteries still require adding water. Watch them in hot weather.

Immobilizers   These are anti-theft devices, required on new cars and light trucks sold in all states, and on <u>any</u> car sold in Western Australia. This law was instituted to dissuade joyriding thefts which had become a wide-spread problem in the mid-eighties.

Immobilizers work by electronically disabling two electrical systems in the car: either starter, ignition, or fuel. This is supposed to make the car impossible to steal. On newer cars, the controls are built into the key, so you don't even know they're there. Older and aftermarket models may be on a separate keychain fob, which is used like an alarm-remote. Others use a sensor on the dash you pass the fob over.

Now casual thieves out for a joyride simply choose older cars that don't have immobilizers. Professional thieves who are after expensive newer cars to strip for parts or to export intact overseas simply drag them onto flatbed trucks and take them away, without having to start them or even break open a door.

Tourist drivers can use their driver's license from their home state or country while visiting Australia.

Migrant drivers can use their home license for up to a year (varies by state), but may have difficulty obtaining

Australian car insurance without an Australian license. All that's usually required to get a local license is to show your old license and take a written test, which is given in English. Study the book. Previously licensed drivers don't have to go through the *L* and *P* stages, or take the driving test.

Special licenses are required for buses, large trucks, and motorcycles [more on **motorcycles** below]. Your foreign motorcycle license will qualify you to take just the *theory* (written) test.

Larger vehicles may require special training. Five-ton trucks which I could legally drive in California with my standard license require special licensing in Australia.

Drink (drunk) driving   Don't have more than one drink an hour if you plan to drive. Better yet, use a designated driver or take a cab.

If you're driving a car and are stopped by a police officer, you'll be asked to blow into a breathalyser—also known as *blowing in the bag*. This is routine; everyone who is stopped *blows in the bag*. If you refuse, you can be arrested on the spot. The limit in most states is 0.05% BAC (blood alcohol concentration) for full-license drivers. It's less for *P* plate drivers.

 Police sometimes set up checkpoints using a *booze bus* (large police van set up as a combination blood lab and holding cell) on busy streets during shopping nights, weekend nights, and around the holidays. They block off a lane and route all cars through a line of officers who administer breath tests. They're usually set up around a blind turn with no way to turn-off to avoid it (police cars are waiting to chase those who try). You have no choice but to *queue* (line up) and take your turn to blow in the bag (they let your keep the straw as a souvenir). If you're under the limit, you drive off. If not, they pull you aside and start the process, which involves a second breath test a few minutes later, a possible blood test, and if you fail those, you'll be arrested on the spot and put in the *booze bus* with the other unfortunates to await transportation to jail.

Car insurance   For tourists, chances are your credit card will cover your rental car. Be sure to check coverage and use the credit card that has the best policy. Travel insurance will cover the *excess* (deductible). If you rent a 4WD, the excess can be surprisingly high.

As for people who are staying longer and are purchasing or leasing a car, you get to buy insurance. *CTP* is *Compulsory Third Party* insurance, which is required by law and covers the other guy if you're at fault. In Western Australia, it's issued as part of your registration. In other states, it's sold separately. This doesn't cover collision, theft, etc. That's sold through independent insurance companies.

All totalled, with the difference in the dollar factored in, car insurance costs about the same as most places in the U.S.

Bicycles are also called *pushbikes*, or simply, *pushies*. All bicycle riders of all ages in all states must wear approved bicycle helmets. In reality, compliance isn't very high, less than 50 percent. This law doesn't apply to riders of three or four-wheel pedal cycles.

An important difference: the front and rear brake levers are switched. In the U.S., the rear brake is actuated with the right hand lever, while in Australia, that lever works the front brake. This might seem minor to the casual rider, but for someone who rides a lot, whether they're road-riders or mountain bikers, this could be hazardous in an instinctual move. If you grabbed what you thought was the rear brake and instead locked the front wheel, you'd be launched over the handle bars and there goes your collarbone—or your skull if you're not wearing a helmet.

Signals Australians are very good about using their turn indicator lights. In fact, Australians will conscientiously use their indicators as they blatantly violate other driving laws.

Hand signals Few people use hand signals anymore, in America or Australia, just drivers of older cars, older motorcycles, and bicyclists.

Since the driver is on the right side of the vehicle, the signal will be made with the right hand. The hand signals are exactly opposite of those used in North America. A straight right arm means a right turn, a bent-up arm means a left turn. Motorcycle and bicycle riders may also signal a left turn by pointing straight out with their left hand.

Motorcyclists riding vintage bikes with no turn indicators

must use hand signals. But since the signalling (right) hand is also the throttle hand, when you take your hand off the throttle to signal, the bike will immediately slow down, putting you at risk of getting hit from behind. You can signal a left turn by pointing straight out with your left hand, but the laws are vague on right turns. Use your turn indicators if you've got them.

Motorcycles are very popular in Australia, just as in the U.S. and Canada. It's great riding country, with good weather and tens of thousands of kilometres of open road—not to mention beating expensive petrol prices, ease of parking and the ability to cut through traffic.

Bikes sold are Aprillia, BMW, Ducati, Harley, Honda, Hyosung, Kawasaki, KTM, Moto-Guzzi, Pagsta, Suzuki, Triumph, Yamaha; plus scooters like Vespa's, and lots of cheap Chinese copies of Hondas and Yamahas..

Learning to ride a motorcycle is a formal affair. One usually takes a course with an instructor or with someone who has been licensed for several years (varies by state). The newly licensed rider is limited to a bike with a 250cc engine or smaller the first year, then with further lessons can move up to bigger bikes.

Your foreign motorcycle license will work without restriction if you're a tourist. If you're from the U.S. or Canada and are staying long enough to need an Australian license, they'll generally let you bring your current rating with you, so all you need to do is pass the *theory* (written) test.

Harleys are as prolific in Australia as in the U.S.. In fact, per capita there are more Harleys in Australia than anywhere in the world. Most are owned by nice people who like loud sounds, lots of vibration, and want to be noticed. Some are owned by *bikies*. Bad-guy bikers are called *bikies* and have a nasty reputation. Several bikie gangs are as notorious as their American counterparts. Don't mess with them.

Dual sport bikes are popular, used both off-road and as commuters in urban areas. Farmers and *graziers* (sheep and cattle ranchers) use four-wheel ATVs for farm work. There are special agricultural two-wheel dirt bikes with low seats and large fuel tanks for working livestock. My Yamaha AG200 is a prime example. It has lots of suspension, but I can still easily put both feet on the ground. It's built for fat-footed farmers in big boots, so neutral is all the way at the bottom—which makes it hard to bail into first gear to get out of a tough situation—but you get used to it. It has crash bars around both the engine and handlebars, so the farmer can literally drop the bike if he has to get off in a hurry, like when trying to catch a sheep or slipping and falling in fresh cow-flop. It also has a squarish tank so you can lay a lamb across it. It runs all day on a few litres of petrol, needs no battery, and in the rough, pulls like a fourteen-year-old. It's the best (and ugliest) trail bike I've ever owned.

Crotch-rockets like Ducatis, Ninjas, and Hurricanes are common, and are commonly used to break speed laws. They get away with it because—currently—speed cameras only shoot a photo from in front and there's no front license plate on a motorcycle, so they can't be caught. Motorcyclists have bragged to me how they've cut across several lanes on the freeway just to get in front of the speed cameras to flip them off as they flash. These aren't just *bikies*, but seemingly normal young men with mischievous grins on their faces. With the new rear-shooting cameras, that era will be coming to a close.

The Australian mail moves by motorcycle. *Posties* (mailmen and women) deliver to city and suburban homes on little Honda trail bikes. They drive on *footpaths* (sidewalks) and dart in and out of traffic. They seem to be above the law. [more in the section on **postal matters**].

A recent trend is *Chondas*: counterfeit Honda and Yamaha enduros made in China. These bikes are such close copies that some parts are interchangeable with the originals. They're sold for half the price of the Japanese originals—often through tool shops instead of bike shops—so many never get licensed. The hoon element has moved in, riding them illegally on footpaths, walking tracks, and bridle trails, which is giving police, park rangers, property-owners, and the public a major headache.

On your return to the U.S.   When you return home, your automobile driving sensibilities may be confused for a short time. Don't be surprised when you find yourself signalling turns with the windshield wipers.

Fuel

Petrol stations work the same as gas stations in North America. They're mostly self-service, though in some rural areas people will actually come out and fill your car for you. The gas pumps, called *bowsers*, work the same, though they measure in *litres* (approx. four litres to a gallon). There are no pay-at-the-pump systems: you have to go inside and *queue* (line up). Most petrol stations have convenience stores and snack bars, so once inside, you can buy a *pie* (hand-sized meat pie) and a *cuppa* (cup of tea or coffee), and do some light shopping before you pay for your fuel.

A feature that's come around in last few years is the supermarket discount *docket* (voucher). When you spend $30 or more at one of the major supermarket chains, you get a *docket* for a four-cent discount per litre at certain allied petrol stations. That's sixteen cents a gallon, and on a larger vehicle can add up enough to pay for your *pie* and *cuppa*.

Note: After you've paid your bill and go back to your car, you'll probably get in the wrong side of the vehicle. This is normal. You'll sit there feeling foolish with your key in your hand and no place to put it. To save face, open the glove box and pretend to rummage around in it for a moment, then get out and go around to the driver's side, as if you meant to do that in the first place.

Gasoline is called *petrol*, and it's purchased by the *litre* (which is about one quart, so there's about four litres to a gallon) and costs about 50 percent more than what you'd pay in the U.S. The octane is higher: regular unleaded is 91, super is 98.

Gas or Autogas   In Australia, if you ask for *gas*, you'll get Autogas or propane, also known as LPG (liquid petroleum gas), the same stuff used in a barbecue. Many cars have been converted to run on *gas*, which costs about half as much as petrol. Gas doesn't contain as much energy as petrol, so it takes about 1½ litres of gas to go as far as one litre of petrol. It's still a significant savings, plus it emits 10–15 percent less greenhouse gases and 20 percent less ozone-forming chemicals. Many conversions are *dual-fuel,* they'll also run on petrol. Conversion installations are eligible for government subsidies, and that, along with the savings in fuel costs over a few years, will pay for the conversion. One drawback is that Autogas isn't generally available outside of urban areas. That's why dual-fuel is the way to go instead of LPG-only. Another drawback is that the LPG tank takes up most of the *boot* (trunk).

Holden makes a dual-fuel version of the Commodore. Ford makes an LPG-only Falcon that's the favourite of taxi companies, due to its cheap operating costs. A bonus: the engine will last a lot longer, since gas burns cleaner. It doesn't fill the crankcase with harsh, acidic vapors that eventually eat up bearings.

Some large truck fleets are converting their diesels over to *LNG*, Liquid Natural Gas.

Diesel is widely used, and many 4WDs and utes run on it. You get better fuel economy with diesel, since there's more energy in it. In the bush and on farms, diesel is more commonly used than petrol. On total fire-ban days during the hot summer, only diesel vehicles are allowed off-road on farms, since they run less risk of starting grass fires

There are disadvantages. Diesels put out particulate pollution, though this has been greatly reduced with better injector technology. Diesels are more expensive to buy, since the engines are built to withstand higher compression. Diesel fuel costs about 10 percent more—it's mostly tax, since diesel is cheaper to refine than petrol—and the vehicles are louder and have slower acceleration. The latter has been solved with turbocharging.

Turbo diesels, especially intercooled versions, are quite peppy. A three-litre turbocharged diesel engine behaves like a normally aspirated four-litre, but with better fuel economy. Turbos work by routing the exhaust gases though a sealed chamber with a turbine fan inside. The pressure of the exhaust spins the fan up to 50,000 rpm. The fan is on a shaft, and on the other end of the shaft, in a separate chamber, is another fan spinning at the same speed, forcing fresh air into the engine intake. This allows more fuel to be burned more efficiently and boosts performance by about 30 percent.

As you can imagine, this produces a lot of heat, and diesels don't like to breathe hot air, so the *intercooler* was invented, which cools the air entering the engine, giving it even more power.

There are a few disadvantages. Most noticeably, the engine is weak if run below 2,000 rpm, the point where the turbo boost kicks in. Also, there's a noticeable lag after you put your foot down while the turbo spins up to boost-pressure. The other disadvantage is that turbos get so hot that if you turn the engine off after a long run, the excess heat can boil the oil and will eventually burn the chamber seals, which are expensive to replace.

To reduce heat, the engine should be idled for 5–10 minutes until the turbo is cooled. This can be a pain if you're late or if you've been driving for a while and have to go to the *loo*. A *turbo-timer* can be installed that will do this automatically, shutting down the engine after a specified time. So if you see someone park their diesel 4WD and walk away without turning off the engine, that's what's happening.

Biodiesel blends are becoming available; check with your vehicle manufacturer's recommendations. As of early 2007, Toyota recommended only a five percent blend (called *B5*) with standard mineral diesel. Some service stations, like Gull in Western Australia, are offering *B20* (twenty percent mix). I've used it in my diesel Toyota Land Cruiser with no problems.

Biodiesel is usually a blend of soybean oils put through a process called transesterification. Homemade fuels from recycled cooking oils can also be made using the same process. The result is a much cleaner fuel that pollutes a lot less, but produces slightly less power. Older engines should have the rubber fuel lines replaced, but vehicles built since the mid-1990s should be OK.

The major downside to running *B100* (100 percent biodiesel fuel) is that it's so clean it scours the impurities left by mineral diesel fuels in the tank and fuel lines, resulting clogged fuel filters. It isn't harmful to the engine; it'll just stop running until the filters are replaced. This means that going back and forth between pure biodiesel and mineral diesel is impractical at this time.

Fuel economy isn't measured in miles-per-gallon or in kilometres-per-litre, but in *litres-per-hundred-kilometres*. Ten litres-per-hundred-kilometres is about twenty-four mpg.

Australian cars

Common Car Terms

Aussie	American
All the fruit	All the extras
Autogas	LPG for cars
Blowing the straw	Breathalyzer test
Bonnet	Hood
Boot	Trunk
Bowser	Gas pump (at a service station)
CTP	Compulsory third party insurance
Footpath	Sidewalk
Gas	Propane
Give Way (sign)	Yield
Hire car	Rental car
Immobiliser	Automatic security system that makes vehicle inoperable
Laneway	Alley
Litre	Measure of liquid, about one quart (four per gallon)
LPG	Liquid petroleum gas, propane, Autogas
L plate	Displayed on learning driver's car
Multanova	Portable speeding camera
No Standing (sign)	No Parking
Peak hour	Rush hour
Petrol	Gasoline
P plate	Probationary driver, displayed for first two years licensed
Roundabout (roundie)	Circular intersection, traffic flows around it clockwise
Servo	Service station
Skimmed	refers to turning the brake rotors
Windscreen	Windshield
Witch's hat	Orange safety cone (because of shape).

Cars overview   Roads are smaller and things are more expensive than in North America. That's why Australian cars tend to be about 2/3 the size of American cars. You won't see Crown Victorias, Ford Excursions, or Dodge King Cab dually pickups. The largest passenger vehicle sold is a Toyota Land Cruiser, which is about 2/3 the size of a Chevy Suburban. Suburbans, powered by diesel V8s, were briefly imported as Holdens in the mid-nineties, but were too big to be practical and were discontinued. Ford sells dual cab F250 pickups— good luck trying to park one in the city. Besides size, fuel cost is a key factor, with prices 50 percent higher than in North America.

Australia has its own car industry, which is amazing for a country of only 21 million people. Three automobile companies build cars in the country: General Motors Holden, Ford of Australia, and Mitsubishi. Holden and Ford have lines of uniquely Australian cars, designed, engineered, and built in the country, plus lines of foreign-produced cars re-badged under the Ford and Holden names for Australia. Mitsubishi makes one model in Australia and imports the rest. Most police cars are Holdens, while most taxis are Fords.

Holden is owned by General Motors, which started exporting engines and chassis to Australia in 1919, contracting with Holden Motor Body Builders to make bodies and to assemble them into finished cars. In 1931, GM bought the company and formed General Motors-Holden LTD. After WWII, Holden began designing and building cars specifically for Australia, starting with the FX model in 1948.

The large, four-door Holden Commodore is the equivalent of an Aussie Chevy, though built tougher for Australian conditions. It's the quintessential full-sized Australian car: rear-wheel drive, powerful, durable, and comfortable. Holden also imports smaller GM cars, Suzukis, and Isuzu light trucks and 4WDs, all re-badged under the Holden name.

While almost all American cars have gone over to being front-wheel drive, the full-sized Holdens and Fords have remained rear-wheel drive, partly because they're often used to pull trailers, but mostly because Australians like them that way.

The full-sized four-door Holden Commodore is soon to be imported into the U.S. as the Pontiac G8.

In 2004, when General Motors decided to revive the famously rear-drive Pontiac GTO for the American market, they realized they didn't have a rear-drive platform in the U.S. Instead of designing a new one, they imported the Holden Monaro, an iconic Aussie two-door, V8 super-car. They redid the trim, swapped the steering wheel to the other side, and called it the "New GTO".

Australian car exports aren't new. Holden yearly exports up to 30,000 of the full-size Commodore four-door sedans to countries in the Middle East, South Africa, Asia, and Brazil. They're a good choice in the third world. Besides being stylish and modern, the cars are tough. Holden has also been exporting hundreds of thousands of engines each year for GM factories worldwide. The 3.8 litre V6 in my '99 Holden Commodore VT was identical to the one in my dad's '92 Buick Le Sabre. The Commodore was the better car: better handling, speed, fuel economy, durability, simplicity, and roominess. Holden also makes luxury versions called the Statesman and Caprice. The prime minister rides in one, sitting in the front seat, of course (Aussie egalitarianism).

One downside of the Holden Commodore's power and rear-drive is the fact that it has become the choice of drivers who do *burnouts*. A burnout is where the driver intentionally spins his rear tires to produce as much noise, smoke, and skid-marks as possible. Burnout drivers, (also known as *hoons*), can all but write their names in skid-marks. The Australian state governments have tried unsuccessfully to stop these hoons. Perhaps the easiest way would be to retroactively ban all Holden Commodores.

Ford of Australia was founded in 1926 as a subsidiary of Ford Canada. Australia is where old American Ford names go into exile. The Falcon, Fairmont, and Futura continue on Down Under. The Fairlane—the big, top-of-the-line Ford—is to be retired in 2008, due to lack of sales. The Maverick name lived as a re-badged Nissan Patrol 4WD until it was replaced by the Ford Explorer in 1997.

The Falcon is the star of Ford's lineup, having won "Australian Car of the Year" several times in a row. It was originally a beefed-up version of the same 1960 Falcon that was America's first economy car, and many of those old 60s Falcons are still plying Australian roads. The Falcon has been entirely Australian-designed and built since the early 1970s and is a heavy hitter, available with a V6 or high performance V8. Mad Max's car was a '73 XB Falcon GT Pursuit Special, the last of the big V8 Interceptors. Smaller Ford cars and trucks are actually re-badged Mazdas and European econo-boxes. Ford also sells an Aussie version of the Explorer, called the *Territory*, built in their Melbourne plant.

The biggest and most powerful pickup trucks available in Australia are the Ford F250 and F350. They're identical to the U.S. models, but built in Brazil, and are powered by a 5.4 litre petrol or 7.3 litre turbo-diesel engine. They're the only choice for pulling very large loads and for use as tow trucks. They dwarf all other cars and light trucks on the road.

Mitsubishi is the only other manufacturer building cars in-country, at two assembly plants in South Australia. The flagship of the line is the 380 VRX, an Aussie version of the Galant, which is built for the North American market. With higher build quality, a more powerful engine, and a heavier suspension than its American counterpart, it's designed to go head-to-head with the Holden Commodore and the Ford Falcon. Mitsubishi has a complete product line that includes tiny econo-boxes, mid-sized sedans, light trucks, and heavy haulers.

Chrysler once had a large presence in Australia. It started importing complete cars from the U.S. in 1935. In 1951, they started building bodies in Adelaide for imported American chassis and drive trains. The cars were based on the American Plymouths, but with Australian restyling. The Chrysler Royal, Plainsman, and Wayfarer were the main models and looked similar to their American fin-mobile cousins. By the 1960s, models were available with V8s and Torqueflight transmissions. Aussie drivers like performance, and they got it with Chrysler.

The same Plymouth Valiant that was sold in North America

was called simply the Valiant in Australia. It was a redesigned Aussie version, since the slant-six engine created problems in converting to right-hand drive. It debuted in 1962 and proved a lot faster than the Holdens, and became an Aussie icon. The Valiant followed American styling and was built into the late '70s. From '71 through '73, they built the Charger, which was a short-wheelbase Valiant V8 muscle car that looked similar to the American Dodge Barracuda. Many 1960s Valiants—wings and all—are still on the road today.

Big Chrysler sedans from the '60s are still around, though they look strange with the steering wheel on the right. Dodge pickups and utes are objects for restorers, and rusted old Dodge trucks can still be seen plodding farm fields and country roads.

Chrysler Australia stopped production in 1981 because they couldn't compete with Japanese imports. They sold the Adelaide plant to Mitsubishi.

Daimler (Mercedes) bought Chrysler in 1998 and ran it as Daimler-Chrysler. They were already importing Mercedes, so they brought in Dodge, Chrysler, and Jeep. The Mercedes line—cars, trucks and buses—were marketed separately.

In Australia—as of 2007—Chrysler was selling the 300c, Crossfire sports coupe, Voyager minivan, Calibre, and PT Cruiser. Jeep is a big seller, including the Cherokee (same as the Liberty in the U.S.), the Grand Cherokee, the Commander, and the Wrangler. In May of 2007, Daimler sold Chrysler to Cerberus, a private equity company. What effect this will have on imports to Australia remains to be seen.

Misc. Aussie auto manufacturers   In the past, several other car manufacturers assembled vehicles Down Under, including VW, Renault, and British Leyland, but all have since ceased.

Imports include BMW, Citroen, Chrysler, Daewoo, Daihatsu, Honda, Hyundai, Jeep, Kia, Land Rover, Lexus, Mazda, Mercedes, Nissan, Proton, Renault, SsangYong, Subaru, Suzuki, Toyota, Volvo, VW, and a few special makes like Ferrari, Porsche, Alfa, Rolls, and MG.

Many imported models are the same as those sold in the U.S., but with different names. The Mitsubishi Montero is called a Pajero (pronounced *Pah-Ger-O*), the Isuzu Trooper is a Holden Jackaroo and the Isuzu pickup is a Holden Rodeo. All three of the above are available with petrol, diesel, or intercooled turbo-diesel engines. Infiniti doesn't exist as a brand, nor does Acura, but the latter are marketed as high-end Hondas. The Mazda Miata is called an MX-5 and isn't marketed as a mild-mannered girl's cruiser like in the U.S., but as a semi-aggressive, British-styled sports car, with a price tag to match.

Nissan and Toyota of Australia have almost entirely different product lines from what they market in America, with the exception of the Toyota Camry and Celica (Australian pronounciation: *sell-eeka*) and the Nissan Maxima. There are many third world models, notably the large Toyota Troop Carrier (also known as the *Troopy*) and the potent Nissan Patrol (arguably the best production 4WD in the world). There are four-door utes (pickup truck chassis with flatbed trays) and large diesel utility vans. The SsangYong Rexton is a Korean-built full-sized luxury 4WD powered by a cloned Mercedes engine. Proton is a Malaysian manufacturer that has development deals with VW and Mitsubishi and sells a full line of cars. There are also lots of small Asian and European cars too tiny to market in the U.S.

Utes   The *ute* (utility vehicle) is a generic name for pickup trucks, but more specifically, ones that have had the bed replaced by a flatbed aluminum tray with short fold-down sides. You can carry a lot more with this configuration.

A popular car-style that has vanished in America but is still being built in Australia is the sedan-based pickup, like the old Chevy El Camino and the Ford Ranchero. Aussies still make them, based on full-sized Holden Commodores and Ford Falcons. They are V-6 and V-8 powered, rear-wheel drive, available in two- and four-door models with beefed-up chassis. Many are set up as work trucks, others as sports-trucks and family cars. Some have pickup beds, some have flat trays.

4WDs   There are many four-wheel-drive vehicles sold in Australia, but when it comes to serious outback performance, there are only a few worth mentioning, and all are diesels: the Toyota Land Cruiser and the Nissan Patrol, with the Land Rover a distant third. Anything else is just a *soft-roader*.

Americans don't appreciate how tough outback conditions can get. The normal American SUV wouldn't make it through the first day on some of the more serious routes. On trips like the three-week Canning Stock Route, travellers routinely get several flat tires per day and have to pull the tires off the rims to fix them each night (that's why they use tall skinny tires on split-rims). Snorkels on the trucks aren't just for going into deep water, they're to scoop cooler, less-dusty air from high above the road surface. Bush-welding is an art: hooking several car batteries in series to stick your vehicle back together. You have to carry all your water, food, and fuel. Serious off-road explorers have *air-lockers* that lock the transfer case and both differentials for unbelievable traction.

Australia is serious 4WD country—and not just for recreational explorers—miners, *pastoralists* (cattle and sheep ranchers), and anybody who has to "go bush" knows it's serious business.

Even in normal highway driving in the outback, you can hit a kangaroo. That's why many cars and trucks have the beefy bar-work around the front end, called *'roo bars*. Heavier duty versions are called *bull bars*. In the bush, you see dead kangaroos laying alongside the road every few kilometres. They seem to come out at dawn and dusk and make suicide runs in front of headlights. If your kids ask you why they're lying there, tell them they're resting.

Towing and trailers   *Box trailers* are the true workhorses of the Australian fleet; it seems like everybody has one. They are usually an inexpensive six-foot by four-foot trailer that instantly turns the family car into an *ute* for hauling furniture, dirt bikes, livestock, firewood, mulch, or taking a load to the *tip* (dump). It's the perfect complement to the DIY (do it yourself) attitude.

Many tradesmen, like *chippies* (carpenters) and *sparkies* (electricians), use enclosed versions of the box trailer to carry their tools and supplies, towing them with the family car instead of buying and maintaining an expensive dedicated work truck. When they're not working, they unhitch the trailer and it's back to being a family car.

It's funny seeing the vehicles people tow with, which is

anything with a motor and a tow-ball. Small pickup trucks tow large boats, family cars tow horse trailers. You see box trailers loaded with yard trimmings headed for the *tip* behind tiny Daewoos, Hondas, and Suzukis, and even fancy cars like BMWs, Jags and Audis.

Motorhomes aren't as common as in North America. Instead, people are more prone to buy a *caravan* (house trailer) and tow it with the family car. This is very popular with the retired.

There are small (by American standards) diesel-powered cab-chassis motorhomes by Maui and Winnebago, but these are mostly *holiday hires* (vacation rentals). Other holiday hires are self-contained campers built into small vans or pop-top Toyota Land Cruiser Troop Carriers. These *Troopy* Campers are great for travel into the bush. Once the odometers on these hire campers hit 100,000 kms. (60,000 mi.), they're sold from the fleet and locals snap them up. Locals also convert small buses, like the Toyota Coaster, into motorhomes.

A budget tourist's alternative to the motorhome is the "Wicked" vans (**www.wickedcampers.com.au**) that seem to appear every summer. These are funky second-hand vans with outlandish hand-painted decorations, designed for the backpacker traveller. They're cheap, they carry a lot of people, and you can sleep in them. They can be hired in one city and dropped off in another.

Camp trailers are heavy-duty off-roaders, towed by a 4WD. Some have built-in tents and can carry an aluminum boat on top. Lighter versions are designed to be towed by a small family car. People tent-camp in Australia, in fact, in a typical *caravan park* (campground), tents will out number motorhomes and *caravans* four to one.

Hitches   Standard tow-balls are 50mm, which is one mm smaller than the standard two-inch American ball—enough to prevent an American ball from going into a standard Australian trailer hitch. There's a smaller 47mm size (not very common) that's slightly smaller than the standard American 1 7/8-inch ball.

Receiver hitches work the same as in the U.S., and an American two-inch bar will generally go into an Australian receiver, but the male part may need the corners ground, since the females are 50mm, about one mm too small.

Why bother to bring your American stuff (like I did)? Why not? If you're migrating and planning on towing boats or *caravans* (travel trailers), and are shipping down a sea-container full of stuff, it's not a bad idea to bring your hitches. The limiting factor in a container isn't weight, but bulk [see section on **shipping your household goods to Australia**]. It'll save you some money, since parts are expensive Down Under.

If you plan on towing a car behind a motorhome, the towbar that is mounted on the car is called a *towing A-frame*.

Grey market refers to a vehicle not originally marketed in the country but imported as new or nearly new [more on **importing cars** in the next section].

Many almost new cars are cheaply available for grey market export from Japan. This is because the Japanese have strict emissions laws, rigorous yearly road test requirements, high depreciation, and strict environmental laws that make it expensive to dispose of cars that are just a few years old. Also, Japan is a right-hand-drive country, so little conversion work is required, and there are regular deliveries of new cars from Japan on roll-on-roll-off ships, so transporting a grey market car is cheap and easy (around A$1000) compared to A$3000 for shipping a car in a container from North America.

The Toyota Prius and some Lexus hybrids are being marketed on a limited basis. Prior to that, they were imported grey market from Japan. One grey market favorite is the Mitsubishi Delica, a sleek 4WD turbo-diesel van built on the heavy-duty Pajero 4WD chassis.

Importing a car from America

There are many advantages and disadvantages in importing a car from America. It can be expensive and a lot of trouble, so there should be a good reason to do it: a unique vehicle, one with sentimental value, a collector car with potential for lucrative resale, etc.

Right-hand drive conversions   Cars have to be converted to right-hand drive, except in Western Australia, where pre-1989 cars don't have to be changed over. Later models can be seen driving around unconverted, but these are using paperwork as a delaying tactic; eventually, they'll have to be changed over. A proper conversion by an accredited engineering firm, complete with an *Australian Compliance Plate*, can cost $30,000. If you're looking to buy an American car already in Australia, beware of older conversions: some merely had the controls run to the opposite side of the car with chains and levers, and could be unsafe. A good conversion sees the entire front end of the vehicle remanufactured, from the dash forward.

Some American cars were converted at the time of sale, as Pontiac, Dodge, Studebaker, and a few others exported cars to Australia in the past. Ford sells trucks in Australia very similar to American models. Jeeps and some Chryslers are currently imported new [see **cars overview** section above].

Legal requirements   Not long ago, it was possible to make a living importing American cars, like Corvettes, Camaros, Cadillacs, and Mustangs. One bought them cheap on the West Coast of the U.S., shipped them across the Pacific four-up in a container, did a few modifications on arrival, and put them up for sale with a big price tag. Now websites like eBay have driven the prices up for classic cars, and individuals can find and import their own cars and cut out the middle man.

Shops are available that do conversions. Before going with one, make sure they can issue an *Australian Compliance Plate*.

Importation is most commonly done by container through various shipping agents along the U.S. West Coast. A shelf system is built inside a sea-container and four passenger cars can be squeezed in, costing about A$3000 per car (in 2007). These shippers can be found through the Yellow Pages in Long Beach, California, and Seattle, Washington. Be careful with the shipper, as it's easy for a car to be damaged in the container.

Then comes the Australian government paperwork.

Before deciding to import, take the time to research the costs and legal requirements. Australian Customs, DOTARS (Department of Transportation) and individual states each have different laws that must all be met. Just getting a vehicle to the country doesn't mean it will be allowed in, and just getting it into the country doesn't mean you'll be allowed to put it on the road. This also applies for trucks, motorcycles, and trailers.

Travel trailers and boat trailers can have additional problems. U.S. maximum width for trailers is 8-foot 6-inches, while the Australian maximum is 8-foot 2½-inches (2.5 metres). If it's wider than 2.5 metres, you'll need a wide load permit to tow it, and will have to display *Wide Load* signs front and rear. The wider you go, the more restrictions there are, like not being allowed on highways at certain times such as *peak hour* (rush hour), at night, or on freeways at all. Do your homework.

Visitors may be able to temporarily import a vehicle for a period of one year, so you can bring a camper or motorcycle into the country to tour with. It'll be on a carnet and will have to be out of the country by a certain date. Check with DOTARS.

Adult migrants to Australia can each bring in one vehicle, be it a car, truck, motorcycle, etc., but it has to have been registered in that person's name for twelve months. If you want to bring in two vehicles, register the other one in your spouse's name and allow a year to qualify.

Note: Even though migrants won't be charged Customs Duty, they'll be charged some additional fees and 10 percent GST (Goods and Services and Services Tax) on the value of the vehicle, including all shipping costs and transport insurance.

If you're migrating to Australia and plan to ship your household goods in a sea-container, you can also put your car or motorcycle in the same container. The vehicle will still need its own paperwork and will be treated at the Australian end as a separate importation from the rest of your goods.

To import a vehicle outside of migration, you have to be a citizen or permanent resident and you have to pay full fees and duties to DOTARS, Customs, and GST.

Importing a vehicle temporarily for racing or rallying purposes requires proper racing licences and homologation with the FIA (Federation Internationale de l'Automobile). The vehicles can only be used for practice and competition.

All of this information is available on the web, at **www.dotars.gov.au,   www.customs.gov.au,   www.rvcs-**

prodweb.dot.gov.au/cert.html, and individual state licensing boards, according to where your imported vehicle will be licensed.

If you still want to import that vehicle, here's what you do.

First contact DOTARS and go through their process, which can take a month, but can be expedited to a few weeks if you're determined or up against a shipping deadline. If you don't have your DOTARS Import Approval, no legitimate shipper will touch the vehicle ("she'll be right" doesn't work in the U.S.) Shipping by sea-container will take five to six weeks. Shipping by airplane takes three to five days, but it's very expensive and there are lots of technicalities—like draining all fuel and scouring the tank with alcohol and dry-ice before it will pass hazardous materials certification. Shipping by airplane is usually only done for race cars or motorcycles.

Once the vehicle has arrived in Australia, it will have to go though Customs. Customs doesn't have anything to do with DOTARS, so have duplicate documentation on hand of everything you sent DOTARS. Once Customs approves the vehicle and collects their fees, you can take it home on a trailer.

Next you get to take it *over the pits*: an inspection at a state government licensing centre. This is to make sure the vehicle complies with the *ADRs* (*Australian Design Rules*). Besides converting to right-hand drive (*RHD*), you may have to change the color of the plastic covers on the lights, change the speedometer to kilometres, and install new *tyres* (tires). Some brake lines may need to be replaced. Cars built before January 1, 1989 can be exempt. Even if it's an older vehicle, state inspectors will pick and probe, and if it's not too bad, will eventually pass it. Then you get to pay for registration, and it's yours to drive. After all that, the darn thing had better be worth it.

The metric system

It should be of no surprise that Australia is on the metric system; the entire world is, with the exception of the U.S., Liberia and Burma. Australia started converting in 1966.

The metric system is more logical than the U.S. system of feet, pounds, and gallons. Think about twelve inches to the foot, three feet to the yard, 5,280 feet to the mile—and that's just distance.

What's the difference between a fluid ounce and a weight ounce? How many ounces are in a quart, a gallon, or a cup? In the metric system you just keep adding zeros, and it's designed so linear and volume measurements mesh

The metric system is foreign to those from the U.S., but it's incredibly simple and well thought-out once you're forced to live with it. Here's how it works:

First: *milli* means thousandth, *centi* means hundredth, *kilo* means thousand.

Distance is measured in *metres* (mtr), which is a little over a yard. In one *metre* there are 1,000 millimetres (shorthand: mm) or 100 centimetres (cm). 1,000 metres make a kilometre. You just keep adding zeros.

Liquid is measured in *litres* (l) which is a little under a quart. In one litre, there are 1,000 millilitres. One millilitre (ml) is equal to one cubic centimetre (cc.)

Weight is in *grams*. A thousand grams is a *kilogram*, or simply a *kilo*, about 2.2 pounds.

All the measurements are cleverly interchangeable: a *cubic metre* (cum) contains 1,000 litres. A *hectare* contains 10,000 square metres. A *tonne* is a metric ton, and contains 1,000 kilos.

OK, you agree the metric system is more logical and you're willing to give it a try, but you've only known the U.S. system of feet, pounds, and gallons: how can you estimate what you are buying, building, or driving? Here are some quick and dirty equivalents:

Quick metric conversions

A litre is about a quart. Four litres are about a gallon.

A kilo is 2.2 pounds (if you went through the sixties, you already knew that). Roughly a pound is half a kilo, minus ten percent. A *tonne* is 2200 lbs.

A metre is a little bit more than a yard (39 3/8 inches or roughly 3.3 feet). Figure 3+ feet to a metre. Three metres are almost ten feet. These are approximations; the easiest way to deal precisely with metres is to buy a tape measure that reads in both feet and metres (most come like this) and use it as a handy converter, like an old fashioned slide rule.

A kilometre is .6 miles. Multiply the kilometres by six, then move the decimal. Example: 50 kilometres an hour is 50x6=300; move the decimal, it's 30 mph.

A hectare is 10,000 sq. metres, or about 2.5 acres. 1,000 sq. metres is approximately one-quarter acre, about the size of a suburban lot. To roughly convert square metres to square footage, just add a zero to the metres and add 7 percent (i.e., 100 sq. metres would be approximately 1,070 sq. feet).

Speedometers in Australian cars built after the mid-sixties are in kilometres. Just watch for the speed limit signs, put the speedometer needle on that number, and you'll be fine. Here's an idea of what the speeds are:

Normal posted speeds (approximate):
40 kph....25 mph   80 kph.....50 mph
50 kph.....30 mph 90 kph.....55 mph
60 kph.....35 mph 100 kph....60 mph
70 kph.....45 mph 110 kph....65 mph

An important note, these are approximate conversions: as amounts go up, the error from the approximation increases. I find it's easy to estimate in feet and build in metres. If accuracy is critical, use a calculator and do a precise conversion. NASA missed Mars with the Climate Orbiter because someone forgot to convert miles to kilometres.

Temperature is measured in Celsius (originally called centigrade). Celsius is more logical: freezing is 0 degrees, boiling is 100 degrees (in Fahrenheit, freezing is 32 degrees, boiling is 212 degrees). There's no easy way to convert, since Celsius degrees are larger than Fahrenheit degrees and the zeros are in different places. You'll have to stoop to rote memorization:

Roughly:
0 C is 32 F
5 C is 40 F
10 C is 50 F
15 C is 60 F
22 C is 70 F

27 C is 80 F
32 C is 90 F
37 C is 100 F
41 C is 105 F

Power is measured in *kilowatts* (kW) and torque in *Newton metres* (Nm), even in cars. It's hard to get excited about a car with 100 kW and 250 Nm (that converts to about 135 horsepower and 185 foot-pounds of torque). A kilowatt is about 1 1/3 horsepower and a Newton metre is about 3/4 foot-pounds (precisely, one kW is 1.341 horsepower, and a Nm is .738 foot-pounds).

Calories aren't just a way of making you feel guilty about eating things that make you fat, but are a measurement of heat energy. Metrically, this is measured in *joules*. A joule is one Newton metre, or the amount of energy required to lift 100 grams one metre, or warm one cc of water ¼ degree C, or create one watt of power for one second. Pretty neat, huh?

By way of conversion, a joule is .22 calories. A calorie is about 4.2 Joules. Large amounts are expressed as *kilo joules*. Just eat-up and forget about it; you're on vacation.

Stationery

Paper size   It's the subtle things that get to you, lulling you into a false sense of confidence, leading you to think you have everything under control, and then "wham": gotcha again. Take a simple thing like stationery. How could anybody change anything about the size of a piece of paper that would have any international significance? They can, and they did, and it's just enough to make American stationery accessories like notebooks and multi-hole punches incompatible in Australia—but don't blame the Australians. It's because America is non-standard to the rest of the world—it's that darn metric system again.

The standard letter-sized paper in Australia—and most of the world—is called A4. A4 is slightly narrower and slightly longer than American letter-sized paper (8.27" by 11.69" vs. 8½" by 11"). It's just different enough so that business envelopes are a different size, as are manila folders, notebooks, and binders. Ring notebooks (called *files*) use A4 paper with two holes instead of three (though some paper is punched for both systems).

Here's where the metric magic kicks in: A3 is twice the size of A4, A5 is half the size of A4, A6 is half the size of A5, etc. The larger the number, the smaller the paper.

Computer printers will have to be reset to print A4 paper. In Windows, go to "File", "Page Set-up", and reset the paper size to "A4". If you're on Mac, just listen to your iPod and wish you'd bought Apple stock in 2002, like I did. Actually, in Appleworks, click "File", "Page Set-up", then choose "A4" from "Paper Size".

Misc.   A ballpoint pen is often called a *biro* (pronounced *bye-row*). It's from a brand name, which came from the inventor, Laszlo Biro.

In the U.S., one signs important documents in blue ink so it's easy to tell an original from a photocopy. In Australia, one signs everything important in black ink.

A *diary* isn't just something you write your deepest thoughts in. In Australia, that's what you call your appointment book or Day Runner.

You can be hard-pressed to find pencils with erasers attached to them, and erasers are commonly called *rubbers*. I'm not making this up. Imagine my reaction the day my ten-year-old daughter came home from school and asked me if she could borrow a *rubber*.

Postal system

The postal system is run by a government-owned corporation called Australia Post. Some post offices are corporately operated while others are franchises.

Mail is delivered to homes and businesses five days a week, Monday through Friday. There's no Saturday delivery. Letters will <u>not</u> be picked up from your home *letter box*; you must drop them in a *post box*. Post boxes are red, with "POST" written on it in large white letters, mounted on a pole in front of post offices, petrol stations, newsagents, etc.

Posties (mailmen) are the men and women who deliver the mail. They don't go on foot or in a Jeep or mail van like in the U.S.; instead they buzz around on little red Honda trail bikes loaded down with huge orange bags *chockers* (full) with mail.

Posties are generally nice people, but with the excuse of delivering the mail they perform the most outrageous moves on their little bikes, darting through traffic, cutting between parked cars, and dodging pedestrians on the *footpaths* (sidewalks). They jump *kerbs*, take shortcuts over lawns, and roll backward down steep driveways. I've seen them drive part way into shops to drop letters on the front counter. So if you hear the putt-putt of a small motorbike approaching, watch out; the *Posties* are above the law.

Postage   In 2007, a domestic letter mailed within Australia cost 50 cents Australian, a post card to the U.S. was A$1.10, a letter to the U.S. was A$1.80. Air mail takes about five days. If sending an item to North America, be sure to write *AIR MAIL* prominently on it or it will take four to six weeks to travel by sea. Stamps can be bought at a post office or newsagent.

Shipping   For larger items or urgent or valuable deliveries that require tracking, go with FedEx or DHL. This is especially true if you are shipping something *into* Australia, since they're set up to deal with customs. In that situation, be sure to have a receipt and a list of contents and their values. An operator for the shipper will call you for details prior to delivery. FedEx Overnight can take two days, plus time in Customs.

On some imported items you'll be charged Customs duty. Some items are duty-free if there are no comparable items manufactured in Australia—professional motion picture equipment falls under this category—but you have to know to ask for your exemption. Check the Australian Customs website, **www.customs.gov.au**, for more information. If you find that your item is listed as duty-free, write down the number of the section that covers it to quote to the FedEx or DHL operator who calls to arrange delivery. Duty-free or not, you'll still have to pay GST (Goods and Services Tax). If you're shipping an item overseas for repair and have to pay for that repair, you'll pay GST on that, too.

Receiving mail from the U.S. and Canada If you're

moving to Australia, notify your senders and put in a change of address form in your old post office, just as if you were moving across town. For greater volumes of mail, rent a private post office box with a forwarding service in your old hometown and have your mail sent weekly, biweekly, or monthly, as needed. That way you don't have to put the burden of forwarding mail on your family or friends. Once you've settled in and everyone has your new address, you can cancel the service. You may want to keep this forwarding system going indefinitely in situations where you're required to have an American address in order to retain American credit cards, bank and brokerage accounts. This is also the best way to receive your favorite American magazines, which may otherwise be unobtainable in Australia.

Telephones

OK, so you've been using the telephone since you were five years old; what's the big deal? The big deal is that the Aussie system of phone numbers is so different and inconsistent that at first you probably won't be able to make a simple phone call without help. Why?

Australian phone numbers defy all logic in the sequence and amount of digits used. In America, phone numbers have long been standardized: you dial 1, then the three-digit area code, then a three-digit prefix, then four numbers. (Example: 1-800-555-1212.) It's the same pattern for landlines and cellulars, businesses or residences; anywhere you go in the U.S. or Canada.

This logic doesn't apply to Australian phone numbers. Australians use different amounts of digits in different groupings in different situations. A home number might look like this: 9999 9999, a *mobile* (cellular) number might look like this 0499 999 999, a *free call* 800 number would look like this: 1 800 999 999, while a *1300* (25-cent inquiry number) might look like this: 139 999 or this: 1300 999 999. And that example doesn't include area codes. There's no consistency so at first it's really confusing.

Here's my American friend Bob's simplified version. My more detailed explanation follows:

Bob's simplified version

1. Domestic Australian calls from within the same area code: Dial the eight-digit phone number (without the area code) if calling a landline, or the 10-digit number calling a *mobile* (cellular)—pronounced "*moe-byle*". A landline number should look like this: 9999 9999; a *mobile* should look like this: 0499 999 999. Any number that begins in 04 is a *mobile*.

2. Domestic Australian calls from a different area code: Dial Area Code (with 0) + Calling Number. The landline should look like this: 08 9999 9999; the mobile will still be 0499 999 999, as the 04 is the area code for all *mobiles*.

3. International calls dialing <u>out</u> of Australia: Dial International Code (0011) plus Country Code (1 for U.S. & Canada) plus Area Code and Number (if U.S. or Canada). It should look like this: 0011-1-800-555-1212.

Buy an inexpensive calling card specifically for the country you're calling, available from a newsagent. Rates are usually less than 5¢ per minute and can be as low as 1¢ per minute. For calling cards, you have to dial a local 8-digit access number, or a 1-800, or 1300 number if calling from outside a city (read the directions on the back of the card), then the calling card number, the international code, then the U.S. number with area code. Have a local help you the first time. You can top-up a calling card with a credit card by calling the access number.

4. International calls dialing <u>into</u> Australia: Dial International Code (011 from US) plus 61 (for Australia) plus Area Code (dropping the zero) plus Calling Number. The home landline we used in #2 should look like this: 011-618-9999-9999. The *mobile* should look like this: 011-614-9999-9999.

Again, shop for the best buy, usually less than 20¢ per minute. Check your long distance provider or buy a calling card at a 7-Eleven.

That's the "how"; here's the "why":

My detailed explanation   Some basic background info on how the Australian phone system works:

A cellular phone in Australia is called a *mobile* (pronounced "*moe-byle*"). Australian telephones, both landlines and *mobiles*, physically operate the same as in the U.S. and Canada. In other words, phones have a key pad with numbers on it and a hand set—but that's where the similarity ends. The telephone system is completely different.

If you dial "0," nothing happens. Directory assistance is 1223, or 12455. International directory assistance from inside Australia is 1225. To reverse charges or charge the call to a third party, dial 12550 and have the number you want to call standing by.

Emergency is <u>not</u> 911, it's *000*, which is pronounced "*triple zero*". If you're on a GSM *mobile* phone, are outside your service zone, and 000 doesn't work, dial 112. This might not work on a CDMA *mobile* phone.

The pound sign (#) is called the *hash key*. Calling card users will be prompted to use this key.

An 800 number is a *free call,* but is called a *one-800 number* and is followed by three numbers, then another three numbers: 1-800-801-800 (this happens to be the number to call to get an overseas operator).

A *1-300* number, or any number that begins with 13, is called a *thirteen-hundred number.* It's an inquiry number for a business and costs 25 cents per call with no time limit. These *1300* numbers sometimes use 6 digits, sometimes 10. For example: the phone company's business number is 132 200. The Western Australian State Emergency Services number is 1300 130 039. There's no apparent rhyme or reason to any of this; you just have to go with it. It gets easier after a few years.

There are *1-900* numbers for specially-charged services, like psychic hotlines, sport lines, weather, etc.

All *mobiles* start with the prefix *04*. They use 10 digits and are sequenced like this: 0499 999 999.

All landlines are eight digits, usually written four and four, such as 9999 9999. The first number (in this case, the 9) varies by city. In Brisbane, the first number in a landline is always 3, Townsville is 4, the Gold Coast is 5, Canberra and Hobart is 6, Melbourne and Adelaide are 8, Sydney is 9, and Perth is mostly 9 (though it also uses 6).

But wait! That doesn't include the area code! When calling a landline from another state <u>inside</u> Australia, you put the area code before the number. If you were calling that same number in Perth from Melbourne, you'd dial *08* 9999 9999. The area codes are generally based on the states:

02 New South Wales, ACT (Canberra)

03 Victoria, Tasmania

07 Queensland

08 South Australia, Western Australia, and the Northern Territory

Note: There's some overlap in the corner where Victoria, New South Wales, and South Australia meet.

To call Australia from the U.S., dial the International Code (*011*), then Australia's country code (*61*), plus the area code (<u>minus the zero</u>), then the number. To call the Perth landline number we used above from the U.S., you'd dial 011 618 9999 9999.

To call an Aussie *mobile* from the U.S., again drop the first 0 and insert the country code. We'll use the same *mobile* number we used above (0499 999 999). It becomes: 011 61 499 999 999.

To call the U.S. or Canada from Australia dial 0011, then 1, the North American area code, then the number. Example: 0011-1-800-555-1212.

To access your U.S. calling card in Australia, try:

AT+T	1-800-881-011
Sprint	1-800-881-877
MCI	1-800-881-100
WorldCom	1-800-881-212
Bell Atlantic	1-800-881-152

Then put in your calling card number and the number you're calling. Some of these access numbers put your call directly into North America, so you might not have to use the country code, listen to the prompts.

The cheapest way to call around Australia and back to the U.S. is to buy a pre-paid calling card from a newsagent. You can replenish it by calling a 1-800 number and charging it to your credit card.

A final note about phone numbers: It might seem as if the number you're trying to dial must be wrong because it has the wrong amount of digits, but forge ahead and try it anyway. There's no logical pattern to Australian phone numbers.

Cellular phones are called *mobiles* (pronounced *moe-byle*), and use similar, if not identical, handsets as those in America. It's illegal to use a hand-held *mobile* in Australia while driving a motor vehicle. You must use a hands-free kit, consisting of at least a headphone/earpiece. This law is enforced.

Mobile calls are billed differently. In American cellular phone systems, both outgoing and incoming calls are charged to the cellular phone owner. In Australia, only the outgoing call is charged to the mobile owner. The incoming call is charged to whoever is calling. There's usually a connection fee and a charge based on airtime. It all ends up on the caller's bill at the end of the month.

CDMA and GSM are the current systems, along with 3G. GSM is more common in the cities, but CDMA has better reception in fringe areas and in the outback, since remote mines use the latter system. CDMA will be phased out by 2008 and replaced entirely by what is being called *Next G*, which is 3G plus wireless broadband Internet capability. It's eventually supposed to have better reception than CDMA.

Bring your American cell phone   If you're travelling in Australia, you might want to bring along your American cell phone If it's a relatively current model, it will probably work, and you can buy a prepaid SIM card (on GSM or Next G) or prepay your CDMA (before phase-out) and have easy communication. The major companies are Telstra, Optus, and Vodaphone; shop for the best deals. Remember to get a voltage-converter and adapter for your charger or bring your car kit [see the section on **electricity—cell phone chargers**].

Some American cellular phones won't work in Australia. If, for whatever reason, your American phone doesn't work, you can pick up a prepaid phone, available at kiosks as you get off the plane in most major airports or in a shopping centre phone store. As of this writing, Telstra has stopped selling all CDMA phones, and Next G prepaid phones are quite pricey, and they've introduced prepay minimums with expiring minutes, so you might want to check Vodaphone and Optus first. Shop the best deal, and after all the discounts and bonuses, you should be able to get an effective 15 cents per minute.

For international calls back home, you can use a prepay mobile phone in conjunction with a prepaid calling card, which you can purchase from a newsagent. Use the *mobile* to call the local access number for the calling card, enter the card number, the International Code, then the number back home. After you've done it a few times, it'll be easy.

Phone etiquette   People often answer the phone by stating their name instead of "hello", even at home. Being a paranoid American, I don't do this, since I don't necessarily want a stranger to know who they've called, in case it's a wrong number or a scam. Ask an Aussie why they answer that way, and they'll generally say it's more businesslike.

Caller ID is very common, so if you call someone and don't leave a message or change your mind and hang up before they answer, there's a good chance they'll call you back, because they have your number on their phone and figure you got cut off.

The Yellow Pages

"Find things fast in the Yellow Pages" might be the slogan in North America, but it's an oxymoron in Australia. Finding anything at all in the Yellow Pages can be a bit trying, because they're not listed where you'd expect them and they're often called by different names.

For example, take automobile services, which are scattered throughout the book. Auto electrics, air conditioning, and wrecking are listed under "Autos", while limos, detailing, and car *hire* (rentals) are found under "Cars". New and used car sales, accessories, and *trimmers* (upholsterers) are under "Motoring", while other car-related items are listed under "Shocks", "Towing," and "Transmissions".

Window screens (called *flyscreens* or *flywire*) aren't listed under either of those headings, but are under "Security Doors and Windows". If you can't find it, keep looking or ask someone for help. Even locals shake their heads and call directory assistance.

Internet

Phone plugs are the same, so the modem in your laptop will plug in. AOL has a local number in most cities. Hooking up is easy and providers are helpful.

Australian websites usually end in *.au*.

DSL is called *ADSL* (for Asymmetric DSL, meaning the data comes in at a faster rate than it goes out)—the same as in the U.S., but just a different name.

Cable broadband is available in major cities. Government-subsidized two-way satellite Internet is available in remote areas. Blackberries and hand-held devices are supported. Wi-fi hot spots are in many airports and business centers. *Internet cafés* (cybercafes), are cheap: $5–6 an hour—and common in cities and resort towns. Some small towns have *telecentres* or Internet facilities in, or adjacent to, their libraries.

Electricity and appliances

Australia uses a different electricity system. In America, electricity is 110 volts at 60 Hz (cycles). In Australia, it's 240 volts at 50 Hz. Note, I said 240 volts. Europe is 220v, Australia is 240v, but most modern equipment can handle the small difference.

What does this mean to you? If you were to plug most American appliances directly into an Australian circuit, there's a good chance they'd blow up, and in so doing, trip the main circuit breakers in the entire building—believe me, I've done it. To prevent this, Australian plug ends are different than American ones. The following is an explanation and a set of solutions to keep you and your gear out of trouble.

Plugs   In Australia, the wall plug used is either two or three prongs. The two-pronged plugs are the same spacing as North American plugs, but are splayed at an angle, "pigeon-toed." The third prong is flat-bladed like the other two, but below and in the center. A determined fool with a plug adapter or a pair of pliers can get around this. If you're bringing something electrical with you, be sure you know what it is capable of (details below) and how you should use it.

Power points   A plug outlet in Australia is called a *power point*. Believe me, 240 volts is nothing to laugh at.

Australia is very safety-conscious; that's why each power point is individually switched. The switches work opposite of those in America: down is on, up is off. If you can see the little red indicator on the edge of the button, it's on.

Why is each *power point* switched? Where a 110-volt shock will bite, 240 volts will bite and burn a lot harder. Volts don't kill, amps do, but if you're suddenly shocked, the amps will surge through your body on the back of 240 volts. With each power point switched individually, you can turn off the power point before you plug in or unplug the cord. Most circuits, especially those around water, like in a bathroom or a kitchen, are fitted with an *earth leakage circuit breaker (ELCB)* to minimize the hazard. In the U.S., this is called a "ground fault interrupter", or (GFI).

FYI: In Australia, a power cord is called a *lead* (pronounced *leed*). The electrical term for "ground" is *earth*. A circuit isn't "grounded", it is *earthed*.

Using American electrical equipment in Australia

If you're moving to Australia, you don't have to get rid of all your 110v lamps, electronics, and tools. Some will switch to 240v automatically, some will work with minor modifications or by using adapters, converters, or transformers, and some won't work at all. If you're coming as a tourist or on a business trip, there are ways to use your laptop computer, cell phone, and iPod chargers.

Electrical converters   Small electrical converters that bump the wall voltage down from 240v to 110v are available in the U.S. from places like Radio Shack and travel stores. Get them <u>before</u> you come over; the converters available in Australian stores are designed to change the voltage in the opposite direction.

When shopping for a converter, check the wattage it puts out: a battery charger for your cellular phone or iPod draws little current, but a hair dryer draws a lot—special converters are made for hair dryers. Make sure you get the proper plug adapters for Australia, as described above. These little converter boxes plug into the power point, you plug your device into it, and everything should work just as it did back home. A tip: Don't put anything on top of a converter; they can put out a lot of heat.

If you're bringing along a lot of electronics for work or are moving to Australia for an extended time, you can get a heavy-duty 300 or 500 watt converter at an electronics supply store (buy them in North America before you leave, they're very expensive in Australia), then you can set up a 110v station in your home or business. This way, you can use larger 110v electronics, like your sound system, projectors, computer accessories, etc. You'll need to bring North American-style 110v power strips and 110v extension cords for that station. Be aware, not all converters change the cycles from 50 to 60Hz, so anything with a motor, including electric clocks, movie projectors, etc., might not run at the proper speed.

Don't bother bringing large appliances like washers, dryers, refrigerators, vacuum cleaners, etc. They draw too much current for a converter or transformer and aren't worth the trouble. Buy or rent them locally. You can rent appliances like TV's, refrigerators, washers, computers and furniture, by the week in Australia.

Computers　　Windows-based PC's are the same as in North America. Prominent makes are HP, Dell, Compaq, IBM, Toshiba, NEC, Sony, Asus, Acer. The operating systems and software work the same.

A Mac is often called an *Apple Mac*, and uses the same OS systems. Apple has the same relative market share as they do in North America: professionals who specialize in graphics, and people who like to be different. The text of this book was written on a PC, the cover was designed on a Mac.

USB 2.0 and Firewire all work. Monitors, keyboards and mouses work the same. The same brand printers are available as in North America, but not all ink cartridges. Bring a supply or be prepared to buy a new printer.

Australian websites end in *.au*. [more in the section on the **internet**]

Most better computer and electronic components are capable of handling both 110v/60Hz and 240v/50 Hz. Read the label on the back of each unit; it will tell you the voltage range. Some appliances, like camera chargers, printers, and scanners, switch automatically. Read the specifications either in the manual or on the back of the device. If it says "110v-240v", you're in luck. All you need to do is get a plug end adapter. Others, like desktop computers, must be manually switched from 110v to 240v. There will be a red recessed switch on the back of the computer, which should be marked 110v-240v. Switch it to the proper voltage <u>before</u> plugging it in. In either case, you'll still need a plug adapter to convert your cable or to buy a new cable.

Australian cables are available that will plug directly into each unit, but they're expensive (A$10-A$20 each). If you have a lot of components, that will add up fast. It's a lot cheaper to put an adapter on the wall-plug end of the old cable. They're cheap (about US$1 each), but you need to stock up on them before you leave North America. Try Radio Shack or travel stores.

Again, beware! Make sure the device can handle 240v or has had the power supply switched to the 240v position <u>before</u> you plug it in!

Wall transformers   Many electronic devices, like musical keyboards, games, radios, phones, etc., have wall transformer boxes that plug directly into the *power point* (wall socket). These supply low-voltage (3, 5, 6, 7.2 volts, etc.) to the device via a cable and connector. This is so the manufacturer can make one device for the world, changing only the external transformer box for each market. Most of these won't switch automatically from 110v to 240v (read the label). If you're a short-term visitor, just get a converter, but if you're moving to Australia, here's the long-term solution:

Once you've arrived in Australia, you can swap the American 110v wall transformer for a comparable 240v version to supply the correct low-voltage for the device. These can be purchased at Tandy's (Australian Radio Shack) or Dick Smith's. These come with a variety of output plugs to fit various devices. However, just getting a unit that supplies the correct voltage isn't enough. It<u>'s crucial that the amperage output of the new wall box matches that of the 110v unit it</u>'s <u>replacing, or is close.</u> If the amperage is too low, the device won't work; if it's too high, it will burn it up (the telltale grey smoke emanating from the device will be the indicator). Read the label, write down <u>both</u> output voltage and amperage, and match it with a 240v model—or just bring along the 110v wall transformer and have the salesperson match it. It's a bit of a hassle, but it's cheaper than buying a complete appliance. Electronics can be expensive in Australia, and some things aren't available at all.

Cell phone chargers   If you're staying only a short while and will be *hiring* (renting) a car, just bring your car kit and charge the phone off the cigarette lighter.

FYI: It's illegal to talk on a handheld *mobile* (cell phone) while driving a car anywhere in Australia unless you use a hands-free kit, which consists of at least an earphone.

Light bulbs are called *globes*. There are two kinds of standard-sized household 240v *globes*: *screw base* and *bayonet base*. Bayonet bases are found on older lamps. The bulb itself looks the same, but the metal part that goes into the socket doesn't have threads; it instead has two small pins that positively lock the bulb into the base. Newer lamps use the conventional American-style screw base—but don't try screwing in an American 110v bulb into an Australian lamp: as soon as the switch is thrown, it will pop.

Florescent lamps are called *floros*. In 2007, the Australian federal government mandated the phasing out of all incandescent globes by 2010, replacing them with compact fluorescents. This will save about 75 percent of the energy currently consumed by incandescent globes.

Fluorescent tube fixtures work pretty much the same as in North America, but one clever addition is an external starter, a little can-shaped component about the size of your thumb that twists into the side of the fixture. If your *fluoro* light doesn't work and the tube is good, pick up a replacement starter at the hardware store. It's cheaper and easier than replacing the entire ballast.

110v lamps   If you're moving to Australia, you can bring and use your American lamps. The wires are identical, as are the screw bases for the bulbs, so all you need to do is swap out the 110v bulbs for screw-base 240v versions and change the plug ends or use adapters.

Light switches   In America, you turn on a switch by

flipping it up. In Australia, you flip it down.

Radios   Digitally-tuned North American radios can have problems with Australian stations. The same frequency bands are used, but the intervals between stations are different. Some can be adapted, some can't; check the manual. Older analogue styles don't have this problem.

Older Australian multi-band radios were called *radiograms*. Early AM radios didn't have frequencies printed on the dials, just the name of the cities, as the only thing broadcasting in those days was the ABC. Aussie component stereos from the 70s and 80s had separate tuners and amplifiers.

TV sets   Tuning a modern TV set in Australia is different than in North America. In Australia, the tuner in the set stores the channels <u>sequentially</u>. In a major city, the ABC, which is broadcast nationally on channel 2, ends up on channel 1. Channels 7, 9, and 10 (the big three commercial networks), end up on channels 2, 3, and 4. SBS (Special Broadcast Service) ends up on channel 5. Anything else, like Access 31, which is broadcast on UHF, stacks up past that. In regional areas, the local country networks will end up in those spots.

When you buy a new TV and put it through "Auto Tune", it does this automatically.

Video   Australia and America use different electronic signals for video. America uses a system called "NTSC", while Australia uses "PAL". Most Australian TVs are multi-format and play both systems, but American TVs aren't and won't.

NTSC is the electronic standard for TV signals in the U.S., Canada, Mexico, and Central and South America (except Argentina and Brazil), along with Japan, South Korea, Taiwan, and the Philippines. The "SECAM" signal is used in France, Russia, and western Africa. Almost everyone else (including Australia and New Zealand) is on PAL. Each uses completely different electronic methods of reproducing a video image and playing sound.

American TVs and video gear will only play NTSC. Your American TV will <u>not</u> play broadcast stations in Australia, nor will it play PAL videos and DVDs. It would be like trying to talk to a spider: not only wouldn't it understand what you're saying, but it wouldn't even know that you were speaking. If you're moving Down Under, sell your American TV equipment or put it in storage until you return.

The good news is that most new Australian TVs, VCRs and DVD players are "multi-format"; they'll play anything: PAL, NTSC, and SECAM. Newer Australian multi-format tape decks will play NTSC American videos, so your NTSC home movies and favorite films on tape will play in Australia on your new Australian multi-format VCR and TV.

Unfortunately, this is not the case when going back to the U.S. PAL videos won't play back in the U.S., since U.S. video equipment plays only NTSC. So if you're moving Down Under, don't get rid of that NTSC video camera just yet. You may want to keep it to send tapes back to the folks you left behind.

DVDs are a different story. Though multi-format DVD players found in Australia will play NTSC as well as PAL, there's also a "Region Code" electronically imbedded in most commercially produced DVDs. This allows them to be played only on machines sold in that region, making it harder to produce counterfeit DVDs.

If you're interested, here are the regions:

Region 1   U.S. and Canada
Region 2   Europe and Japan
Region 3   Southeast Asia
Region 4   Australia, New Zealand, Central and South America
Region 5   Russia
Region 6   China

So, you ask, what does this all mean? If you buy a DVD in Japan, you figure it should work in the U.S., because Japan and the U.S. are both on NTSC—but it won't work, because they have different Region Codes. But if you're in Australia, again you're in luck: many DVD players sold in Australia are multi-format <u>and</u> multi-region, so they'll play everything. If you're buying a new DVD machine in Australia, make sure you get one of these.

Either way, if you're moving to Australia, you can bring

your old NTSC DVD player, run it off a 240v-110v transformer, and play your old NTSC Region 1 movies on your new Australian multi-format TV. The cables will plug right in. *No worries.*

Hard drive video recorders like TiVo, appeared much later in Australia than the U.S., around 2005. They're called *hard drive digital recorders*, and often come with built-in DVD player-recorders.

Video rentals   A video rental store is sometimes called a *video library*. Chains are Blockbuster, Civic Video, and Video Ezy, and work just like those in North America. Most of what is for *hire* (rent) are American films. In fact, it's hard to find a good selection of Australian movies. For that, you need to go to an independent shop. DVDs have almost completely replaced videotapes. DVD's can be ordered on the Internet and delivered by mail from <u>bigpondmovies.com</u> and <u>quickflix.com.au</u>.

High definition/wide screen/digital   Australia is broadcasting wide-screen (16:9), and widescreen TVs are common, but it's not necessarily high definition. High def is marginally available, and shouldn't be confused with digital TV. The complete changeover to digital (where analogue will be shut off altogether) has been put off until 2008 in Australia, and probably will be pushed back farther. Digital set-top boxes are available, as are cable TV and satellite.

Cable & satellite TV (see **media**)

Health Care

Medicare   Australia enjoys universal health care, called *Medicare*, administered by the federal government. This means everybody in the country can get medical care at little or no cost, depending on the doctor or hospital. The overall level of treatment is good, though waits for elective surgery can be lengthy—that's why there's private coverage for those that can afford it. Private health care premiums are tax creditable. Not covered are: ambulance, dentistry, glasses, prosthesis, and cosmetic surgery.

Some doctors advertise *bulk billing*, which means they'll bill Medicare directly and accept whatever Medicare pays as total payment, so the patient pays nothing and owes nothing. This isn't just generosity, as a doctor friend has informed me. With bulk billing, the doctors are guaranteed payment and don't have to chase deadbeats who don't pay their bills. Public hospitals work the same as bulk billing. X-rays are covered 100 percent, a CT scan about sixty-five percent.

On the surface, the health care system looks a lot like the U.S. system. Doctors have private offices (called *surgeries*), by themselves or in groups. You book an appointment over the phone, you wait in a waiting room, you see the doctor. If they don't bulk bill, you pay the bill and get a form to turn in to Medicare. The difference between what Medicare pays and what you're charged is called the *gap* (usually about 1/3 of the bill).

To get reimbursed, you send in a form to Medicare and a check will be mailed to you, or you can have a direct payment deposited into your bank account, or you can go into a Medicare office in a regional shopping centre and receive cash on the spot.

The *Pharmaceutical Benefit Scheme* (*PBS*) covers prescription drugs with a deductible. This is automatic at the *chemist's* (pharmacy) when you pay for the prescription.

The bottom line is that all Australians have basic health care: listen-up, USA!

General practitioners and specialists   The hierarchy is: doctors, physicians and surgeons. The first two are addressed as "doctor", the latter as "mister". If you find yourself *in hospital* and are introduced to a doctor-ish looking person who is referred to as "mister", he's your surgeon. The doctor above him is called "professor".

In the U.S., if you have a medical problem, you can start with your general practitioner or, if you choose, go directly to a specialist; it's up to you. A woman might see her gynecologist for a yearly checkup. Someone with back pain might go directly to an orthopedist. You don't have to waste time— yours and the doctor's—just to be told what you already know, that you need to see a specialist. In Australia, GPs are the gatekeepers of the healthcare system. You need to go to one and get a referral before you can see a specialist. If you went directly to a specialist, Medicare wouldn't cover it. This is dictated by the Medicare system to keep costs down.

In Australia, there are fewer specialists, so GPs handle a lot of the load. A woman is more likely to go to her GP for routine female checkups and to see a gynecologist only if there is a complication. If you're suffering from clinical depression, you'd see a psychologist for counselling and your GP for an antidepressant; and only if that wasn't working would you see a psychiatrist.

Private health coverage   Many people opt for supplemental private health coverage, which uses private hospitals with shorter waits for elective surgeries. These can also be offered as job perks. Private policies receive a 30 percent rebate from the federal government toward the premiums, filed with your year-end tax return. Typical private policies are about $2,500/year for a family of four—about what you'd pay per month in the U.S. These policies can cover dental with limits.

If you have a private policy and get sick or are injured and have to go to an emergency room, you'll enter the public health system. If you need to be hospitalized, you then can go into the private system. If you chose an elective surgery, you'll enter the private system directly.

Australian medical terms

One doesn't go "to a hospital" they go "to hospital", as if being in one was a condition, not a location.

A *junior doctor* is one who has completed his/her twelve-month internship and is undergoing further training to receive *fellowship* from the medical training college. This is similar to a "resident" in the U.S.

A *registrar* is a doctor with a few years of training beyond his or her residency.

A *consultant* is a doctor who is a specialist.

A surgeon is called *mister*, not doctor.

A nurse is sometimes called a *sister*, with no religious implications.

Normal body temperature: (98.6 degrees F.) is 37 degrees C.

Australians tend to call any cold the "flu". They'll say, "I'm feeling *fluie*." *Crook* also means sick, as in "I'm feeling *crook*."

If a medicine or other substance is labelled *Not to be taken,* it means it isn't to be taken <u>internally</u>.

An intravenous injection is called a *jab* or a *needle*.

Out-patient surgery is called *day surgery*, or *same day surgery*.

Ibuprofen (Advil) is called *Nurofen*.

Acetaminophen (Tylenol) is called *Panadol*.

Aleve is called *Naprosyn* and requires a prescription.

Mononucleosis is called *glandular fever*.

Estrogen is spelled *oestrogen*.

A Caesarean section is also called a *Caesar*.

Women who opt for Caesareans because they don't want to go through normal childbirth—for whatever reason—are called *too posh to push. Posh* means elegant.

Health care for travellers   Visitors to Australia have a few options if they need medical assistance. For simple office visits, just go and pay; it's cheap. For serious emergencies, you might have to pay up front and hope your medical policy will cover things. Make sure you get receipts for everything and submit a claim to your insurer when you get back home. Another option is Traveller's Insurance, which covers medical costs, including air-evacuation from a dive boat, which is required on some live-aboard dive boats on the Barrier Reef. It also covers trip cancellation, lost luggage, and the *excess* (deductible) on your hire car.

If you have permanent residency or have a parent, spouse, or child who is an Australian citizen or resident, you'll automatically have Australian Medicare coverage. If you're from Ireland or New Zealand, you have full reciprocal coverage. If you're from the UK, Sweden, the Netherlands, Finland, Norway, Italy, or Malta, you're covered for *immediately necessary* treatment.

If you've migrated on a permanent residency visa or are on a work visa and have applied for permanent residence, you can get a Medicare card. The latest info is on the Medicare website: **www.medicare.gov.au**.

Flying doctor service

This is an Australian icon. The Royal Flying Doctor Service was established in 1928. It's partly funded by the state and federal governments, but the air fleet is supported entirely by charitable donations. It maintains a network of shortwave radios at remote settlements and pastoral stations throughout the Australian bush and provides communication, health care, advice, and air-evacuation when necessary.

The brave doctors, nurses, and pilots have saved thousands of lives in the eighty years since it was founded.

Social assistance

Australia has a social welfare system that helps citizens with lower incomes, seniors, the unemployed, the disabled, and families that need counselling. There's also a system of allowances and benefits to supplement working people with low wages. It's a safety net, insuring that no one starves or becomes homeless. The centralized welfare, employment, and family assistance agency is called Centrelink, a part of the Department of Human Services, and can be contacted on the web at: **www.centrelink.gov.au** or at 1 800 050 004.

Public housing for low-income and disadvantaged families is provided by the individual states. There are high-rise U.S.-style projects in Sydney and Melbourne, and low-density detached bungalows on master-planned estates located in the suburbs of other eastern cities and towns. In Western Australia, Homeswest owns 39,000 properties, including many houses in mainstream neighborhoods. Homeswest provides varying rent subsidies to families who would otherwise be on the streets.

The homeless problem in Australia isn't as widespread as it is in major American cities. You rarely see people sleeping on the streets.

Concessions/concessionaires

Concessions are special rates that seniors and the disabled receive on pharmaceuticals, transportation, car registration, phone bills, utilities, and admission to entertainment events. One needs to apply for a *concession card.*

Students can also qualify for some concessions for reduced prices to events, train tickets, etc., by showing their student ID cards.

Education

The school year runs from February to December. There's a six-to-eight week summer break from just before Christmas until after Australia Day (Jan. 26). There's a two-week term break around Easter, another in mid-January, and a third in October.

Primary schools have *kindy* (preschool), *pre-primary* (kindergarten), then years one through seven.

High school is years eight through twelve. Years eight through ten are mandatory until a student reaches age sixteen. Some students leave after year ten for independent apprenticeships or to train for a trade at a TAFE (state trade school). Some just drop out and get a job or go on the *dole* (welfare), some finish and then go onto apprenticeships, TAFE, or university.

For those students who plan on going to university, years eleven and twelve are spent studying for university entrance exams.

High school graduates are called *leavers*. Students in the last month of their twelfth year are *schoolies* and go on a raucous celebration much like spring break in the U.S. There are resort areas you might want to stay away from in late November when the *leavers* are on the loose.

Through a strange loophole in the law, students in some states could, as recently as 2006, drop out of high school after year ten and apply for the *dole* (welfare) and get paid to do nothing at the age of sixteen. A person who did this was called a *bludger*. Imagine dropping out of school and receiving several hundred dollars a week to sit around the house and play video games. This is being eliminated, and staying in school until year twelve will be mandatory.

HSC, TEE, TES, TER, OBE High school *leavers* who pass their final exams receive a *Higher School Certificate (HSC)*. There are no SATs. Students take classes and are tested in subjects that directly apply to their chosen field of university study. University admission is based on grades and scores on the *TEEs* (*Tertiary Entrance Exams*), *TERs* (*Tertiary Entrance Ranks*), or *TESs* (*Tertiary Entrance Scores*), depending on the state.

As of 2007, Western Australia was going through an embattled change from their old system of TEEs to one called *OBE* (*Outcomes Based Education*). It's designed to standardize the testing and grades with the eastern states. Some educators think it's a dumbing-down of the education system.

School terminology

Semesters or quarters are called *terms*.

Grades are called *years*. First grade is *year one*, second grade is *year two*, and so on.

"Home room" in high school is called *form room*, or just *form*.

A high school is sometimes called a *college* (example: Trinity College is a high school).

College is called *university* or *uni*.

Mathematics is called *maths* (for some reason, they put an "*s*" on the end, which actually makes sense, since it's mathematic**s**, not mathematic).

The *head boy* and *head girl* are the popularly elected student leaders of a school, like student body presidents.

Dux is the honor awarded to the top student in the school.

A *cohort* is a group of students at the same level.

The *Parents and Citizens (P & C)* is the equivalent of the PTA.

VET is *Vocation Education Training*.

LOTE means *Language Other Than English* (a foreign language program).

Substitute teachers are called *relief teachers*.

Alumni are called *ex-students*.

S&E stands for *Society and Environment*, the equivalent of Civics or Social Studies.

Rock Eisteddfod is a bi-yearly modern dance/drama competition held between schools as part of the Global Rock Challenge to promote healthy lifestyles.

Steiner schools are innovative education systems, similar to Montessori schools.

Government schools in Australia are generally pretty good. They aren't completely free. There are yearly student fees of about $250 (it increases as the student progresses), which cover expendables in cooking, science, and physical education classes. Though fees aren't mandatory, the money has to come from somewhere, and the students that pay end up making it up for those that don't.

Government schools are run from the state level. This means there's less local control over assigning of teachers and required curricula, though individual schools have a good amount of independence when it comes to day to day operations and programs.

There's a different air about Australian high schools. American schools can be the center of activity for teenagers, with weekend football or basketball games, marching bands, cheerleading squads, proms, dances; after school clubs, like science, chess, and journalism; and weekend fundraisers, like car washes and carnivals. Aussie schools do little of that. There are sports, like a school *footy* team, but the games take place after school with little fanfare. There is a Year Twelve Ball, but that's about it. Once school is out for the day, the school is like a ghost town.

Private schools are a common alternative to public schools. They're usually prestigious institutions, often run by churches, which can be K-through-twelve or just high school. Some are all-girls, some all-boys, many are co-ed.

Many parents believe it's easier to get into a university from a private school and they feel it's worth the trouble and expense. They would rather put the money into high school, knowing the hard part is getting the good *marks* (grades) to be accepted into *uni;* the easy part is paying for it [more in **university tuition**].

Yearly fees for private high schools range from A$3000 for Catholic schools to A$6000 for mid-range colleges to A$13,000 for the most prestigious high schools.

Private schools in Australia receive government subsidies. For example: in 2006, the State of Victoria provided A$30 million in additional funding for private schools. Most, but not all private schools are run by churches: some are prep schools, like the prestigious, all male Guildford Grammar in Western Australia. Most non-church schools have affiliations with a church.

Getting a good education is just one reason to send your child to a private school. Just as important—at least in the minds of the parents footing the bill—are the "contacts.". It's assumed that the friendships made at a private school will be essential later in building a career. Keep in mind, Australia has a relatively low population, and once a person is in their career they'll keep running into the same people, many of whom they knew in school, and if it's a prestigious school with kids from the "best" families...

Important alliances developed in a private high school can benefit one in later years—or so the theory goes. In practice, the "Old Mates" networks do make it hard for an outsider to break in to some fields.

Uniforms   All students in primary and high school— both public and private—wear uniforms. State schools usually have polo shirts and *jumpers* (long sleeve jerseys) with school crests on the breast as tops; shorts or long pants for the boys, and shorts, long pants, or skirts for the girls.

Private school students have shirts, ties, and blazers; long pants or shorts for the boys, skirts for the girls, and knee socks for both.

The uniforms look very formal, regimented, and English; but it simplifies the choice about what everyone is going to wear to school.

A **gap year** is a year taken off school, usually between high school and university, to travel and work. There are many programs in Australia and abroad that cater to young people out to expand their horizons before settling into the serious business of building careers.

Universities   There are forty-one universities: thirty-eight government-funded, three private. There's no equivalent of an American junior college or community college. However, there is *TAFE* [next section].

The typical undergraduate course is three years for a bachelor's degree, with an optional fourth year for *honours* or for a specialized degree.

The reason for three-year undergraduate programs in Australia versus four years in the U.S. is that there's a different attitude about general education courses. Basically, that you should have had them in high school. Take veterinary schools, for example. In the U.S., one does four years of undergraduate for a bachelor's in Science, taking general education classes and basic sciences. As you approach graduation, you apply for entrance to a vet school and hope you get in. If you do, you enter a four-year program, for a total of eight years. However, if you aren't accepted, you then (at age twenty-two) have to re-think your entire education program.

At Murdoch University in Western Australia, one applies for the veterinary program right out of high school and if accepted, goes directly into a six-year program. If you don't get in, you can re-apply in another field, and since you're only eighteen, little was time wasted.

Once accepted into the veterinary program at Murdoch, the student does a year of general science, three years of study for a BSc in Veterinary Biology, followed by two more years for a bachelor's in Veterinary Medicine and Surgery. At twenty-three, the student is ready to start work as a registered vet in Australia or New Zealand. Murdoch is also accredited by the American Veterinary Medical Association.

University tuition By U.S. standards, the tuition is cheap, and much of that is covered by student loans. In the U.S., you save your money for university; in Australia, many people spend the money on private high schools because they know the hard part is getting into *uni* and the easy part is paying for it. This is because the *Higher Education Contribution Scheme (HECS)* system provides cheap loans that are payable once the graduate's income reaches a certain level.

At the University of Western Australia, for example, these are some approximate tuition estimates for a domestic student working toward an undergraduate degree in 2006 (prices are in Australian dollars; the source is the UWA website):

Humanities	$9,250/year
Law	$9,750/year
Mathematics	$12,150/year
Agriculture	$24,100/year.

TAFE   Since not everyone intends to go to *uni*, many students leave high school early to learn a trade, either through a private apprenticeship or at one of the TAFEs. (*TAFE* stands for *Technical and Further Education*). They're set up like community colleges, but without the general education classes (which one is supposed to have gotten in high school). They teach specialized programs in a wide choice of professions, including: art, hair dressing, fashion design, auto mechanics, computer programming, computer repair, carpentry, business, electrical contracting, drafting, engineering, public relations, plumbing, video production, brick laying, radio announcing, pottery, forklift driving, farming, livestock-raising, welding, etc.

Media

TV   There are two categories: *free-to-air* and *cable/satellite*. In 2007, only 25 percent of Australian homes had cable or satellite pay-TV. Most viewers watch only free-to-air, so everyday references about "what was on the *telly* last night" are more apt to be about shows on the broadcast networks rather than paid channels. Talking about what was on the Comedy Channel or Sky News is a bit snobby (beware the *tall poppy* syndrome), and most people wouldn't have seen it anyway.

Free-to-air   The two government networks, ABC and SBS, reach most of the populated areas in the country. In the major cities, there are three nationwide commercial networks: 7, 9, and 10. In smaller cities, the country, and the bush, there are regional networks that are affiliated with the commercial networks.

There was a time when American TV series aired in Australia a year or two behind the U.S. Now, with next-day podcasts of shows plus airings on You-tube, Australian broadcasters are being forced to air first-run episodes the same day as in North America.

Channels Seven, Nine, and Ten are available in Brisbane, Sydney, Melbourne, Adelaide, Darwin, and Perth, and are on the same channel as their names imply (Simple, eh? Not. See the section on **tuning a television**). The commercial networks are each part of a media conglomerate.

Seven Network also owns one-third of Sky News Channel, which is on cable/satellite and owns a long list of popular magazines.

Nine Network also owns one-third of Sky News, plus Nine MSN on cable/satellite, one-quarter of Foxtel, which is cable/satellite in Australia, plus magazines, sports stadiums, and the Hoyts theatre chain.

Ten Network was recently bought by Canadian conglomerate Can-West. It produces a string of popular Australian shows, like "Big Brother Australia", "Neighbours", and "Australian Idol".

All three carry Australian dramatic, news, and *chat* (talk) shows; plus drama, comedy, and chat shows from the U.S. and the UK. They are based out of Sydney, where most of the production originates. Their individual stations in the capital cities of each state produce limited local shows and news.

WIN, Southern Cross, Prime, and GWN are media companies that own rural and regional TV networks with some original local programming. They are affiliates with the three big networks and carry their shows. Some regional networks also own radio stations around the country.

There are two free-to-air government-owned networks.

ABC (Australian Broadcasting Corporation) is often called Channel 2. It's commercial-free and carries documentaries, local and national news, and public affairs programming, children's programming, American and British drama and comedy series, and a few game shows. While not snobby, it's a more intelligent alternative: the thinking person's channel. ABC also has a cable/satellite network called ABC2, that broadcasts documentaries, educational, news, and public affairs programs.

SBS (Special Broadcasting Service) is the other government-owned free-to-air network, not affiliated with the ABC, and carries documentaries, movies and TV series in sixty foreign languages and English, some with subtitles; along with foreign news programs from all over the world in native languages without subtitles.

Cable & satellite   Foxtel and/or Optus TV cable is

available in most areas of major cities. Foxtel satellite service is available in the cities and in some rural areas. With a population of only 21 million spread out over a huge area, the Australian market is relatively small, so there isn't much room for competing systems. Foxtel is a three-way partnership, owned one-quarter by Nine Network, one-quarter by Rupert Murdoch's News Corporation, and half by Telstra (the national telephone monopoly).

On Foxtel you get CNN, BBC, Fox, Sky Channel, Disney, E!, Nickelodeon, Discovery, Biography, History, TCM, Showtime, three Comedy Channels, Animal Planet, ESPN, three FOX Sports channels, and twenty channels of Fox Box Office Movies—about 100 channels in all (and still there's nothing to watch). Most carry U.S. content, with Australian announcers that make it seem a bit less American, with the exception of s*port* (sports), which are mostly Aussie and European.

There are a few bonuses. Being on the opposite end of the day, you can watch the "CBS Evening News" on Sky Channel while having breakfast in Perth at about the same time it's being aired in New York—a full three hours before it's seen in LA. On the other hand, "The Tonight Show", "The Colbert Report", and "The Daily Show" air on the Comedy Channels with a one-or two-day delay. The same goes with "Late Night with David Letterman" which for some reason is is on Biography Channel.

When it comes to sports (*sport*), it's mostly cricket, *Footy* (Australian Rules Football), rugby, soccer, lawn bowling, and motor racing. Some American sports are aired by tape delay, due to the time difference. FOX Sports 1, 2, and 3, and ESPN show baseball, NBA, NFL, and college football, but often late at night or early in the morning.

One or two major league baseball games are broadcast each week—live in the morning, which is game time in the U.S.—and replayed later that night. The Aussie networks take the liberty of shortening the tape-delayed games: they cut out the teams changing the field, the relief pitcher's long walk in from the bull pen, and the seventh inning stretch—and if nothing happens in the eighth inning, they skip it altogether and go to the ninth. They wouldn't dare treat cricket like that, and those *tests* (games) can drag on for five days.

One shouldn't complain, though. Before cable and satellite, there was almost nothing in the way of American sports on Aussie TV, and what little there was was broadcast in the middle of the night. On my first trip to Perth in 1989, I turned on the *telly* one Saturday afternoon to find that three of the four stations were showing the same thing: lawn bowling.

The Super Bowl airs live on Monday morning, due to the time and day difference. It's the international feed, so you have to put up with some second-string American sportscaster trying to explain the game to people who have lived their lives knowing only footy, rugby, and soccer. You also miss the great ads. Keep in mind that almost no one in Australia watches the game on a Monday morning in the middle of summer, so no sponsor wants to waste money advertising on it. On the 2006 Super Bowl, when the network in the U.S. was charging a million dollars a minute, the Australians couldn't give away spots. They ended up running the same tired Chrysler ad every commercial break. By 2007, the Super Bowl was aired on Fox Sports, ESPN, and SBS. SBS, which is dedicated to foreign broadcasting, carried it with the U.S. commercials as a "cultural experience".

Radio   The ABC has three AM networks, all devoted to news, talk, and features. One is a twenty-four-hour news network. Besides Australian news, it broadcasts BBC news, and the English language editions of Deutsche Welle (German) and Radio Netherlands (Dutch), plus National Public Radio's "All Things Considered" (American). It also carries live coverage of Parliament when it's in session.

ABC also has a talk station that is produced locally out of each state capital and rebroadcast state wide.

ABC's third AM network is Radio National, a country-wide arts and journalism network.

ABC has two FM networks: one is mostly classical music with a few weekend jazz programs; the other is youth-oriented.

The SBS radio network carries foreign language programming.

There are various commercial AM and FM stations, mostly

Top 40 rock and roll and a few country stations. These are owned by national media conglomerates and can originate from central studios in the eastern states or from local studios in state capitals and regional cities.

There are also *community stations* of various sizes. Some are small niche stations, broadcasting in Russian or Greek, and are often run by unpaid volunteers. Some are quite large and sound commercial. These community stations are allowed to play limited advertising, which must be identified as *station sponsors*, while maintaining non-profit status. These stations have varied programming.

And then there's *Racing Radio*—the bookie's dream—twenty-four hours a day of horse and dog races [more in **gambling**].

For Americans hankering for the sound of home who can't always tune into NPR's "All Things Considered" on ABC-AM, there's radio on the Internet. Use your computer to tune in American and international radio. You'll have 10,000 stations at a mouse-click. If you really want to get fancy, plug your living room stereo into the headphone jack of the computer and rock out.

Newspapers There are two national newspapers: a daily, "The Australian", and a business-oriented weekly, "The Australian Financial Review".

In the capital cities there are twenty-one daily/weekend metropolitan papers. There are also over 450 regional papers, including more than 100 ethnic language papers.

Many of the major papers are tabloids that have opinion blended with journalism. There are two major papers in Melbourne: "The Age" is a serious paper, but more people read "The Herald Sun", which is a tabloid and is Australia's biggest selling daily.

The "West Australian" is the only major Perth daily and is a good example of a tabloid. Objectivity is secondary to selling papers, and opinionated headlines are common. A front page headline about the then state *Premier* (Governor) Geoff Gallop read: "Fat cats flourish under Gallop." Another one read: "How scam scumbags rip us off." (Note that Australian papers don't capitalize all the words in headlines.) A story about Jane Fonda speaking at a 2007 Washington peace rally referred to her as "Hanoi Jane" (without the quotation marks). Another story led with "Spoilt WA jobseekers...are creating unemployment pockets...". These aren't on the opinion page or labelled as opinion, but are presented as straight news. The worst thing is that there's no alternative for statewide news in WA, since it's the only paper in town.

In the tabloids, *the cricket* often bumps major news from the front page. A bad car accident is described as a *horror crash* or *road carnage*; a sex offender is a *sex fiend*; and the word "alleged" is rarely used. Some cover photos are shocking, if not completely disgusting. The inside front cover is opinion, gossip columns, and political cartoons. Car crashes, murders, political gaffes, and scandals fill the next ten pages, followed by a few pages of world news, more opinion pages, then business, racing, and *sport*.

Ironically, most of the news on the Perth pop radio stations is lifted from the first five pages of that morning's West Australian, so people who get their news between music sets only know the paper's take on the news that day. As an alternative, many people in Perth read the national daily, The Australian, and get their local news from the ABC.

Magazines include the same wide range of topics as in North America. The best place to shop for magazines is at a newsagent's. Many imported magazines are available from the UK and the U.S. There are Australian versions of "Vogue", "Cosmo", and "Men's Health". The "Time" magazine sold in Australia is the Hong Kong edition, half as thick as the U.S. version with only the international stories. If you're moving to Australia and want true American editions, rent a post office box in the States and have the magazines forwarded [see section on **receiving mail from the U.S. and Canada.**]

Gambling

Gambling is an Australian tradition and is promoted privately and by the government. There are legal forms in all states: state lotteries, casinos in capital cities, betting parlors in neighborhood shopping centres and pubs, and horse and dog tracks.

Horse and dog racing is so prominent that there are *Racing Radio* stations throughout the country that carry nothing but race results.

Gambling is state regulated, and the states rely on profits to fund many community programs, including programs for people who gamble too much. Gamblers are also called *punters*.

Pokies is short for *poker machines* (slot machines). Australian slot machine designs are used worldwide. One of the world's largest manufacturers is the Australian company, Aristocrat. Just about every bar and private club in Australia has some.

Let's use Western Australia as an example, where the average citizen loses $500 per year gambling—such is the price for dreaming of the big win.

The Burswood Casino complex is across the Swan River from the Perth *CBD* (*Central Business District*). Picture a medium-sized Las Vegas strip casino/hotel/resort. It's about halfway from the CBD to the airport and just across the freeway from the Belmont Horse Track. Burswood not only attracts Perth locals and visitors from around WA, but lures tourists from Asia who want a holiday in a western country.

Like a Vegas hotel/casino, Burswood has a convention centre, two hotels (unlike Vegas, the hotels aren't cheap), a half-dozen restaurants and bars, a golf course, a pool and spa, tennis courts, night clubs, a legitimate theater, and, of course, a casino. Curiously, unlike American casinos, the slots don't ding and chime; it's a relatively quiet casino. Poker, baccarat, blackjack, craps, and roulette are played, along with *Two Up*.

Two Up is as basic as a game can get—kind of like pitching pennies against a wall—more at home in a bush camp than a casino. It's an old Australian coin-flipping game, played with two pennies. Players place bets on how they'll come up, both heads or both tails. There's no playing table; the coins end up on the floor.

When you first come upon the *Two Up* game in the casino, it looks a bit strange. You see a crowd standing in a circle and assume there's a gaming table in the middle, but when you get closer, you notice there's no table. They're just standing around an open space in the middle of the casino floor. Before you can laugh, you notice how intent everyone is. One of the players puts the two pennies tails up on a little flat piece of wood called a *kip*. He or she throws them up a certain height— the pennies must turn properly—if not, the *ringkeeper* will make the player do it again. When the pennies fall to the floor, the ringkeeper leans over them and reads if they're both heads or both tails. He then picks up the coins, everybody pays off, and they toss again. Pretty basic.

TAB   If you can't make it across town to the casino, there are opportunities right in your neighborhood: the *TAB* (*Totalizator Agency Board*) betting shops. TABs are in shopping centers throughout Australian cities. There's also PubTAB and BistroTAB, which are in local taverns and eateries. Here one can place bets on horse races, dog races, sports games, etc. In Western Australia, TAB generates A$1 billion annually—in a state with a population of 2 million. Some eighty-three percent goes to the winners, a percentage goes to support the racing industry, and about 4.5 percent (A$48 million) goes to community services. TAB also sponsors a program called *Betcare* for people who can't control their gambling, which, of course, is most of their customers.

That's not all: the WA state lottery (Lotterywest) has multiple games, such as Powerball, Scratch and Win, Soccer Pools, Daily Draws, etc. These can be purchased from local newsagents, and some afternoons you'd think selling lottery tickets was all newsagents did.

The profits from WA's Lotterywest, funds arts programs and concerts, builds and maintains nature trails, bankrolls community events, and more. The state film board, Screenwest, is Lotterywest-funded, and not only promotes filming in WA, but also provides seed money for local production and educational programs like the Film and Television Institute (FTI) in Fremantle. FTI not only teaches filmmaking in a traditional setting, but also provides filmmaking programs that travel to remote communities at the far ends of the state to teach video storytelling to indigenous people.

The social fallout from gambling is a concern to some, but the dependence on generated revenues seems to far outweigh any remorse. Gambling is deeply ingrained and accepted in the way of life and is unlikely to be eliminated.

Tobacco

Cigarettes share the same problems as in North America, and smokers face the same kinds of laws. Smoking has been banned in—and near—most public buildings throughout the country. Smoking in restaurant *alfresco areas* (semi-enclosed outside dining patios) is still allowed in some states: Queensland makes smokers go outside, Northern Territory has no restrictions at all, and the other states fall somewhere in the middle. Queensland has even banned smoking on patrolled beaches (ones with lifeguards). Smoking seems to be on the decline. The only bright spot for smokers is that Havana cigars are legal—but not cheap.

Alcohol

Beer   Australia is famous for beer—drinking it, as well as making it. Amongst some social classes, beer is almost a religion. Beer drinkers tend to be loyal to their brew.

One major misconception is that all Australians drink Foster's. Chalk that one up to advertising—in America. Fact is, you rarely see Foster's, except in Queensland, though you see a lot of Foster's products: *VB* (Victoria Bitter), *Crownies* (Crown Lager), Carlton, Sterling, Cascade, etc. The Foster's you get in North America is actually made in Canada (read the label, mate).

Other major beers are XXXX (called *4X*) from Queensland, Swan Lager from Western Australia, Boags from Tasmania, Tooheys from New South Wales, Victoria Bitter (VB) from Victoria, and many more. There are many smaller breweries, like Western Australia's Little Creatures and South Australia's Coopers, plus micro breweries, like Feral, Bootleg, and Mountain Goat. Hundreds of boutique breweries have sprung up throughout the country, each making their own brew to their own recipes, served fresh to locals and tourists.

Domestic beer isn't cheap—about twice the U.S. price. You can expect to pay A$30–50 for a *carton* (case), or A$12–15 for a six-pack, depending on the brand. If you hanker for the taste of home, Budweiser, Miller, and Corona are available as expensive imports, along with many beers from Europe. When it comes to a good brew, what's a few dollars? Besides, one doesn't buy beer; one just rents it for an hour or so.

Beer terms   A *stubby* is a bottle of beer. A *stubby holder* is an individual bottle cooler made of wetsuit material that keeps the contents cold. The stubby holder is another Australian icon; many Aussie males travelling abroad make sure to pack theirs because you can't count on finding one just anywhere. If hosting a group and you want to fit in, have a supply on hand. Most Aussie working class males don't drink beer out of a glass unless drinking *draught* (draft) in a pub. ("Out of the bottle is just fine, mate. Ya got a stubby holder?")

When you do go into a pub, tavern, or hotel and ask for a glass of beer, you'll need to know the correct terms, which vary from state to state and city to city. A small (eight oz.) glass is called a *pot* in Queensland, a *middy* in Western Australia, and a *schooner* in South Australia; while a large glass (sixteen oz.) can be a *schooner* in Queensland, but a *pint* in WA .

And then there's a *yardie*. A yardie is a yard-long beer glass, spherical at the bottom, with a narrow neck that flares to a wide horn at the top. It holds up to a half gallon of beer. If you Google *yardie,* you'll find the first two pages of listings are websites about how the former Australian prime minister, Bob Hawke, once held the world speed record for drinking a yardie. It's truly something any Aussie would be proud of.

Besides being a stubby, a bottle of beer can be a *coldie*. A big bottle can be a *tallie* and a small bottle can be a *throwdown*. A can of beer is a *tinny*. It's all confusing, but don't be intimidated. The first time you order at a pub in a region, you're bound to get it wrong; just ask the bartender for the right term and by the second round you'll be ordering like a local.

If you want to buy the next round, you say "it's my *shout,*" which means "the beer is on me."   A *Yankee shout* is where everyone pays for themselves.

A case of beer can be a *carton, box,* or *slab*. If you make a stupid mistake at work you might get *slabbed*, which means you have to bring a case of beer to share with your work mates the next day.

A pitcher can be a *jug* or a *handle*. I once went into a pub after a hot twelve-hour drive up the west coast from Perth to Exmouth and ordered a pitcher of beer. The bartender didn't seem to understand what I was talking about.

We went back and forth over it for a bit, and were both starting to get pissed off when a young woman sitting at the bar next to me said quietly, "Ask for a *jug*."

I did so.

The bartender looked at me and said, "Why didn't ya say so in the first place? I thought ya wanted me to get a camera and take a picture of beer," and he served me my *jug* of beer.

Had he just been *havin' a go at me* or was he serious? At that point, I didn't care, I was thirsty.

In the great Aussie *DIY* (*do-it-yourself*) tradition, you can also make your own beer with home brew kits available at supermarkets. There are also shops that cater to do-it-yourself brewing. They provide the materials and tanks, you do the work, and when it's all done, you bring home a large quantity of your very own concoction.

Wine   Australian wines are wonderful, world class, and relatively inexpensive. Some eighty percent are from the Barossa Valley in South Australia and the Hunter Valley in New South Wales. There are cottage industries in almost every state, most notably several areas in Tasmania: Piper River, Derwent Valley, Tamar Valley, etc., and in Western Australia: the Swan Valley, the Southwest, and Margaret River.

Almost all varieties are grown. Sirah is called *Shiraz* (pronounced *sheer-azz*). Blends are common, such as Cab-Merlot, Cab-Shiraz, Grenache-Shiraz-Merlot, etc. Whites include Chardonnay, Chenin Blanc, and Gewurtztraminer.

Dessert wines are quite good. Try *cane dried*, which means the cane is cut leaving the bunch in place on the trellis for a few weeks to intensify the sugars.

Foster's owns a large percentage of the big wineries after buying Southcorp in 2005. Their wineries include Wolf Blass, Penfold's, Rosemount, Black Opal, and a few dozen more. They also own Matua Valley in New Zealand, Beringer,

Souverain, and Staggs Leap in the U.S.; plus more in Italy. There are too many to list.

Chateau Cardboard is Dame Edna's favorite: wine packaged in two- or four-litre cardboard boxes.

Mixed drinks in a can are called *RTDs* (*Ready to Drink*). There is Jack Daniels and Coke, Bacardi Breezer, Vodka Cruisers, and many more. You drink them like any canned drink and they're easily transportable and handy for barbecues, beach picnics, and BYO restaurants.

Hard liquor   North Queensland is sugarcane country, and that's what rum is made from. Bundaberg (*Bundy*) is the most famous rum, made in the town of the same name. There are several types and ages of Bundy rum, some so smooth you'd almost think you were drinking scotch.

Various small label whiskeys are produced throughout the country. Imported booze is expensive—grab some duty-free on the plane or at the airport. Jack Daniels seems to be the most popular American whiskey.

The esky is an ice chest (from Eskimo cooler). They come in all shapes and sizes.

When Australians are invited over to a barbecue, they might show up with a small *esky* full of their regular brew, and perhaps a bottle of wine. In America, when one brings a six-pack of beer to someone's home as a guest, one usually leaves what's left at the end of the night. Aussies, at the end of the evening, will take any unconsumed bottles home in their *esky*.

Drunk driving in Australia is called *drink driving*. My advice: don't. They are extra-vigilant. Any time you're stopped by a cop—and they don't have to have probable cause like in the U.S.—you'll be asked to *blow in the bag*. There are road blocks in major traffic areas on shopping and weekend nights for *RBTs* (*random breath tests*).

Drugs

Abuse of non-prescription drugs is very similar to North America, and to make a laundry list of them would be tedious and undoubtedly of little interest to the readers of this book. Getting caught with a small amount of marijuana will result in a caution or minor fine, depending on the cop and the state.

Heavier drugs (coke, heroin, speed, ice and ecstasy) will see you in court. You read about date rape drugs in the newspapers. One bad option among the poor is solvent sniffing—*petrol* (gasoline) or paint—as not only do they get wasted, but they end up with permanent brain damage. Let's move on.

Dress

Business   Australians are casual dressers, but they dress up for business.

Business suits are common in the *CBDs* (*Central Business District*) for lawyers, accountants, and businessmen. This is usually a two-piece or vested suit, black or with an understated stripe, four-button or double breasted. Once in the office, the coat generally comes off, but the tie stays on.

Engineers and less-formal white collar workers will wear slacks and a pressed, button-front shirt. Ties are rare.

Many workers who come into contact with the public wear uniform shirts. Real estate reps, bank workers, etc., wear ironed, button-front shirts or blouses with the company logo embroidered on the breast—name tags are common. Salespeople, counter clerks, car dealers, etc., wear golf or polo shirts with printed or embroidered logos on the breast. The color is usually the same for everyone in a particular shop, so finding a salesperson is easier.

One reason for the widespread use of uniform shirts is because Aussies are very casual dressers, and with required uniforms they are forced to dress presentably.

Tradesmen will commonly wear *hi-vis* (florescent) yellow, lime, or orange-colored shirts, for high visibility and safety. This is especially true for *truckies*, heavy machinery operators, road crews, or construction workers. These will commonly have logos on the breast and are UV-resistant (the southern sun is merciless). Shorts are common for working men. *Blokes* (men) under forty wear long ones that go below the knee. Older blokes wear them short, just below the *bum* (butt).

School kids wear uniforms, too. Public schools use a polo shirt with the school logo, a heavier *jumper* (sweater or sweatshirt) with logo for cooler days; matching shorts, long pants, or skirts for girls, and shorts or long pants for boys. Private schools often require school blazers, button-front shirts, and ties; slacks or shorts for boys, skirts for girls; knee-socks for both.

After work   Perhaps because of the uniforms, both at school and at work, when an Aussie is on their own time, he or she usually dresses very casually. The standard fashion seems to be beach togs, even though they might be hundreds of kilometres inland. *Boardies* (sloppy, loose-fitting shorts), untucked T-shirts, or a *singlet* (tank top) are common. For footwear: thongs, or in the case of Western Australians and Queenslanders, barefoot. Dark socks worn with *joggers* (sneakers) are the norm.

Many Aussie males seem to be impervious to rain and cold and dress lightly in singlet, shorts, and thongs, even on the coldest days. In deference to a bad storm you might see a bloke wearing a jacket with shorts and thongs. Few people dress differently for the rain; most ignore it. Don't worry about them, *they'll be right.*

Going out   In the cities, many businessmen and women will dress up to go out. Black seems to be the color of choice. In the suburbs, many men go out in beach clothes, and it's common to see a well-dressed woman in a nice cocktail dress or slack outfit accompanied by a man wearing baggy shorts, thongs, and a T-shirt printed with an art logo, a car logo, or just an off-color saying. This has become institutionalized to the point where it's intentionally used in the wardrobe on TV commercials—I know this for a fact because I've worked on them and asked the Agency people about it.

Footwear deserves mentioning. I've seen people at the *tip* (city dump) wearing nothing but thin rubber thongs on their feet, up to their shins in debris. At least they weren't barefoot.

Nikes and Adidas can be pricey, over A$200 for a fashionable pair, though Chinese imports are cheaper.

The traditional work boot is a short, pull-on with elastic sides, water- and oil-proof leather, sometimes with steel toes. They're made in Australia by Blundstone and Rossi, and in Asia by some others not worth mentioning. They're relatively inexpensive and sturdy. You can easily slip them off when going in the house so as not to track in dirt.

Multi-story buildings

The bottom floor is the *ground floor*, the floor above that is the *first floor*, and on up. The area below the ground floor, as in a building on a hillside, is called an *undercroft*.

Some buildings are wholly owned, some are *strata-titled* (co-ops), with individual offices separately owned. This provides investment opportunities for owner-occupiers or small investors [see section on **real estate**].

Australians like to formally name otherwise ordinary buildings. Sometimes it's after the original builder, sometimes after the occupant. The Asthma Foundation in Perth is in a modest office building called *Asthma Foundation House*. Wesfarmers, a multi-billion dollar corporation, is in a fifteen-story skyscraper called *Wesfarmers House*.

The Australian home

A tour   Most Australian homes have several smaller rooms instead of fewer, larger rooms. One reason is that it's easier to heat in winter, as most homes don't have central heating. A typical home might have a *lounge* room (living room), a family room, a games room, a screened-in veranda, a kitchen, bedrooms, bathroom, and a toilet or two.

The toilet itself isn't in the same room with the bath, shower, or sink, but in a separate room. This makes sense for a family, as one person can be washing in one room while another person is using the toilet in the other.

Toilets and bathrooms have tile floors with drains in the center; useful if there's an overflow or when it comes time to mop, but short on aesthetics as the sink and shower drains are plumbed common with the floor drain, which means the stuff that goes down them can be seen passing by under the floor drain. Thankfully, toilets are on separate lines.

To save water, Australians use two-speed toilets: one button for a half-flush, the other for a full-flush. On some toilets, it's pull for half, push for full; on others, it's by duration—hold it down two seconds for half, longer for full.

Don't forget to observe if the toilet water spins the opposite direction as in the Northern Hemisphere.

Bedrooms in older homes don't have built-in closets; instead they'll have a freestanding *wardrobe*, often called a *robe*. If you rent an unfurnished older home, you might have to buy a *robe* or two.

Electric blankets in Australia are heated electric pads that are placed <u>under</u> the sheets, immediately on top of the mattress. American-style electric blankets that go on top are unavailable, and if you ask for one and describe how it works, you'll receive dumbfounded stares.

Kitchens typically have a meals area in addition to a separate, more formal dining room. In the kitchen, you'll find most of the *mod cons*, (modern conveniences) you're used to: double sink (usually stainless steel), microwave, and lots of appliances, like toasters, juicers, ice cream makers, etc. The stove can be gas or electric or both, with a gas top (sometimes called the *hob*) and an electric oven. Refrigerators tend to be about two-thirds smaller than those in North America; some have an ice maker and cold water spout. Often there's a second fridge on the back porch, and sometimes a deep-freeze. Dishwashers aren't as common as in the U.S., and there are no garbage disposals or trash compacters, but you can be certain of finding an electric kettle in every kitchen. This is just what the name implies: a vessel you plug into a power point, flip the switch in the handle and it heats the water for you. When it's boiled, it switches off automatically. These are as common in an Aussie kitchen as the sink itself.

When hand-washing dishes, Aussies use soap, but typically don't rinse the dishes with fresh water before putting them in the drying rack.

Garages   Aussie houses often have carports instead of garages. Some of these have lockable garage doors, but are open to the sides and back.

The shed is another Aussie icon. Located in the backyard, it's usually a simple galvanized structure for tools and storage. This is where Dad retreats when he's had enough pleasant family life. It's no surprise that this is also where the *beer fridge* is usually located.

Air con (*air conditioning*) is common, and there are several kinds used.

Window-mounted units have largely been replaced by *reverse-cycle* (also called *split-systems*) installed in individual rooms. A vented panel is mounted flat on an interior wall with hoses going through the wall to an outside heat pump. These units can run in one direction as an air conditioner and, at a touch of a button, can be run in reverse as a heater. Most have TV set-like remote controls.

Large centrally-located forced air systems like those found in suburban American houses, are rare in Australian homes. Some newer homes are being built with these, and are called *ducted system.*

You'll find many homes will have whole-house evaporative coolers—called "swamp coolers" in the U.S. They're simply a big blower box on the roof with water plumbed to it. The water soaks into pads in the sides of the box, an electric fan pulls air through the pads, evaporation cools the air, which is then blown throughout the house. The trick is to leave a few windows open so the air can flow through. These don't work well in humid regions.

Water heaters   Though conventional hot water systems using gas or electric-heated holding tanks are available, *instant-on* water heaters are more common. It's a box about half the size of a microwave, mounted on an outside wall near a bathroom. It super-heats the water in a small (about a half-gallon) copper tank before delivering it into the house. This system is energy efficient but can produce an irregular hot water mix in the shower. The trick is, turn on the hot water, then once it's at full heat, blend in the cold water to the desired temperature. Properly set up, these systems work as well as the large water heaters used in North America, but with considerable savings from not having to keep a large amount of water constantly heated.

Another energy efficient alternative to the instant-on systems are solar water heaters mounted on the roof. Normal city pressure pushes the water up to the heater, where it flows through a solar collector (a radiator made of copper pipes in a black box), then into a large water storage tank, where it continues to circulate by convection. They have an electric or gas booster to heat the water on sunless days, They're on time clocks, so heat can be boosted automatically for early morning or late night needs.

Washing machines are as essential as in North America, but dryers tend to be smaller and only used in the winter or in rainy weather, as Aussies line-dry most of their wash. Because of this, dryers are often kept outside on the back porch or in a nearby shed.

The *Hills Hoist* is a four-sided, rotating clothesline on a central pipe with a crank in the middle so you can lower it to hang the clothes and then raise it so the kids and the family dog can't get at them. It's a homegrown invention Aussies are proud of.

Misc.   Window screens are called *flyscreens* or *flywire*. Security screens are common to prevent burglaries.

A trash can is called a *rubbish bin*. An outside trash can with wheels is called a *wheelie bin*.

The kids' playhouse is called a *cubby*.

A hand rail is called a *balustrade*.

Hanging pictures   When attempting to hang pictures on plaster walls, don't use nails. Unlike *gypboard* (sheetrock), plaster crumbles and leaves big holes. Use a masonry drill and a wall anchor insert. For heavy items, use *Dynabolts*.

House   architecture   in   Australia   developed pragmatically. Early *humpies* (native shacks) led to mud brick cabins, galvanised steel shacks, then timber plank homes. Today there's a *hotchpotch* (hodgepodge) of styles.

Australian cities are mostly vast suburbs. Cookie-cutter tract homes aren't common; homes are generally individually built [see section on **real estate**], so there's more variation than in suburban America. That said, the basic suburban brick home is relatively boring, but there are some interesting styles if you look for them.

Federation refers to the style of building at the time Australia federated into a nation, around 1900. It's generally red brick and white mortar, with high peaked roofs covered in corrugated steel, often *bullnose* (curved down over the veranda), with Queen Anne filigree around the corners. The windows are tall and slim, multi-panelled, often with *leadlight* (stained glass) patterns and artwork. There are many examples of these still standing, plus new versions being built reminiscent of the age.

Italian immigrants built brick houses with a series of arches across the fronts, often supported by Roman columns. Short columns support *balustrades* (handrails).

Some homes are split-level with the garage and a few rooms on the lower floor. Broad exterior steps lead up to second-floor entrances where the living areas are. This split-level style is called a house with an *undercroft*.

Scattered in the older big city suburbs are colonial farmhouses, English country cottages, Mediterranean villas with tile roofs, Californian Craftsman bungalows, and ultra-modern white cubical homes in multi-story arrays.

However, most newer suburban homes are practical, boring, double brick.

Construction   Older houses are made of wooden planks, *cladding* (siding) or *weatherboard* (also called *Hardiplank*, after the manufacturer, the John Hardie company). Weatherboard is a fibre-cement plank still in use today and used like shiplap. Some were made of pressed asbestos sheets—called *fibro*—which has been illegal since the late 1980s.

Asbestos was a common building material until its cancerous side effects were discovered. Corrugated asbestos fencing was common throughout Australia, and a lot of it is still around. They say it's safe as long as you keep it sealed in a coat of paint. Beware: don't break up old *fibro* boards or fence materials.

In the southeast and west, brick construction is now very common. Some brick houses in the eastern states are merely a veneer of brick. True brick houses have outer walls that are *double brick* (two layers with an air space in the middle), which keeps inner walls dry and insulated. Inside walls are single-thickness. Masonry is un-reinforced, since earthquakes are uncommon. The inside of brick houses is often left raw brick or *rendered* (plastered). In very dry weather, the mortar in brick homes can crack, and homeowners are advised to water their walls.

Timber (wood) framed houses aren't as common as brick. As wood studs becomes more expensive, hollow steel beams for framing are being used. Wood is also subject to *white ants* (termites).

Rammed earth (which looks like poured concrete) is a new trend: cool in the summer, warm in the winter. *ECO block* is concrete poured into four to eight-inch wide hollows in foam forms with rebar inserted. It's energy efficient and sturdy [also see **real estate, new homes**].

In the northern tropics, homes with broad verandas are built on poles called *stumps*. This construction allows air to circulate underneath and provides additional storage. It's also good in a flood and to protect the houses from termites. Queensland houses typically have lots of air circulation and sometimes have fancy filigree around the verandas.

Roofing is either fired-cement tiles in various shapes and colors or sheets of corrugated galvanised steel. The steel can be either factory painted (*Colorbond*) or left with the shiny galvanised finish.

Tile roofs are supported by narrow toe-rails. Tiles interlock and rest on top, and a lip on the tile hooks over the top edge of the rail. Only every fourth-or-so tile is nailed to the rail, so be very careful walking on these rooves; it's easy to crack a tile and fall through. Step where the tiles overlap; it's the strongest part. The advantage of these rooves is that they ventilate well and are waterproof, and it's easy to remove a section to replace tiles if needed or to gain access under the roof.

A *timber and iron* house is a wooden house with a corrugated sheet steel roof. To Americans, corrugated steel roofs might seem cheap, like they belong on a mining shack. Indeed, they go back 150 years in Australia. Early settlers would build their entire houses, including the walls, out of it, since it was easily transported and lasted a long time.

It still is and does. Many new houses are roofed with steel, in galvanized finish or *Colorbond*. *Bullnose* sheets are pre-curved sections that give a classic *Federation* look.

Corrugated steel sheets are relatively inexpensive, light, sturdy, and easy to work with. One man can roof a house in two days, and the sound of rain falling on it is pleasant, especially in dry country. When installing it, put in a lot of screws to hold the panels down in strong wind. If you have to walk on the roof, walk where the screws are; the support beams will be directly underneath.

White ants (termites) are virulent in Australia. They'll eat through unprotected pine in a few months. Anything wood should be off the ground on steel footings and the bases painted with creosote if possible. In the northern regions of Australia, termites will make mounds that can grow to two metres (six-and-a-half feet) high.

Wood dimensions come in either metric or imperial. When you refer to a wood size, the order of the dimensions is reversed. The common two-by-four is called a *four-by-two*, a one-by-eight is an *eight-by-one*, etc. Dimensions are also in millimetres, so 19mm is about ¾ inch, and 40mm is about 1½ inch. Most tape measures are in both metres and inches and can be used as a handy converter. I find it easier to estimate in feet and then build in meters. Millimetres are clearer to read on a tape measure and easier to work with than fractions of an inch.

Lumber is called *timber*. Be wary when you price timber in the shop, as it's sold both by the length and by the metre. Look closely; shelf placards will read $X per *len.* (length) or $X per *mtr.* (metre).

Pine, spruce, or fir is also called *oregon*, though it usually refers to Douglas Fir which was imported and grown as a forest crop. Plywood is very expensive. Native woods like jarrah are also expensive, though incredibly hard and strong—so hard that you sometimes have to a drill lead hole before you can nail into it.

Jarrah, a eucalypt native to southwest Western Australia, is such tough wood it is often recycled, salvaged from demolished homes. Hundred year old wharf pilings have been made into beautiful table tops. You can mill off the outer layer, revealing a beautiful polished red surface ready for another hundred years of life as furniture.

Wood glue, like Elmers, is called *PVA* glue.

Gardens   Aussies love their backyards. The Australian dream is a four-bedroom house on quarter-acre *block* (lot) with a Holden in the carport, a wide-screen TV in the lounge, a shed out back, and a lawn all around.

They love their lawns and their flower beds. Unfortunately, in the past decade there has been a countrywide drought. The "El Nino" that brings rain to the U.S. robs it from Australia. Water rationing is normal, with watering days mandated and fines levied if violated.

Garden hoses, sometimes called *hose pipes,* are innovative. Instead of having the American screw-in fitting on the ends, they have plastic quick-releases. Any hose will pop onto the fitting at the faucet and any nozzle will pop onto the other end. If you're migrating, don't bother bringing the hoses; buy them there.

Sprinklers are also called *reticulation.* Drip irrigation is common. Many suburban *blocks* (lots) have *bores* (wells).

Nuts & bolts   Though Australia has been on the metric system for forty years, standard (USA measurement in fractions of an inch) nuts and bolts are still as common as metric, so hang onto your tools.

Fixings (nuts, bolts, screws, and nails) are pricey, so if you're *shifting* (moving) over and have room in the container, bring a supply. Also bring your favorite adhesives. Many materials easily obtained in North America aren't available in Australia or are very expensive.

Swimming pools

Ninety-five percent of Australian backyard pools are saltwater. It's not ocean water, but fresh water that has had salt added to it (ocean water is eight times saltier). Saltwater pools are far superior to normal chlorinated ones. The salt is actually good for your skin and is a recommended treatment for eczema. Most noticeably, it's much nicer to swim in than stinky, eye-stinging chlorine. Public pools, because of their size and the large numbers of people that use them, utilize the same conventional chlorination systems common in North America.

How do saltwater pools work? If you remember your high school chemistry, salt is a molecule containing sodium and chlorine, $NaCl$. An electrical unit in the pool's filtering system electrolyzes the NaCl molecule, producing NaOCl, sodium hypochlorite, a safe form of chlorine that purifies and sterilizes the water. Instead of pouring jugs of chlorine into the pool, you occasionally add a twenty-lb. bag of salt. The sodium pulls the acidity down, so you also have to add small amounts of hydrochloric acid to keep it balanced, but it's still easier to maintain and better for swimmers than chlorine-only systems.

If you rent a house with a pool, get a simple ph test kit and follow the instructions.

Real estate

Methods of land ownership   *Freehold, leasehold* and *Crown land* are the basis of land ownership in Australia.

Freehold means privately owned land. This can be bought and sold.

Crown land is government owned land and can be used for parks, utilities, airports, government facilities, granted to individuals or corporations, sold as *freehold* land, or leased. The *Crown* originally referred to the Royal Family, but it now applies to any government land ownership, be it state or federal. The land is held in the *right of the Crown*, and *the Crown* has legal rights as an individual land owner. About half of all Australian land is *Crown* land, including ninety-three percent of Western Australia.

Leasehold is where an individual or corporation buys a long-term lease on Crown land, usually ninety-nine years, and can treat the lands as if they owned it privately. Throughout the interior, huge tracts consisting of hundreds of square miles of Crown land are leased as cattle and sheep stations. The backbone of the economy—the mining industry—is entirely on leased land.

All the privately occupied land in the *ACT* (*Australian Capital Territory*) is *leasehold*. This was done to avoid speculation in undeveloped land. The city of Canberra had been created as the nation's capital from scratch in the bush in 1908 because a compromise couldn't be reached to base the capital in either Melbourne or Sydney. Cheap leases were issued to stimulate home building to jump-start development of the city. An individual was issued a lease and had to build a house on it within a year. The leases are now sold as if they were private land, and a nominal annual fee is paid to the government.

Real estate terms   The equivalent of a U.S. real estate agent is called a *real estate representative* (or *rep*), while the equivalent of a U.S. real estate broker is an *agent*.

Escrow is called *settlement.* An escrow officer is a *settlement agent* (or a *conveyancer*). Minimum settlement time for a cash sale is about three weeks.

Home loans work similar to those in North America.

Mortgage payments are called *repayments.*

A lien is called a *caveat* and can be placed against a property without the owner's knowledge.

Strata refers to condominium-style ownership, either private residential or commercial [more in **strata titles**].

When land is condemned for public use, it's called *resumption.* The land is said to have been *resumed.*

A model home is a *display home*; model homes are *display villages.* A housing tract is called a *housing estate.*

Buying off the plan means buying anything that hasn't been built yet. This can be an unbuilt tract home, *strata* (condo-style) development, office, or commercial building.

Reno means renovated or renovations.

An open house is called a *home open. Home opens* are generally held on Sunday afternoons, are advertised in the papers, and last only about one hour. The short session means a *rep* can open several homes that day, while *stickybeaks* (looky-loos) are minimized and homeowners aren't inconvenienced for the entire day. Temporary signs are posted at cross streets to lead you to the house.

House and *block* (lot) size are expressed in square metres. For an <u>approximate</u> estimate, just add a zero to the square metres, plus a little (i.e., 200 sq. metres is about 2,000 sq. feet). A quarter acre is about 1,000 sq. mtrs. Another common measurement is the *hectare*, which is 10,000 sq. mtrs., or about 2.5 acres.

Foreign investment in real estate   Only citizens, legal permanent residents, citizens of New Zealand, and foreign nationals married to an Australian can automatically buy residential property in Australia. All others must apply to the *Foreign Investment Review Board* (*FIRB*). With approval, foreign nationals may be able to buy <u>new</u> residential property, but when they eventually sell it, it will have to be sold to an Australian. Commercial property is easier for a foreign national to purchase.

Under the Australia-United States Free Trade Agreement (AUSFTA), it's easier for U.S. citizens to buy commercial property. For specific information, try the website at **www.firb.gov.au.**

Home sales   Just like in the U.S. and Canada, owning your own home is the Australian dream. The process of buying a home is similar.

Commissions are around 2–3 percent and aren't necessarily split between buying and selling reps. When commission splits do happen, they're called a *conjunction*.

Frequently there's <u>no</u> buyers' rep, only a sellers' rep serving both (<u>buyer beware</u>!).

On the east coast of Australia, homes are often sold by public auction. The auction is held on the front lawn in open bidding, and if the minimum price isn't met, there's no sale. On the west coast, auctions aren't as popular, but do occur.

In some areas, home prices are sometimes listed in a *price-range*, not at a fixed price. For example, a house might be listed as $350,000–380,000. This might seem a bit strange, and it doesn't necessarily mean the seller will take the lower amount. It means the seller will entertain offers in that range, hoping for offers from several potential buyers that will push it toward the upper end. It also gets buyers to look up into the next price bracket. Sometimes commercial realtors won't state a price, but will ask for *expressions of interest* or *price on application*. This means you make a blind bid; the highest bid over the seller's minimum (which they're not making public) gets it. In a hot market this can really drive the prices up.

An important aside: Buyers are on their own when it comes to researching their properties. There's some requirement of disclosure by the seller and the rep, but buyers should make an effort to research the property during the *due diligence period*, which can be a week or two, negotiated in the *purchasing offer*. During this period, the potential buyer can check out the titles and contracts, talk to the local shire or city governments to find out what's planned for the area, talk to the neighbors to find out what's not visible or apparent (i.e., a loud road nearby, airplane noise, a bad smell from a factory when the wind shifts, a neighbour who races dirt bikes in the back yard, etc.), and read the association agreements if strata-titled [see **strata titles**].

Australian developers can be every bit as cutthroat as American ones. People have purchased land to build their dream home next to what was listed on the developer's plans as a "water conservation reserve"—envisioning a placid marsh or lake—only to discover it meant a future sewage plant. Likewise, people have been sold rural land only to discover that a high-density subdivision was planned nearby and their quiet country lane would soon be a busy thoroughfare.

Home financing   As in North America, home loans come from banks, credit unions, and mortgage companies. Privacy laws prohibit buyers from being pre-qualified for loans by agents, so the seller won't know whether a buyer will actually be able to borrow the money to buy their home until the financing is either approved or disapproved. A buyer can obtain a verbal or written pre-approval, but banks usually won't be held responsible in case conditions change.

Most loans are for part of the purchase price, but 100 percent loans are available at higher interest rates.

In some states, first-time home buyers can receive a grant to help make their purchase or can have the *stamp duty* waived.

Stamp duty is a tax that applies to home buying in some states. It can add several thousand dollars to the purchase price. Stamp duty can be tiered, meaning the percentage increases as the house price goes up.

New homes   Housing tracts aren't common as in America; most homes are individually built on sub-divided land. A developer will clear a piece of ground and put in the basic infrastructure, like roads, water, power, and sewers; and sell it ready to build on. Instead of signs proclaiming "New Homes", you see signs advertising "*Land Sale*".

Buyers then have an architect design a house and hire a

builder to construct it. The upside is that every fourth house isn't identical—each is an individual design, reflecting the character of the inhabitants. The downside is that homes aren't mass-produced in an assembly-line system, and therefore cost more and take longer to build.

Strata titles refer to condominium or co-op style ownership, where one has title to the space but not necessarily to the land. Owners control a share of the total area, proportionally based on how much of the total property they own.

Strata titles can be on a townhouse in a residential development, an apartment in an apartment building, a retail store in a shopping center, a warehouse or factory in an industrial center, or an office in a business center or a skyscraper. It's a *scheme* (system) that allows a small investor to get into a bigger market

A suburban strip mall with a half-dozen stores might not be owned by one person or company. Each individual shop might have a different owner—and not necessarily the proprietor of the business in that shop. In large office buildings, individual floors and offices can be owned on a *strata* basis by separate small investors who either occupy the space themselves or rent it out.

It's a kind of investor egalitarianism. One might not have the leverage to buy a $35 million high-rise building, but you might be able to put together $500,000 to buy an eighth of a floor of that building. The investor then rents it out at a 6–10 percent annual return, hoping for a long-term financial appreciation of the property.

Strata companies manage the properties—usually those with ten or more units—and there's a set of rules and regulations. Each title is assigned a *unit equivalent,* to be used for voting, tax and maintenance levy purposes, in proportion with the percentage of the property owned. There's an *annual general meeting (AGM)* and minutes are kept. If you're planning to buy a unit in a strata building or complex, you can ask for a copy of the minutes to see the current situation and what's planned for the future.

Commercial real estate   There are real estate

investment trusts, and a lot of real estate is foreign-owned, especially by Japanese, Chinese and European offshore investors. Commercial leases are usually five years, and most improvements, *rates* (taxes) and building management fees are paid by the lessee.

Renting   *For Let* means either "for rent" or "for lease". At first glance, house and apartment rental rates look really cheap. On closer examination, you'll discover the symbol *p/w* after them, meaning *per week*. You can also pay per *fortnight* (two weeks) or per month.

Property management companies usually handle rentals. They'll carefully screen new tenants and will request references. They may meticulously photograph the property before you move in, and you'll be asked to put up a *security bond* (deposit), which is put in a government-controlled escrow account. You may even be restricted as to how many pictures you can hang on the walls or whether you can hang towels on the outside veranda railing. Managers are allowed to occasionally inspect the interior—they'll make an appointment—and when you move out, you'll be required to return the place to an immaculate condition and to have the carpets commercially cleaned.

Month-to-month renting is called *periodical tenancy*.

Labour (labor) and business

The Australian minimum wage is about twice that of the U.S., and the basic work week is thirty-eight hours. Employees get nice workplace benefits: an average of four weeks per year of *holiday* (vacation), paid *sickies* (sick days) long-service benefits, and *superannuation* (also known as *super*—what they call retirement funds).

Basic wages agreed upon though negotiation are called *award rates*. These are set by the government with a list of entitlements and minimum wages for specific jobs. One can check to see if the job they're seeking is covered by an *awards rate* or what the *historical rate* has been for that job. The website is **www.workchoices.gov.au.**

Penalty rates are higher than normal rates paid for work performed outside normal working hours—this can mean for overtime or for working on a weekend or holiday.

An employee isn't fired; he's *sacked*. One isn't laid off; one is *let off, stood down*, or *made redundant* (the latter meaning your job has disappeared due to restructuring). *Rationalisation* means eliminating staff or equipment to make a business more efficient. An employee who feels they were wrongly *sacked* or *made redundant* can usually appeal to a state appeals board. Information can be found at **www.workplace.gov.au** or through the individual states.

The Australian workplace has been transformed in the last twenty years. At one time, the unions were very strong. They overplayed their hands in some major work stoppages in the 80s (airlines, wharfage), and the government legislated limits to their powers. The unions are still formidable and frequently flex their muscles, but have decreased significantly in size. Management can now sue a union if workplace disruptions can be proven unjustified. The government can also levy fines on unions and deny their representatives access to workplaces. In some cases this has tamed the unions, in others it has made them more defiant and aggressive.

The federal government has pushed through *IR* (*Industrial Reforms*), which created the *Australian Workplace Agreements* (*AWAs*), further eroding the strength of the unions and tilting power toward employers. This was done by the Howard government in 2006, trying to make the Australian workforce internationally competitive. Individual workers now negotiate their own rates, and not everyone has the bargaining skill to get themselves a good deal. Workers in commissioned sales, like real estate, have to be paid a wage and have it deducted from their future commissions, which can be difficult for the employer.

Employees can now become independent contractors. The employer gets the work done but doesn't have to pay benefits or worry about government oversight. The contractor has to supply his/her own tools, vehicle, workers compensation insurance, and *superannuation* contributions, but they can charge more and have a degree of independence. There are also significant tax benefits for contractors, since they can deduct their expenses and are taxed at a lower corporate rate. Many former employees are doing the same job at the same company, but are now functioning as independent contractors or consultants. Generally, only the best workers are allowed to do this, and their job security is in knowing that they're in demand.

Take, for example, what happened in Western Australia in the early 2000s. The mineral resources boom in the Pilbara region up north absorbed much of the local workforce from Perth in the south, and it was hard to find good people to hire. In conditions like this, independent contractors can get themselves a good deal.

The downside is simple: can an individual get himself a reasonable deal negotiating in private? Can a nineteen-year-old worker who really needs a job negotiate successfully with a fifty-year-old manager who is under pressure from his superiors to cut costs?

It's hard to find something funny on this subject, but here goes: My favorite Australian union name is the *Liquor, Hospitality, and Miscellaneous Union.*

Religion

In order of numbers, they are: Catholic, Anglican Church (Church of England, or Episcopal Church in the U.S.), Uniting Church (a merger of Methodist, Congregational Union, and Presbyterian), Presbyterian, Greek Orthodox, Baptist, Pentecostal, Jehovah's Witnesses, Church of Christ, Salvation Army Church, Seventh Day Adventist, Latter Day Saints (Mormon), and Brethren. Other Christian religions are present and represented in smaller numbers. Non-Christian religions include (in order of numbers): Islam, Buddhism, Judaism, Hinduism, and others.

Despite all that, Australians aren't particularly religious as a nation, especially when compared to the U.S. This can be partly traced to the original settlers: in the U.S., many were religious refugees, in Australia, they were mostly convicts.

Australians love to question authority, such as government, the legal system, the police, etc., and religion is no exception. Church attendance isn't high, only six percent attend regularly. A lot of people will proudly proclaim their atheism. It's been said that in the absence on religion, Australians have turned to their sport teams as repositories of their faith.

Post 9-11 Note: Though there is isolated agitation within the Islamic community, most Muslims consider themselves solid members of the greater Australian community, and most non-Muslim Australians remain typically tolerant. There have been a few exceptions on both sides. Some clerics have made volatile statements, and there were the so-called anti-Muslim beach riots in Cronulla, near Sydney in 2005, but these were isolated instances, and generally everybody gets along.

A curiosity: You might occasionally see a six-pointed Star of David displayed or used in advertising, especially on handwritten signs. This isn't a mark of Judaism. In Australia, the six-pointed star is commonly used as Americans would use a five-pointed one—for decoration or to attract attention. Jews are in such a small minority that most Aussies aren't aware of their presence.

Weddings & funerals

Many Australian weddings are held in churches, with ceremonies performed by appropriate clergy, but since a large percentage of Aussies are non-religious, many marriages are performed by a *celebrant*. A *celebrant* can be described as a justice of the peace with a major in charm and a minor in philosophy. They also lead non-religious funerals. Celebrants are specially trained and are registered with the government. Some celebrants are justices on the peace, but not all JPs are celebrants.

Weddings are big events just as in North America (if you want a primer, watch "Muriel's Wedding"). A bachelor party is a *bucks night;* a bachelorettes party is a *hens night*. Both involve much alcohol and as much embarrassment for the honored person as can be arranged.

Marriage, partners and de factos   Marriage is treated a bit differently than in North America. While traditional marriage still exists, many good, enduring relationships have never had the blessing of the church or the legal system, which is why the term *partner* is widely used.

It's common to meet families where the couple has been

united for years and have had several children together, but have never chosen to formalize the relationship with a ceremony. The feeling is that what exists between the couple is no business of the state or any religious organization.

These individuals are referred to under the term *de facto*, as in his *de facto* wife, or her *de facto* husband. In South Australia, de factos who have been together for three years or have a child together have all the legal rights of marriage if the relationship breaks up: child custody, support payments, division of assets, etc.

Prostitution

Prostitutes are also called *sex workers*. Prostitution is legal in most of Australia. The exceptions are South Australia, where it's illegal, and Western Australia, where it's technically illegal but "*informally tolerated*" by the police.

In the other states and territories, restrictions apply, but vary state to state on street work, pimping, and brothels. Brothels tend to be small and are often called *massage parlours*. In Tasmania, only *sole operators* are legal. Most states require health checks and supervision.

Taxes

Australian income tax law provides protection from double taxation if you have assets in two different countries. We pay tax on our U.S. income to the U.S., and on our Australian income to Australia. We file a copy of our U.S. form with our Australian taxes [more on **U.S. taxes in Australia** below].

The **tax year** is July 1st to June 30th. If you have tax liability in both the U.S. or Canada, and Australia, this makes coordinating your taxes a bit difficult. You have to pick a starting point, and we've found basing it on when you entered the country is as good a method as any.

Australian income tax   Australia has a reputation of having high taxes, though there are frequent noises in Parliament about lowering them—usually just before an election. There are no state income taxes, just federal. The federal government sends money back to the states, but it can withhold funds as ransom to get its way on issues. It's been holding back billions of dollars from Western Australia because WA won't loosen its weekend trading hours ban and because it hasn't eliminated the stamp duty on cars and homes.

Tax returns need to be filed with the *ATO* (*Australian Tax Office*) by October 31, unless you're using a tax agent, when you need to have consulted with him/her by that date. If you're not on a *PAYG* (*Pay As You Go*) withholding system, you pay quarterly installments. First payments are due November 21, or if that's on a weekend or holiday, the next business day after.

Income Tax Table

The 2006-7 tax schedule is: (in Australian dollars):

$0–6,000	No tax
$6,001–25,000	15 percent for each dollar over $6,000
$25,001–75,000	$2,850 plus 30 percent of earnings over $25,000
$75,001–150,000	$17,850 plus 40 percent of earnings over $75,000
Over $150,000	$47,850 plus 45 percent of earnings over $150,000

GST means *Goods and Services Tax*. It's a national ten percent sales tax on <u>everything,</u> with a few exceptions, such as some medical expenses and food bought in grocery stores (except hot takeaway food and beverages).

GST is levied on everything along the supply chain, from manufacturing through distribution, sales, and even installation. Retailers generally include GST in their prices, so there's no figuring at the counter; the marked price is the final price.

Carpenters charge GST, as do mechanics, pool cleaners, etc. When taking a bid from a tradesman, be sure you know whether he's including the GST. When you receive a bill it will have *Tax Invoice* written prominently on it to make it a legal GST document. Likewise, if you issue an invoice as a result of a service you have provided, you must write **Tax Invoice** on it. You must be registered for GST with the *ATO* (*Australian Tax Office*) to collect GST.

Here's how GST works. Businesses pay the *ATO* (*Australian Tax Office*) the GST they collect on sales, <u>minus</u> the GST they paid for the merchandise, materials, and services to make the sales. In this way, the GST is passed down the line. At the end of the line, it's consumers who end up paying the tax, because they have nothing to charge GST on.

GST is paid monthly, quarterly, or yearly, depending on the business.

Why GST? The rationale was to create a new revenue stream so other taxes could be eliminated: taxes that were perceived as holding back economic growth—but many of these taxes haven't been eliminated. The states don't want to give up stamp duty and other indirect taxes. The states and the federal government have been fighting over it for *yonks* (a long time).

Stamp duty is a state tax paid on special purchases, like houses, cars, and insurance policies, but since it's a duty and not a tax—it isn't tax-deductible. In Western Australia, for example, there's a sliding rate for stamp duty on cars, with the top rate of 6.5 percent on cars over $40,000. The duty on used trucks is five percent. Stamp duty on leases in WA was finally abolished in 2006.

Real estate stamp duty varies by state. If you bought a $400,000 house in Melbourne, you'd pay almost $20,000 in stamp duty, while in Brisbane you'd pay about $12,500. These stamp duties were supposed to be eliminated by the GST, but somehow haven't gone away.

PAYG stands for *Pay As You Go*, what Australia calls payroll withholding tax. This is a federal tax.

Payroll tax is a state tax businesses pay on their payrolls. It only applies to businesses with annual payrolls over a certain amount, usually around $800,000. It can be seen as a dis-incentive to grow a company.

Business tax is a federal tax. The tax form is called a *BAS* (*Business Activity Statement*). Some people call it the *baz*. It covers quarterly payments on business profits, plus payments of GST and PAYG withholding. If you have a business, get a proper accountant.

Rates are what Australians call property taxes. They work the same as in the U.S., You receive a bill from the local government (shires, towns, or cities) who use the money for local roads, civic improvements, etc.

Superannuation is the national retirement system, commonly called *super*—a privately administered, mandatory retirement plan where the employer contributes an amount equal to nine percent of the employee's income. An employee can add more, as can the self-employed. This is called *salary sacrifice*.

You can go with an administered plan or run it yourself. It's the Republican's dream: an independently managed Social Security system. This is in addition to any government pensions.

Of course, if there's a system, an Aussie will figure a way around it. Retirees once parked their money intentionally in low-interest-paying accounts to fudge their way around the income qualifications for pensions and allowances. The Tax Office decided to counter that by setting their own rate for what the market minimum should be and called it a *deeming rate* (the government *deems* what the minimum market rate should be). *Deeming rates* are set below market rates, so *pensioners* (retirees) can still achieve a high return on their investments while qualifying for allowances. For tax purposes, actual income is still assessed.

Super fund income is taxed at a lower level than conventional investments (15 percent), and from July 1, 2007, investments can be withdrawn tax-free once the owner is over age sixty. Some conditions apply.

Trusts   If you have substantial assets, look into forming a trust. Trusts are more financially flexible and they aren't taxed—instead, beneficiaries are, and at a lower rate. There are many advantages to having a trust; check with an accountant.

U.S. taxes in Australia   Americans working overseas get a dollar-for-dollar credit for income taxes paid to foreign countries to offset American income taxes. They also get a US$82,400 (in 2006) exclusion from the income they report to the IRS. If you're married, that exclusion is per couple.

Don't get excited; you still owe tax to the country you earned it in, but there's no double-taxation between the U.S. and Australia, so you won't be taxed on the same income by both countries. This doesn't apply to some American states that collect state income taxes.

Another wrinkle: a U.S. law passed in 2006 says Americans working abroad must include employer allowances for additional expenses as income. This includes free housing, trips back to the States, and private education for their kids. It gets complicated, and when in doubt, hire a good accountant who knows both systems.

Government

Australia is a Commonwealth, formed by the six former British colonies on the Australian continent, plus the Northern Territory. It is a parliamentary-democratic monarchy. Like most of the former English colonies, Australia uses the Westminster system of government, which means it's ruled by an English-style Parliament elected by the people. The Royal Family of England has statutory power, but it's mostly a stabilizing presence and is very rarely exercised. Australia is also an independent member of the Commonwealth of Nations (the successor to the British Empire), a league of fifty-three former British colonies, including Canada, South Africa, India, Bermuda, etc.

In the U.S., there are four levels of government (federal, state, county, and city); in Australia there are three levels (federal, state, and local). We'll start at the top and work our way down.

National capital   The capital is Canberra, in the *ACT* (*Australian Capital Territory*). The city is patterned in concept on Washington D.C., in that it was created from scratch as a national capital city. Like Washington, it has parks and malls between the government buildings. Where Washington was built on the banks of a river, Canberra was built on the shores of a lake. It was even designed by an American, Walter Burley Griffen of Chicago, Ill.

Canberra lies halfway between Sydney and Melbourne and

was a compromise between political forces in those two dominant cities, each of which wanted to be the capital. Canberra is the only major city in Australia that isn't on the coast. By law, all states and territories must have access to the sea, so the ACT has a 3,000-acre non-contiguous holding at Jervis Bay, where the Naval Academy is located.

Federal   The federal government is also known as the *Commonwealth.* Governmental power lies in the Parliament, consisting of a House of Representatives (150 members) and a Senate (seventy-six senators). Members of the House represent districts called *electorates,* which are established by population. The Senate has twelve senators from each state, regardless of population, and two from each of the major territories—the Northern Territory and the ACT.

Members of the House are elected by popular vote from their *electorates.* Senators go through a *proportional* voting count in each state, which makes it easier for smaller parties to elect a senator than a member of the House [more on this in **elections**].

Whichever political party ends up with the most *MPs* (*Members of Parliament*) in the House of Representatives becomes *the government* and elects the *prime minister* (*PM*). The prime minister then appoints other MPs to head the various ministries, such as Foreign Policy, Treasury, Defence, Education and Training, etc. Ministers can also be from the Senate.

So, unlike the U.S., where there are three branches of government (executive, legislative, and judicial), in practicality, Australia has only two, with the executive and legislative combined into one. Technically, the Queen and her *governor general* (the *vice regent*) are the executive branch, but most policy is led by the prime minister [more about this in **the Queen of Australia** and the **Governor general**].

Either the House or the Senate can originate bills, but only the House of Representatives can propose or amend legislation on any bill that authorises expenditures or imposes taxation, so in effect, the Senate is an advisory body, but both houses have to pass all bills before they become law. Since the de facto head of government is also the head of the Parliament (the prime minister), veto power is unnecessary, though technically the Queen or King, acting through the governor general, can veto bills or laws.

Checks and balances are called *swings and roundabouts*.

There are no term limits, as long as they get re-elected to Parliament and have the seats to carry the majority, a prime minister can keep serving. Prime Minister Robert Menzies served over twenty years.

An interesting feature of the Parliamentary system occurs if the prime minister decides to resign, for whatever reason. A special election isn't called, instead a successor is elected from amongst his party in Parliament. This is also true with the premier in the individual states. This has happened twice in recent years. WA premier Geoff Gallup (in 2006), and NSW premiere Steve Bracks (in 2007), each resigned for personal reasons. In both cases a successor was in place within the week. It is also practice for a retiring prime minister to step down a year before the next election to give his successor a chance at establishing himself as a worthy incumbent.

The major national political parties are, in order of size: the Labor Party (intentionally spelled American-style with an *o* instead of an *ou*), which is liberal and *labour*-based and roughly equivalent to the U.S. Democrats; the Liberal Party, which is conservative and roughly equivalent to the U.S. Republicans; the National Party, which is rural-based, conservative, and represents farmers and *pastoralists* (ranchers), and has formed a coalition with the Liberals to have enough seats in Parliament to take on Labor; the Democrats Party, which is social-liberal and centrist; the Greens Party, which is left wing and pro-environment; One Nation, which is right wing; and Family First, which is conservative Christian. The Country Liberal Party is a Northern Territory party, a combination of the Liberals and the National party, in effect its own coalition. They have a few members in the federal Senate who sit with the Coalition.

The smaller parties have little power (with the exception of the Nationals in their minority role in the *Coalition*), but as Don Chipp, a founder of the Democrats, once said, "Our job is to keep the bastards honest."

Naming the conservative party the "Liberals" was unintentional irony. Robert Menzies, who was Australian Prime Minister 1939-41 and 1949-66, founded the party in 1944. At that time the semi-socialist Labor party was dominating Australian politics. Menzies wrote about forming a new party that had "a liberal, progressive policy and are opposed to Socialism with its bureaucratic administration and restriction of personal freedom". He meant "liberal" in the sense of freeing individuals and companies from socialist restrictions and governmental meddling.

The Commonwealth government is currently (2007) run by an alliance of the Liberals and the Nationals, called the *Coalition*, and has been in power since 1996. The Coalition was formed to defeat Labor which had been running things for the previous ten years. The state governments have parliamentary systems similar to the federal government. The head of each state is the *premier*, and he (or she) is elected from amongst the state parliamentary body. Currently (2007), all the states have Labor-run governments.

Since there's no executive branch, the various *ministers* (Defence, Foreign Office, Treasury, etc., equating to the U.S. President's Cabinet), tend to be the most powerful members of the party(s) currently dominating Parliament. These ministers are called the *front-benchers*. All the other ministers are *back benchers*.

The lesser parties are called *the Opposition*, and they elect a *shadow government*, ministry by ministry. The *shadow ministers* attend all the meetings of their respective ministries as observers and speak out—usually just knee-jerk criticism— about what goes on in each ministry. The advantage of this shadow system is that there's constant oversight of each ministry, as the unwritten duty of *the Opposition* is to keep putting pressure on *the Government* to deal with issues properly. And if the government were to have a sudden shake- up and power shifted to the other party, the new ministers would already be up to speed on administration and issues.

Senators serve a six-year term. Elections for the House of Representatives have no set date, but must be held some time before the end of the third year since the last election. That election is called by the prime minister and is usually timed to his advantage, like when things are going well, when things are about to go bad, or when the opposition is in disarray. Because of this, the official campaign season is short, just a few weeks, though all *pollies* are constantly campaigning, just as in the U.S.

Throughout the three-year term, the ruling party—which controls government spending—withholds funds. Then, just before the election, they free those funds and lavish generosity and largess upon the electorate by announcing popular programs and tax cuts, hoping it will be fresh in the minds of the populace just before they go to the polls. Everybody knows they do it, but it still works.

Campaign funding is strictly limited, so there's no two-year bombardment of TV commercials like in the U.S., nor are there astronomical amounts of money being spent with numerous strings attached—with a population of just 21 million, the money isn't there. That's not to say there are no strings or string-pullers, they're just lower-profile—until they get caught. There seems to be a bribery scandal every few years.

Parliament meets a few weeks a month. Aussie lawmakers in session make the U.S. Congress look like a bunch of chaste librarians. It's really a debating society. Decorum in Parliament is like the British model, where members argue and harass and interrupt each other's speeches with shouts and jibes. The presiding officer of the House of Representatives is the Speaker of the House, who is elected from that body and acts as a referee, constantly telling members to sit down and be quiet.

Before each vote in the Federal House, a bell is rung. Exactly four minutes later, the doors are locked. No members are allowed in or out until the vote is over.

A verbatim transcript of all Parliament debates is called a *Hansard* and is available shortly after each session. *Hansards* are kept by all countries that use the Westminster form of government, so Canadians already know about them. For folks from the U.S., it's the equivalent of the Congressional Record. By checking the *Hansard* on the day of a key debate, one can see which side of an issue any representative took.

One of the most interesting things in Parliament is a session called *Question Time*, where the MPs ask each other questions that must be answered publicly. It's broadcast live on ABC radio and Sky Channel TV. Some questions are merely set-ups for self-congratulation or promoting policy, while others are vicious ambushes. Members of Parliament are exempt from slander laws while in the House Chambers, so they can get away with saying almost anything. They frequently harangue each other with shouted interruptions from the opposing sides. Many citizens tune in to Question Time as entertainment—a reality show with a notable, clever, dependably contentious, cast.

The carryings-on can sometimes sound so childish that you wonder if Question Time should be followed by Nap Time, Milk and Cookies Time, and Make Up and Be Friends Time.

States   There are six states and one territory (two, if you include the tiny ACT). They're all run by parliamentary systems consisting of two houses: an upper house and lower house. The exception is Queensland and Northern Territory, which each have just one house.

The upper house is called the Legislative Council and has a review function for the laws created in the lower house.

The lower house is called, depending on the state, the Legislative Assembly or the House of Assembly, and has the power to authorize expenditures and levy taxes. Members of the Legislative Council have the letters *MLC* after their names; Members of the Legislative Assembly have *MLA*. The majority party in the Legislative Assembly elects a *premier*, the equivalent of the U.S. state governor. He forms a cabinet— *front benchers*—just as the prime minister does in the federal Parliament, and the opposition elects *shadow ministers*.

The states have a great deal of autonomy when it comes to urban planning, roads, utilities, education, law enforcement, basic infrastructure, and levying stamp duty, but the federal government has been chipping away at the states' power, and the feds collect and control income tax and therefore a lot of programs. The Commonwealth tried to establish a country-wide education curriculum and the States knocked it back. The Commonwealth passed a national sales tax, the *GST* (*Goods and Services Tax*), with the proviso that the states eliminate many of their taxes. The states refused, so the ratepayers get double-taxed. It's a constant battle.

Local government is also run differently than in the U.S., where there are counties, and within them, cities, each with their own government and police force. In Australia, there's only one level of government below the state. These can be *shires*, *cities,* or *towns*. Shires tend to be rural, cities are suburban, and towns are urban. They're run by elected councils, headed by a president or mayor, and managed by a CEO (Chief Executive Officer). They are funded by *rates* (property taxes).

These handle local roads, building permits, recreation facilities, rubbish collection, local roads, and community festivals. They regulate urban planning and development to some degree,, but the states supersede them.

There's a state Minister for Local Government overseeing them who can overrule or suspend councils if they act illegally.

Rate payers and progress associations are neighbourhood or homeowners groups. Since the cities, towns, and shires can be quite large, local groups form within them to deal with issues in smaller areas. This might be a suburb in a city, a community in a semi-rural area, or a town in one of the vast outback shires. They advocate for their members to the shire councils. They can become activists on controversial planning issues like urban development or zoning change issues. These associations have formalized constitutions set out by the states, they must hold regular *Annual General Meetings* (*AGMs*), and they have the option to incorporate so individual officers can't be sued if the group steps on the toes of developers, businesses, or council members.

Another local organization are Friends Groups, which are volunteers who take care of natural reserves and parks.

Police and crime   If a police officer stops you, he can ask your name, address, and date of birth. If you withhold this information or get caught lying about it, you can be arrested. The police need no probable cause to stop and question you.

The Australian Federal Police handle interstate and international duties, counterterrorism, and national security, and are the police force for the ACT (Australian Capital Territory).

Each state has one centrally-controlled police force that is deployed throughout that state. There are no separate city forces, nor are there country sheriffs or state troopers like in the U.S. One state police force serves all communities: dense cities, sprawling suburbs, rural farmland, and some of the most sparsely settled regions on Earth.

There are advantages and disadvantages to this system. Administratively, it's efficient, since all elements can easily communicate and resources are maximized, with little duplication or waste. Conversely, there's little local control over how many officers will serve their area, since those decisions are made at the state level.

An example: The first house we rented in Australia was in what we thought was a quiet beach suburb north of Perth. We soon discovered *hoons* would race their cars and motorcycles on our street every night. We called the local city to complain, but they told us they had nothing to do with law enforcement and that we should call the police. The police made a lot of excuses, but said they'd look into it. Before they could do anything, the police commissioner down in Perth decided to transfer a dozen officers from our city to a gang patrol in another city thirty kilometres away. After that, when we called the police to report street racing, we were told there were no officers available to respond. Our city's government had no say in the matter, their response was to shrug-off the matter. As soon as the lease was up we moved away.

Australians have a different attitude toward policing: less is more. Unlike the U.S., where off-duty officers are armed and always ready to go into action, Australian police leave their weapons and attitude at work. They're far less gung-ho and militaristic. It isn't that the officers are lazy or cowardly; they're trained to be less aggressive. Rules prohibit high-speed auto pursuits. Though the cops are armed, if one pulls out a gun, it's a big deal. They first resort to non-lethal methods, like *capsicum* (pepper) spray and Tasers. The state governments are always asking for more officers on the street, but want to keep the level of conflict low. This isn't a completely baseless idea.

Another example: During the G20 conference in November 2006 in Melbourne, protestors attacked the police guarding the conference venues. I happened to be in town at the time, and was surprised to see news footage of police officers in regular uniforms—no helmets or chest protectors—going toe to toe with club swinging rioters wearing helmets and padded jackets. A taxi driver explained to me that the police once wore riot gear, but found that it escalated the situation. If the police looked like bullies, more protesters joined in. By using minimum force at the G20, the police not only kept the protestors at bay and defused the situation, but they also won the sympathy of the citizenry.

It's not always that easy. In rural Aboriginal communities, white officers often get a bad reaction; notably the riots of December 2004 on Palm Island, off the coast of Queensland. An Aboriginal man died under suspicious circumstances while in police custody, and a white officer was accused of beating him to death. Islanders became enraged. They burned down the *watch house* (police station) and the few officers on the island had to barricade themselves in the hospital until reinforcements arrived from the mainland. The fresh officers had little riot training and clumsily returned the island to order. Resentment continues to this day. The state is reviewing its practices and a court case continues about the death.

Other states treat these situations differently. In Western Australia, there are Aboriginal police specialist units that are deployed in areas with large indigenous populations. They handle problems with greater sensitivity before they get out of hand.

In mainstream Australia, day to day crime is mostly non-violent burglaries and car thefts. Robberies are usually committed with non-firearm weapons, like knives and clubs. A Perth liquor store hold-up in March 2007 was typical: the local newspaper reported the robber used a green shovel to threaten the shop owner into emptying the till. The robber got away with a few hundred dollars and a bottle of Jim Beam. The police put out a bulletin for a drunken man carrying a green shovel.

For a wealthy, educated country, Australia surprisingly

suffers with a significant number of idle and angry youth. Young Australian men will sometimes get so drunk they commit unmotivated violent and vicious attacks on each other. The attackers get off by pleading they were so drunk they didn't know what they were doing. Judges seem to buy this as a valid excuse.

It's hard being a cop in Australia. People tend to instinctively side with the underdog, and that's usually the bad guy. The judges are notoriously lenient, and many times the criminal is out of jail before the police officer is finished with the paperwork. Many officers retire early.

Individual rights   The Australian Constitution contains no Bill of Rights. Personal freedoms, like freedom of speech, religion, right of assembly, gun ownership, etc., are determined only by convention and precedent. These are assumed, but not guaranteed rights, and if push comes to shove, individual cases would have to go to court.

The reasoning is that, unlike the U.S., where cabinet members—who are the heads of most of the government bureaucracies—are appointed, in Australia all equivalent ministers in the parliamentary government are elected members of that body, and if they were to violate the basic assumed freedoms, they'd be ejected from office. In a parliamentary system, if there's a major deadlock, Parliament can be dissolved and early elections can be called. There's also the assumption that the members are all basically decent Englishmen who'd do no wrong, and if they did, the impartial Monarch would "still the troubled waters." In actuality, Australian personal freedoms are guaranteed on faith.

This faith is sometimes strained. A 2005 federal law made it illegal to discuss suicide or euthanasia over the phone, Internet, or fax.

Despite that (or because of it), there's a perpetual movement to enter a Bill of Rights into the Constitution, but it isn't seen as a national priority and is seldom mentioned. *She'll be right* seems to apply here, too.

The Queen of Australia   It's not Priscilla; it's Elizabeth II of England.

Australia is a *Constitutional Monarchy*, which means the

Queen (or King) of England is the actual head of state, her *vice regal* (the *governor general*) runs the state, and the Parliament exists at the pleasure of the Queen. It's all in the Australian Constitution; get a copy and read it yourself. When Australia became an independent nation, it didn't sever all ties with Mother England—they never threw the figurative tea into the harbor.

All elected members of Parliament take an oath to "be faithful and bear true allegiance to Her Majesty Queen Elizabeth the Second." Further: "the Queen may disallow any law...and annul the law." All she has to do is notify both houses of Parliament of her decision.

Yes, the Queen of England still technically owns the place. Her picture is on all the coins and her photo is on the walls of all government offices, but tradition deems a hands-off policy—that's what the governor general is for.

The governors general   The prime minister, his cabinet, and elected members of Parliament run day-to-day matters, but over them is the Queen's representative, the vice regal: the governor general. The Constitution of the Commonwealth of Australia, Section 2, reads: "A Governor General appointed by the Queen shall be Her Majesty's representative in the Commonwealth." Therefore, if the Queen has total power, the governor general, by law, does also.

The governor general is technically the executive branch, the commander-in-chief of the armed forces, and has the power to approve the results of elections, allow the appointment of ministers, ratify treaties, appoint ambassadors and federal judges, form commissions of enquiry, and has the power to overrule anything the elected rabble in Parliament might decide upon. Governors general rarely exercise this power.

In actuality, the governors general almost never act on their own and generally follow the lead of the prime minister. In fact, you rarely hear anything about either the governor general or the Queen when it comes to the day-to-day functioning of the government, but they're there.

The Queen appoints the governor general on "advice" of the prime minister. The PM can also advise the Queen to dismiss the governor general and appoint someone else.

Though this has never been done, they came close in 1975 [more below].

Governors general are prominent public servants who have led distinguished careers. Many have been *knighted* or are *peers* (Lords) and are former judges, archbishops, and high-ranking military officers. In the last fifty years, seven out of the eleven governors general were Australian-born—the rest were English. Two, including the first Australian-born governor general, Sir Issac Issacs, were Jewish, which is a good example of multi-ethnic attitudes. They traditionally serve a five-year term. Each state also has a state governor general, serving the same function on a state level.

Though the governors general (both federal and state) are mainly ceremonial positions, they can wield power. This was last done in 1975, when the Federal Parliament reached a deadlock over a key appropriations bill that threatened the financial shut down of the government. The governor general fired the prime minister before the prime minister could ask the Queen to dismiss the governor general. The governor general then appointed the Opposition Leader as prime minister. Later that day, when the new PM couldn't get a consensus, the governor general fired <u>him</u>, dissolved Parliament, and called for new elections. It was a very controversial move, and there's doubt as to whether it would ever be allowed to happen again. But, the Australian Constitution clearly states: "The executive power of the Commonwealth is vested in the Queen and is exercisable by the Governor General, and extends to the execution and maintenance of this Constitution, and of the laws of the Commonwealth." Strange in this modern day? Not so to an Englishman (or woman) who exercises such privilege and power with true British restraint.

Monarchists & Republicans   Aussies have a love-hate relationship with the Royal Family. They like being part of the historical tradition, but dislike and distrust anyone held over them, especially ones who make a lot of money just for being born. What probably irks them most: they hate having the same ruler as the *Poms* (British).

Why not change to a republic and throw the Royals out? It's not that easy. You'd have to rewrite the Constitution and change the entire method of government.

Monarchists are people who believe in the constitutional monarchy. They feel the Monarch is a stabilizing force, a non-political influence that keeps things on an even keel. They point to the simple fact that the current system has worked for centuries.

Republicans are those that believe in chucking off the reins of the Royals and replacing them with an elected President.

There was a referendum in the general election of 1999 to do just that, but it was narrowly defeated. Some people think the government rigged the referendum in such a way as to make it difficult for the "yes" vote to win. It was written so that the President wouldn't be directly elected by the people, but by a two-thirds vote of Parliament. This split the pro-republic vote and led to the referendum's defeat. In the end, the electorate chose to stay with what they had: a known quantity. The fear is, once you open the cage and start changing the Constitution, a monster could emerge and you could end up with something unintended. In 2007, the Labor leader intimated if elected he will hold another referendum on the subject.

The bottom line is that the Royals are a stabilizing force in the Australian ship of state, Parliament is the rudder, and the Monarchy is the keel.

Elections

Australia had two important election firsts: the secret ballot (1856) and allowing women to vote (1894).

Voting age is eighteen. Voting is mandatory in all Australian national, state, and some local elections. A $20 fine is levied if you don't show up to vote. But my friend Karen tells me from her experience working at the polls that once you've been ticked off the list, you're free to vote, to not vote, to throw away, to deface, or to eat your ballot.

"You'd be amazed," she told me, "how many people vote for Mickey Mouse."

So, in actuality, voting isn't mandatory; showing up at the polls is.

Voting law in Western Australia recently went through a fundamental change to a *one vote, one value* system.

Previously, country people's votes counted two or three times as much as those of city voters. This was achieved by making the population of the rural electorates smaller than those in the city. The reasoning was that since most of the population was in the city, rural voters were powerless to have rural issues passed in Parliament. This was overturned in 2005, and the electorates were balanced out so each vote counted as one: *one vote, one value*. A effect is that, by 2007, rural areas were losing hospitals and police services.

[More information on frequency of elections is in the section on **government**.]

Political parties   As mentioned before, the Liberals aren't liberal, Labor is, the Greens are left wing, One Nation is right wing, and the Democrats say they're in it "just to keep the bastards honest." The Nationals are supposed to represent the rural voters, but they're the minority part of a coalition with the Liberals, so they're barely a party.   Family First has one elected member in the federal government, less than those calling themselves independent, and the Country Liberal party is just another name for the Coalition.

Not every voter who votes along party lines is a member of that party. Just because you say you vote Liberal doesn't mean you're a voting member of the Liberal party. There's a formal admission process.

In the U.S., it's a lot looser. You're a member of whatever political party you say you are. You could be a Democrat on Monday and decide to become a Republican on Tuesday—if you feel strongly about it, you can change your registration.

In Australia, it's much more formalized: you can vote for whomever you wish, but in order to actually be in a political party, you must apply, and the party members then decide if they'll accept you. Once in, you pay yearly dues and can vote, but you must also do what the party leadership says. If you cross them, they can throw you out.

Take what happened in Western Australia in early 2007. There was a huge scandal involving an ex-Premier (equivalent of the state governor) who'd gotten caught back in the early 1990s taking bribes from big business and had been thrown out of office and into jail. In 2007, he got caught again, this time doing the bribing. The State Corruption and Crimes Commission released the findings to the public and it all blew up in the press, resulting in a lot of high-level resignations and possible indictments. There were daily leaks about what had happened and what was coming next. The current Premier realized his administration was failing. He put out a gag order on all the members of his party, decreeing that no member could talk to the press, that everything would come from the official spokesman and any violation would mean instant expulsion from the party. The order was instantly effective; the leaks stopped immediately and so did the scandal's momentum, all because nobody wanted to risk being thrown out of the party. Stopping leaks on a dime like that could never happen in the U.S.

Preselection of candidates is what the Westminster system uses instead of holding primary elections.

Australian political parties have more control over their members and proceedings than parties in the U.S., and not only about who says what to the press, but also about who gets to run for office. In the U.S., almost anybody can declare their candidacy, get enough signatures to qualify, and run in a primary election for the nomination of their party. They might not get many votes, but they can run. In Australia, there are no open primary elections, just the final election. Potential candidates must put their name up before a closed party committee (called a *council* or an *executive*) for *preselection*. These committees have total control over who gets to run for office, and therefore who can get elected, and who ultimately runs the government.

One can run as an independent, but without a political machine behind you, it's difficult to get elected. In some electorates that are *safe seats* (securely one party or the other), whichever candidate the *preselection* committee chooses is guaranteed to win. The candidate doesn't even have to be from or live in the *electorate*. The term is *parachuting into a safe seat*.

For example, take Judy Moylan, the Federal Member for Pearce, in Western Australia (electorates have names, not numbers as in the U.S.). Judy is a Liberal, but she broke with

Liberal Prime Minister John Howard over an immigration detention reform bill in 2006, in what was called a *back bench rebellion*. She came close to losing her seat over it because she'd gone against the PM. The Liberal party leadership was going to *stand her down* for preselection for the next election and replace her with someone more loyal. It made no difference that she was the incumbent, very popular with her electorate and could win re-election easily. The party wasn't going to let her run as a Liberal because she'd pissed off the PM. She could have quit the party and run as an independent, but Pearce is a secure Liberal seat and she would have lost to anybody the Libs put up against her because they control the votes (through the leverage system of *preferences*—more about this later). She narrowly beat the challengers for preselection and was allowed run again as a Lib in 2007.

As Brian Costar, Professor of Victorian Parliamentary Democracy at Swinbourne University, said about preselection, "The winner is effectively chosen by a small number of people behind closed doors who may or may not be electors of that district and may, in some cases, not even be Australian citizens."

Australians argue that it makes for a more dependable, stabile election environment. For an American observing this system, it rankles one's sense of independence, despite the chaos in some recent American elections.

Preferential and proportional voting   If the preselection process wasn't enough, the way votes are counted is really out there. It's called a *preferential system*, and it's complex and unique to Australia.

On their ballots, voters are asked to write a number of *preference* next to each of the candidates' names, starting with the one they want to win, which they must mark as #1. They mark their second choice as #2, and so on down the list. If there are five candidates, they rank them one-to-five in order of preference.

The counting of the *first preference* votes is called the *primary vote*. If the candidate with the most votes doesn't have an absolute majority, then the candidate with the least number of votes is eliminated. The ballots that had the eliminated candidate listed as #1 are then awarded to the candidate who was listed on those ballots as #2, and then they're recounted. If there still isn't an absolute majority, they keep going down the line until someone wins. It's complex, but logical.

It gets even more complex in the way the preferential votes are counted for the Federal Senate and the upper houses of NSW, Victoria, South Australia, Western Australia, and the lower houses of Tasmania and the ACT. It's called a *proportional vote*: winning candidates must secure a quota of the vote. The quota is calculated by dividing the total number of ballots by one more than the number of senators to be elected and then adding "1" to the result. That way, the parties each get a proportion of the vote. The upside is that it's easier for a candidate from a small party like the Greens to get elected; the downside is nobody but a Parliamentarian understands how it works.

The ramifications of *preferential voting* are interesting. By having to rate the candidates one-to-whatever, voters are forced to express a preference for a candidate they may thoroughly despise, and the winners can be the most preferred or least disliked. The worst part is that parties can *exchange preferences* for political favors. The parties not only tell their voters to vote for their candidate as the #1 preference, but whom to vote for as the #2 preference, the #3 preference, etc. The result is even if your candidate loses; whoever wins will play ball in Parliament with your other winning candidates. This means there's secret collusion between the parties.

In some states the parties form *tickets*, which have a pre-formed list of preferences: you actually vote for the list and not the candidates. An example: In 2001 in Western Australia, the minor right wing conservative party One Nation wanted to counter the power of the two big parties (Labor and the Liberals), so they put the smallest party, the Greens, on their *ticket* in the number-two position just to spite the two big parties, not figuring it would matter. They underestimated their own popularity and the left wing Greens ended up with five seats in the state's upper house.

Why should it matter that a small party can get a few seats in Parliament when the big parties hold the rest? The small parties can become the deciding or blocking factor on tight votes and can trade power in such situations by getting the big parties to back the small party's otherwise unviable issues. For example, in Western Australia in 2007, during a period of notorious scandals, there was a move by the government (run by the Labor party) to lessen the power of the commission that administered the Freedom of Information Act (*FOI*), the instrument that countered secrecy in government. The Green Party, with only two seats in the upper house and none in the lower house, effectively blocked the move by siding with the opposition (the Liberals). And the Liberals ended up owing the Greens a favor.

Despite being confusing and complex, with *preferential voting* there are no run-off elections and close votes are resolved automatically. Also, voters can support a minor candidate as their #1 preference as a political statement and vote for a more likely winner as #2, knowing if it were to be a close ballot, their vote would go to their #2 candidate. This avoids splitting a crucial vote. (Think how Ralph Nader split Al Gore's vote in the U.S. presidential election of 2000, resulting in the Bush presidency.)

Is the Australian voting system better than that of the United States? That remains for future historians to decide. Both systems show how any system, no matter how well thought out, can be subverted. Humans are political animals, and it's a dog-eat-dog world.

Legal system

The legal system is similar to the U.S. and Britain, with the accused being innocent until proven guilty. Juries, drawn from voter roles, decide major trials, just as in the U.S. On the other hand, judges and *barristers* (trial lawyers), wear flowing robes and little white powdered wigs, just like their predecessors did 300 years ago.

Courts are arranged in a hierarchy. The *High Court of Australia* is equivalent to the U.S. Supreme Court. The *Federal Courts* decide tax laws and federal violations. *Magistrates Courts* were designed to ease the large caseloads on the Federal Courts.

Each state has a *Supreme Court* that deals with serious crime, like murder, armed robbery, etc., These are called *indictable offences*, which equate to felonies. Below them are the *District Courts*, which hear crimes except murder and treason. From there on down are *Magistrates Courts* (also known as *Courts of Petty Sessions*), which were designed to deal with the overburden on the higher courts, and *Family Courts*, which deal with divorce and child issues. Serious crimes are heard by judges and juries; less serious infractions by magistrates. In rural areas, police officers (called *police prosecutors*) present the state's case to Magistrates Courts.

Though crime is every bit as serious as in North America, the names of some of the offences are straight out of Monty Python. Arson is called *Lighting a fire likely to injure or damage*. Kidnapping is *Deprivation of liberty*. A police officer may detain an intoxicated person who is *behaving in a disorderly manner or in a manner likely to cause injury to the person or another person or damage to property*. If you give someone an illegal drug you can be charged with *administering a drug of dependence*. If you attack someone you could be arrested for *an unlawful act with intent to harm, assault occasioning bodily harm*, or *assault by kicking*. And there's the charge of *conspiracy to pervert the course of justice*.

Funny names of laws aside, sentences are notoriously lenient by American standards, and rights of self-defense are restricted. An example: in Sydney in 2003, three men robbed and terrorized a disabled man in his home on several occasions over a period of months. On the last occasion, they murdered him. The trial took three years and they were found guilty. They got an average of twelve years in jail, with the possibility of early parole. It's likely they'll be out in eight. In the U.S., they'd be on death row. Ironically, if the victim had obtained a gun and used it on his attackers to defend himself, there's a good possibility he would have been charged with using *unlawful force* [more on this in **guns**].

Aboriginal tribal law is still practiced in some remote communities. The state police allow elders to try, judge sentence and administer punishment to some degree. When the crimes get serious, police step in and the perpetrator goes into the traditional court system.

Lawyers   There are two types of lawyers, *solicitors* and *barristers*. Solicitors are contract lawyers, Barristers are trial lawyers. Barristers of prominence are appointed *Queen's Counsel* (or *QC*). In New South Wales, the Northern Territory, and the ACT, QCs are called *Senior Counsel*. They're also known as *silks*, after the silk robes they wear in court.

So, if you find yourself in need of legal help, you start with the *solicitor* for advice. If you end up in court, you'll have a *barrister,* and when the guy in the powdered wig and red robe walks in, don't laugh at his get-up; he can put you away—but probably only for a little while.

Military

Being an isolated colony surrounded by oceans, there wasn't much need for a large organized military force. The first armed forces were English Marines, who came as guards with the convicts in 1788. They were more a police force than a strategic military. English regular troops came in 1810. Colonies and towns had volunteer corps, formed in case the convicts revolted. The convict years ended in the mid-nineteenth century.

After that, volunteer units grew and faded as England went through various wars: the New Zealand Maori wars, the Crimean campaigns, Napoleon III's threat to invade Britain, and the African wars in the Sudan. Gradually, volunteer groups became more organized, with professional soldiers as leaders. Periodically there were miners revolts and shearers strikes, and citizen-soldiers were mobilized to deal with them.

There were no large-scale native revolts as in North America. The Aboriginal actions were sporadic and localized. Rarely were there overt battles in the open; most were guerrilla acts, and the British didn't see them as sufficient threat to bring in troops—they were dealt with as police actions.

Australia federated into a nation in 1901, and colonial military forces came under Commonwealth command.

For a country with a relatively small population, Australia has always punched well above her weight in military affairs. First as a colony, then as an independent member of the

Commonwealth of Nations, she (like Canada) supported Great Britain, providing men and material to the British Imperial Forces. Australians distinguished themselves on the African Veldt in the Boer War; on the bloody beaches and cliffs of Gallipoli, and in the trenches of France in WWI, and across the deserts of North Africa and in the defense of Singapore in WWII.

Then came the Japanese War in the Pacific. In 1941, while Australian troops were engaged fighting Rommel in North Africa, the Empire of Japan stormed the British fortress of Singapore, taking thousands of British, Indian, and Australian troops prisoner. This act, more than any other single incident, signalled an end to the British Empire.

Then the Japanese invaded New Guinea, which was Australian territory. Darwin, the capital of the Northern Territory, was bombed. These weren't a few token raids, but repeated strikes by the same Japanese fleet that had attacked Pearl Harbor. Darwin was levelled. More than a dozen ships were sunk, hundreds of civilians were killed, and thousands were wounded. Britain was busy fighting Germany and couldn't help. For the first time, Australians were fighting alone, on their own doorstep, with their backs against the wall.

The *Top End* (northern Australia) was evacuated as the Japanese bombed north Queensland, the Northern Territory and the north coast of Western Australia. Australians reasonably considered they were about to receive a full-scale Japanese invasion, and they had neither the manpower nor equipment to do much about it. Things were looking grim, but help was on its way.

Two months earlier, on the other side of the Pacific at Pearl Harbor, the U.S. had also been attacked by the Japanese. By early 1942, American forces were being pushed out of the Philippines. Australians welcomed the Yanks, and invited them to establish bases in Australia. Australia soon became an impregnable citadel from which to counterattack. Younger Australians might not want to hear about it, but *oldies* gratefully remember that the U.S. saved Australia from being invaded. Since then, the U.S. and Australia have maintained close defensive ties.

Australia emerged from WWII bloodied but battle-tested, wiser, and more worldly. Since then, Australia has maintained an active independent presence both politically and militarily in the region: campaigning in Korea, Vietnam, Malaysia, Indonesia, East Timor, the Solomon Islands, Iraq, and Afghanistan. Australia supplies forces for UN peacekeeping missions worldwide.

ADF   The Army, Navy and Air Force are collectively called the *Australian Defence Forces*, or *ADF*.

National Service or *Nasho* (the draft) ended in 1972. All Australian forces are now volunteer. As for officer training: the Royal Australian Naval College is at Jervis Bay, the Army's Royal Military Academy is at Duntroon, and the Royal Australian Air Force Officer Training School is at Pt. Cook. College degrees for officers are optional; the Australian Defence Force Academy at the University of New South Wales provides Officers in Training with academics for college degrees.

Navy   Australia is an island nation, so having a potent navy is fundamental. The Royal Australian Navy has fleet of thirteen guided missile frigates, fourteen 187-foot Armidale fast patrol boats, six deep-water non-nuclear submarines, plus amphibious assault, mine warfare, and support ships. The Navy no longer uses aircraft carriers; the *HMAS Sydney* and *HMAS Melbourne* were retired in the 1980s.

The *Sydney* was turned into a troop transport; the *Melbourne* was scrapped to make way for the *HMS Invincible*, to be bought from Great Britain. Unfortunately, the Argentines decided to invade the Falklands and the Brits decided to hang onto *Invincible*. By then it was too late to bring back the *Melbourne* and too costly to build a new carrier, so now Australia has none. As consolation, the U.S. has twelve carrier groups and can provide one if necessary.

Australia provides forward support to U.S. Navy vessels operating in southeast Asian waters. The U.S. Consulate in Perth has a full time naval liaison officer, usually a Lt. Commander, specifically assigned for this duty.

In 2007 Australia ordered three Spanish-designed air warfare destroyers, and two amphibious warfare ships capable of launching helicopters and jump-jets. The hulls will be built in Spain and the ships finished in South Australia. They are scheduled to be delivered between 2015 and 2017.

The air arm is currently limited to a fleet of helicopters, mostly Sea Hawks, Sea Kings, and Super Sea Sprites. The Royal Australian Air Force handles fixed wing duties.

Air Force   The Royal Australian Air Force Air Combat Group consists of 145 aircraft including American F18/Bs and F111C attack bombers, British Hawk 127 close support fighters (which double as trainers), and PC9/A trainer-reconnaissance aircraft. The F18s and F111s are due to be replaced by the F35 Joint Strike Fighter around 2010.

The Airlift Group flies C130 Hercules transports, DHC-4 Caribou, and various other support aircraft, with Airbus A330 aerial tankers on order.

The Air Surveillance and Reconnaissance Group flies P3 Orions, with Boeing 737-7ES Aerial Warfare/Surveillance planes on order. The group also operates ground-based radar.

There are several kinds of helicopters: the Blackhawk, Kiowa, and the UH-1H. These will soon be replaced with the more modern Eurocopter Tiger and MRH-90.

Army   The Royal Australian Army consists of 25,000 men and women on active duty and 17,000 in reserve units. Active duty strength is to be increased to 30,000 by 2016. They're organized in two divisions; one deployable overseas, the other for home defense. The Army has seventy-one German Leopard main battle tanks, with fifty-nine American M1-A1 Abrams tanks on order. There are about 1,000 light armored vehicles, armored personnel carriers, Land Rovers, and artillery. There is a fleet of helicopters consisting of the same models as the Air Force.

SAS stands for *Special Air Service* and is the special forces. This experienced, highly respected unit is the match of any on the planet.

ASIO stands for the Australia Intelligence Organization, the equivalent of the CIA. It's based in Canberra, has a staff of about 1,000 and is growing, expecting to almost double by 2011.

Australia originally had a branch of the British "Central

Counter-Espionage Bureau" as part of a British Empire-wide system. In 1949 ASIO was formed in response to the Cold War and is entirely Australian, though one can assume it cooperates with allied countries' counterpart services.

Strategy   The idea is to keep any fight offshore. Australian forces, though not large in number, have a reputation as an able fighting force and are technologically superior to any in the region. The Navy is based in the Pacific and Indian Oceans, and along the north coast. The Air Force has pre-supplied bases around the country and can deploy air wings of fighters and attack bombers as needed. The Army, Navy, and SAS usually have forces overseas running operations as peacekeepers or working with allies in active theaters, such as Afghanistan, Iraq, and East Timor. The rest of the troops are in training or in support.

Out of curiosity, I once asked a friend who is an Australian Reserve Army officer what would happen if one of the large Asian nations to the north managed to fight their way past the Navy and Air Force and invaded somewhere along the vast northern coast.

"We'd let them penetrate into the red centre," he said smugly, "then cut them off and wait for them to die of thirst."

Of course, if push comes to shove, there's always the U.S. Navy's Seventh Fleet. Australia provides forward-support for U.S. Navy ships. The U.S. has several facilities in Australia, mostly communications stations and lightly manned training bases—and then there's Pine Gap.

Pine Gap is located near the geographic center of Australia, not far from Alice Springs in the Northern Territory. It's a top secret U.S.-Australian base called the *Joint Defence Facility* (notice the Australian spelling of *defence*, with a "c").

Pine Gap has about twenty radome antennas and a computer complex, and houses about 1,200 American and Australian personnel. It's top secret, so few people know what goes on there, and those that do aren't telling.

Rumors as to its purpose and activities know no bounds: everything from a UFO base, a five-mile deep hole to tap the earth's magnetic field, a huge nuclear generator to power death-ray space weapons, or a new headquarters for a World

Dictatorship.

One thing is certain: it's a very secure base in the middle of nowhere. Is it run by the CIA and NSA? Probably. Is it controlling satellites over the southern hemisphere? Probably. Nobody is saying for sure, but it shows how close the relationship is between Australia and the U.S. when it comes to defense (American spelling with an "s").

Antarctica

The Australian Antarctic Division claims and manages almost half of the 14 million sq. km. (5.5 million sq. miles) Antarctic continent and maintains several bases. There are three permanent research stations at Casey, Mawson, and Davis; several temporary summer stations; a sub-arctic marine station at Macquarie Island; and a research icebreaker ship, the *Aurora Australia*. As the only other continent completely within the Southern Hemisphere, Australia feels she has a right and duty to occupy and protect the fragile frozen land.

Since 1947, Australia has had a presence on the continent, performing research and scientific studies, living year-round, inventing techniques and technology to survive the harsh environment.

A vital air link was opened in March 2007 when Australia initiated regular air service between Hobart, Tasmania, and Casey station via the newly constructed Wilkins Runway. This was built 70 km. from Casey station, carved out of blue glacial ice and capped with pavement made of compressed snow. It's a full certified aerodrome, so it can potentially handle future commercial flights.

The runway wasn't the only technical achievement. A specially built Airbus A319 has been leased, which carries 20–40 passengers plus cargo and enough fuel to fly round-trip without refuelling. Prior to this, slow C130 aircraft flew the route, much less frequently. This new air link will open up the Antarctic continent. For what? Good question—or as the Aussies might say—*"good ask."*

New Zealand

New Zealand is the sister country to Australia and therefore deserves some mention in this book. Geographically and historically they are as close as two countries can be, even closer than the U.S. and Canada. Aussies and Kiwi's enjoy quasi-citizenship in each others' countries: citizens can travel between the countries without visas and can obtain jobs and own real estate in either, without legal complications. But while the countries are similar, they are not identical, nor are the people.

Where Australia is huge, about the size of the continental U.S., New Zealand is actually two islands about the size of California. Australia is closer to the equator, is flat and mostly dry—with the exception of the northern tropics. New Zealand is closer to Antarctica, is mountainous, receives a great deal of rain and, on the South Island, quite a bit of snow. Australia is an old continent with smooth, worn topography. New Zealand is newly-formed, with jagged peaks, fjords and active glaciers.

Australia separated from the rest of the continents and had numerous mammals, birds and reptiles. New Zealand was thrust up from the ocean depths and had no native land mammals at all, only birds and one strange lizard called a tuatara.

The Aboriginals migrated to Australia 40-60,000 years ago, while the Polynesian Maori settled New Zealand merely 1,500 years ago. Australia was settled by the British as a penal colony and met only token resistance from the scattered indigenous people. New Zealand was settled by free British pioneers who fought several wars for the land against well organized Maori warriors. The Brits ended up buying much of the land from the Maoris. Because of these different origins, the people have a different way of looking at things. Though both have typical British reserve, Aussies seem more distrustful while Kiwi's seem more engaging.

New Zealanders seem to have an inferiority complex toward Australia, as Australia seems to dominate the relationship. This is probably due to the sheer weight of numbers: Australia has 21 million people and a land mass of 7.7 million square kilometres, while New Zealand has barely 4 million people and 269,000 square kilometres. In actuality, New Zealanders have nothing to feel bad about: the scenery is breath-taking, the economy is strong, the food is good, the culture sophisticated, the people well-educated. Politically, New Zealand is more left-wing than Australia, and has declared a non-nuclear status. She is less likely to project power in the region, leaving that up to her big sister, Australia.

The modern Aussies and Kiwi's are steadfast rivals and love to make fun of each other, especially over their accents. To an American ear they both sound like a derivation of British, but the Aussie accent is full of broad vowels and sounds cockney, while the New Zealand accent has clipped vowels and sounds a bit Scottish.

Rugby union is the national sport, and the Kiwi *All Blacks* and the Australian *Wallabies* fight out the bitterest grudge match on the planet since the Dodgers and the Yankees. Though rivals on the sports fields, they fought as a unit in the ANZACs (Australia and New Zealand Army Corps) in both world wars.

All of this is the subject of another book, which I just might write someday. I couldn't think of a better excuse to live in New Zealand for a few years.

International relations

Australia has a limited role alongside the British and American forces in Iraq and Afghanistan. Closer to home, she has projected her limited, though high-tech power [see section on **military**] into the Pacific and Asia, intervening militarily in Indonesia, East Timor, and the Solomon Islands. She also provides advisory, leadership, and economic assistance to the poorer countries in the Pacific region.

Economic realignment from American and European markets to Asian-Pacific trade has been partially successful. Australia is western historically, socially, and demographically, but geographically she's in Asia.

Fitting into Asia is important for more than economic reasons. Just to her north are two billion Indonesians, Malaysians, Chinese, Vietnamese, Japanese, and Koreans, going about their lives indifferent to what goes on in Australia.

To maintain her security, she must be both socially and economically useful to her neighbors.

Living in a bad neighborhood   After the Bali bombings in 2002, Australia awakened once again to the reality of living in a bad neighborhood. With a small population and a huge, mostly unoccupied northern coastline, Australia is in constant fear of illegal immigration, and with it the side effects of smuggling, degradation of the environment, and the possible introduction of disease.

Australia constantly struggles to maintain good relations with Indonesia and Malaysia, her immediate neighbors to the north. Indonesia seems to be unable (or unwilling) to control its fishing industry, which constantly poaches into Northern Australian waters, decimating fish stocks and killing reefs. Australia has had to increase sea and air patrols. Negotiations with the Indonesians are ongoing.

The otherwise rational Japanese annually send a whale-hunting fleet into southern waters to harvest a few thousand whales under the guise of "research". The meat ends up in Japanese meat markets. Australia officially objects, but ultimately does nothing but watch. When it comes right down to it, with 21 million Australians versus 2 billion Asians, there's only so much they can do.

Trade with China is in the multi-billions of dollars, and not just in imports. Australia exports millions of tons of iron ore to China from the vast deposits in the Pilbara region of Western Australia. These mines, built and run by Rio Tinto, BHP Billiton, and others, and partly financed by the Chinese, supply China with the iron she needs to keep America's Wal-Marts fully stocked. There are also large alumina deposits, along with gold, lead, nickel, uranium, oil, and natural gas. As long as Australia manages China's raw material needs, she's worth more as a client than as a colony.

Economics and the future

By the early 1990s, Australia was in danger of becoming what one Chinese premier described as "the poor white trash of Asia." What he meant was—through protectionist economic policy—Australia was stagnating and falling behind. Labor

Prime Minster Bob Hawke and his Treasurer, Paul Keating, forced unpopular reforms on the country, reducing all import tariffs to five percent while phasing out protection for the textile, clothing, and motor vehicle industries. This was both risky and out of character politically, because the Labor Party was the party of the workers, not the capitalists. Australia reluctantly went into what Keating called "the recession we had to have."

By the end of the decade, the reforms had been successful, and to quote Gregory Hywood, former editor-in-chief of Melbourne's "The Age": "Hawk and Keating had transformed the Australia economy from closed and protected to open, vibrant and global."

Keating was elected prime minister in 1991, but was defeated by John Howard in 1996. The economic good times continue because of those reforms.

A major factor driving the economy is the mining industry. Australia has huge deposits of raw materials: iron, nickel, aluminum, gold, lead, uranium, oil, and natural gas. The Chinese have invested billions of dollars in Western Australian iron mines, and huge super-carriers transport millions of tons of ore to steel-hungry Chinese, Korean, and Japanese factories. As sophisticated as Australians consider themselves, to Asian business people, the country is merely a quarry, a market in which to sell electronics and cars, and someplace different to go on holiday.

Though Australia produces substantial oil and natural gas, domestic oil is priced at international rates, so fuel costs are high, about 50 percent more than in the U.S., and a good portion of this is tax. An interesting side note: in 2006 the premier of Western Australia (where most of the natural gas deposits are located) forced a deal with the developers of the huge Gorgon gas field, securing rights to twenty percent of its output for future use by the state in generating electricity and for use as fuel.

If mining is king, agriculture is queen: wheat, sheep, and cattle are exported on a large scale.

Besides processed meat products, an interesting side industry of sheep production is the live animal business.

Australia ships significant amounts of live sheep and cattle to the Middle East. Strict Muslim Halal laws require the local slaughter of animals for religious purity reasons. Giant transport ships, with twelve-story high pens holding upward of 10,000 sheep, make regular runs from Western Australia to the Arabian Gulf.

Because Australia is an island, it's been able to keep out diseases like Mad Cow, but with cheaper production costs, the Chinese are beginning to undercut Australia's market.

One perpetual problem is a general drying of the climate. Agriculturally-dependent Australia has been suffering through a prolonged drought. Over-farming, excessive clearing of native bush, and too much pumping of subterranean water has created areas where the soil has become too saline to work.

Wheat is still a major export, but U.S. government-subsidized exports are squeezing Australia out of many markets.

The Australia-United States Free Trade Agreement, signed in 2004, was heavily one-sided—favoring the U.S. Though it was a major topic in Australia at the time, few in the U.S. outside of Congress were even aware of its passage. As a minor trading partner, Australia had to settle for whatever it could get. The agreement opens Australia for the entry of U.S. products and investors, but ignores Australian exports like Queensland sugarcane and West Australian wheat. Australia was promised eventual equality, but had to settle for whatever the U.S. decided.

An interesting trade tale: the innocuous Ugg boot. The ankle-high fleecy sheepskin boot was an original Australian beach classic, made from abundant sheepskins and worn by surfers worldwide. An American company, Deckers Outdoor Corporation, discovered that the name was considered generic in Australia and hadn't been copyrighted. They registered the name and forbade anyone, including Australians, from using it—not just in America—they brought suit against Australian manufacturers selling Ugg boots in Australia. Then Deckers had cheap imitation Ugg boots mass-produced in China and opened stores at U.S. malls marketing the boots, using images of kangaroos, boomerangs, and the Australian map. When

Aussies tried an end-run and continued making and selling Uggs as "Ughs", Deckers went after them again. Backed against the wall, a small family-run Western Australian company took them on and beat them in the U.S. courts. The name is back as a generic; anybody can use it. It was a rare victory.

Guns

Despite a frontier history, a U.S.-style gun culture never got started in Australia. Guns were around, mostly in the bush, but they were never a part of the national character as they are in the U.S. This probably comes from the British tradition, where even the police were unarmed until the 1960s.

That's not to say there isn't violence, but someone is more likely to hold up a convenience store with a knife (or even a shovel) than a gun.

Australia's modern turning point on guns occurred in Port Arthur, Tasmania, on April 28, 1996, when a lone gunman with an assault rifle opened fire on innocent tourists and townspeople. That afternoon, he killed thirty-five and wounded two dozen more—many of them women and children. Australians were appalled and the government re-examined the gun laws. Gun owners were encouraged to turn in their weapons, which they did in huge numbers. A system of tightly regulated gun licenses was introduced. Each state has its own system of gun regulation. Let's take Western Australia as an example. In 2007 in Western Australia—population about 2 million—there were 85,000 licensed gun owners, of which 14,000 owned handguns.

When you think about it (besides target shooting), the purpose of a long gun is to shoot game and vermin, while the purpose of a handgun is to shoot people. Because of this, handguns are tightly regulated.

Handguns can be owned only by members of approved gun clubs, and then only after a police background check, six months of training, and the approval from the applicant's *partner* (spouse, live-in boyfriend or girlfriend, etc.).

Rifles and shotguns can be obtained for a specific purpose, either for target shooting or to shoot varmints. For the former, you have to be a member of a qualified gun club. For the latter, you must either be the owner of a large property or have the owner of such a property write a letter stating that you'll be using the rifle to control pests on that property. Self-loading (semi-automatic) rapid fire rifles are prohibited. Pump action shotguns are allowed only for *primary producers* (full-time farmers who must control pests). Therefore, only bolt-action rifles and single- or double-barrelled shotguns are available to the public. A state licensing fee is assessed annually.

Here's the procedure in Western Australia to get a gun. First you obtain the letter stating what it will be used for. You fill out an application with the local police stating what calibre gun you want to buy, pay an administrative fee, and pass a written gun owner test. Then you go the gun dealer and pay for the gun. You go back to the police with the receipt and a form listing the specific weapon you're buying by serial number. You pay your licensing fee, install an approved gun safe, and have it inspected by the police. Then you take the police paperwork back to the gun shop and they'll release the gun to you. You then take the gun back to the police, where they'll inspect it and verify the serial number. Then it's yours. You'll need to carry your license whenever transporting your gun outside your home and will need to bring the license to the gun shop in order to buy ammunition.

If that isn't enough to put you off, guns are expensive to buy. They cost about twice what you'd pay in the U.S., plus the mandatory safe—a good idea—fees, and yearly licensing.

That said, there's a small black market for stolen or smuggled handguns, since professional criminals seem to get them. These illegal handguns are the exception rather than the rule. Street violence is usually not committed with guns. Most Australians are appalled by guns and don't understand the acceptance of them in the U.S.

Sport (sports)

Sport is very serious stuff in Australia, and people's support of their teams is deeply felt. It's been said that because Aussies aren't very religious, they place their faith in their sports teams. American sports like football (called *gridiron* in

Australia because *football* means soccer in much of the world) and baseball are played peripherally, but not commonly.

Cricket, when played amongst friends in the backyard, is just cricket, but when it's played professionally, it's *The Cricket*.

The Cricket is a major sport, enjoying a status much like baseball in the U.S. It's a British game, played throughout the Commonwealth. In Australia, there are leagues in each state, and the Australian national team plays in *test matches* (five-day games) and the more modern *one-day* form of the game, against the British, Indians, Sri Lankans, South Africans, Kiwis, etc.

What follows is a (perhaps) too detailed description of how cricket works. If you're not interested, let it suffice that it's British baseball and move on to the next section.

Still with me? Here goes: the traditional long form of the game is called a *test* and is played across a five-day period on a oval-shaped field called an *oval* or *cricket ground* about 140 meters (460 feet) long. There are twelve players on a side, although only eleven may take the field at any time. The player designated as the twelfth man is used only as a substitute for fielding and may not bat or bowl. A *batsman* (batter) *faces* the *bowler* (pitcher). The object is for the *bowler* to throw a one-hop pitch toward the *wicket* (three waist high sticks called *stumps* that have a piece of wood called a *bale* balanced on top). The bowler may take a *run-up* (which is like a baseball pitcher's windup) and must use a straight arm action unique to the game: if the arm is bent, the *delivery* (bowl) is considered a *no ball* and must be bowled again. Each bowler bowls an *over* (six balls/pitches) before he's replaced by another at the opposite end of the pitch who bowls their *over* in turn. Around ninety overs are bowled in a typical day's play.

If the *bowler* knocks off the *bale,* the *batsman* is out (or *bowled*). The batsman protects the wicket and tries to hit the ball with the bat, which is about the size of a baseball bat but with flat sides. He can hit the ball in any direction and if a fielder catches it, he's out. If the ball goes away from the fielders and he's not in peril of being *run out* (caught outside of the *crease* or area around the wicket when the ball is live) he can run to the opposite wicket, which is *one chain* (twenty-two yards) away at the opposite end of the *pitch*. There's another batsman at the opposite wicket, and he has to run to the other wicket. This gains the team one run each time the batsmen cross and reach the opposite wicket. They may run as often as is safe. If the ball reaches the *boundary* (the line around the outside of the field), four runs are scored. Clearing the boundary gains six runs. In these cases running isn't required and won't add to the score. The fielders try to hit the bale with the ball before the batsmen get to the other side. Each inning sees the entire *side* (team) get to bat, each *side* bats twice in a five-day match if time permits.

Instead of a seventh inning stretch, they stop for lunch and tea breaks. A typical test score is 8–231 with a two-wicket win on the fourth day. Don't ask for an explanation, I haven't the foggiest...

I do know this, It's not as easy a game as it looks. It's hard to hit the ball coming off the ground on a bounce with the flat bat. The field of play is 360 degrees around the batsman and the fielders are bare-handed.

There's also a one-day form of the game. Each team is given fifty *overs* to score as many runs as possible (the side with the most runs wins), and the rules are generally the same as in a test match. Some fielding restrictions are imposed to encourage the batsmen to go for big hits, and each player may only bowl a maximum of ten overs each. The one-day form is extremely popular, crowd friendly, colourful, and exciting—or so they say. A World Cup of Cricket is held every four years with many non-Commonwealth countries participating; the one-day form is used. The last World Cup was held in the Caribbean in March and April 2007—yes, it took two months to get through all the games. Australia won.

But cricket isn't just a fancy professional game. People play weekend pick-up games in city parks, at barbecues, on the beach, out camping, in the backyard, even on boats; anywhere.

Australian Rules Football (*Footy*) is a uniquely Australian game. It was originally designed in the 1850s for cricketers to play to stay in shape during the off-season, so it pre-dates American and Canadian football. The AFL

(Australian Football League) was founded in 1896.

Based on rugby, with similarities to basketball, soccer, and *gridiron* (American football), it's played on a cricket oval, which is a lot larger than an American football field. The field size varies, usually around 135 metres wide and 165 metres long (150 by 180 yards), with four tall posts at each end of the field.

The ball is oblong, like an American football, but the ends are less pointed and more rounded, similar to a rugby ball. The object is to kick the ball through the inner two posts (*goal posts*) for a six-point goal. It can pass though in the air or on a bounce, but must remain untouched by opponents to score a six-pointer. If it goes through the outer posts (*point* or *behind posts*), it's a one-point *behind*. Scores often go above 100 points and are displayed as goals and points (example: G 6 P 17—53.) In this case, there were six goals at six-points each, plus seventeen *behinds*, for a total of fifty-three points.

Footy works much like soccer, but the players can use their hands. There's a forward pass (*hand pass*), delivered like a volleyball serve using an underhanded fist-hit.

The players can run the ball forward but must bounce the ball once every fifteen meters (fifty feet) as they run. This isn't as easy as dribbling a basketball, because the ball isn't round, the playing surface is grass, and they're running flat-out dodging opponents. There's a technique of throwing the ball ahead and down with a forward spin so it will bounce up to where the player will be as he runs.

Players can also do a punt-like kick (called a *foot pass*) to move the ball downfield to a team mate. An intercepted pass or a tackle is the only way to stop an advance. When a runner is tackled, the ball immediately goes back into play, without pauses between plays. The tackled player tosses the ball back to a team mate and the play resumes. It's a fast-paced game with few time-outs or stoppages in play. The game runs continuously for four twenty-minute quarters, plus time to account for play stoppage. This can seem strange to a first time observer as the clock goes past "0" and keeps going until the excess stoppage time is used up.

There are eighteen players on the field for each side, with

four on the bench who can be rotated in at any time. They don't wear pads or helmets—safety gear consists of knee socks and a mouthguard. The players tend to be tall, lanky, and tremendously fit, since they must run the huge field continuously for more than an hour. Since the game is constantly running, there are no elaborate plays as in American football; it's more up to the individual player, which suits the nature of the independent Australian.

The *AFL* (*Australian Football League*) is a national league made up of sixteen teams that battle each year to a *premiership* (championship). There are also state leagues with teams from smaller cities and within urban areas, and there are suburban leagues. Like soccer and rugby, supporters can become dues-paying club members and get season tickets. Drinking beer in the stands with the members during a game is a memorable experience—and a great source of Australianisms.

Terms: The *fixture* is the league game schedule. A special game between rivals is called a *derby* (pronounced "darby"), such as between the two Western Australian teams the Eagles and the Dockers, which is *The Western Derby.*

One doesn't *root* for their favorite team; one *barracks* for it. To *root* means to have sex, so don't ask a girl if she *roots* for her favorite team, she's liable to slap you.

One isn't a team fan; they're a *supporter*—one *supports* their team.

A rookie is called a *debutante*. It's hard to think of a six-foot-four-inch, two-hundred-ten pound, sweaty, muddy Footy player as a *debutant*, but there it is.

Footy is played by kids and adults, in the park, backyards, the beach, and at school.

Rugby traces its roots back to *caid*, a primitive Celtic game originally played with an inflated bull's scrotum as a ball—really—you can't make this stuff up.

Modern rugby began in 1823 at Rugby School in England, using a manufactured ball similar to a footy ball. Rugby is more popular than footy in the states of NSW and Queensland—the rugby states—with *Rugby League* (also known as *Super 14*) and *Rugby Union*. They started as one, but became two very different games.

Rugby League, as played in the Southern Hemisphere, is an international game, consisting of fourteen teams from Australia, New Zealand, and South Africa, under a consortium called SANZAR.

The game lasts eighty minutes, the playing field is 100 metres by 68 metres (110 yards by 75 yards), with thirteen players on a side. They get six tackles to run the ball downfield to *ground* the ball in the goal, which means the player runs between the goal posts and throws himself on the ground. This is a four-point *try*. When a player is tackled, his team mates drop ten metres behind him, he tosses the ball back to them, and it's back in play. The ball can only be advanced by kicking and running.

One of Rugby League's legends is John Hoppoate, a player who used to play for the Balmain (now West) Tigers. He was *turfed* (thrown) out of the league for fingering another player's *ring* (anus) during a *scrum* (pile-up). It was dubbed the "Crouching Tiger, Hidden Finger."

Rugby Union is also an international league. The Australian national team is the *Wallabies*. The New Zealand team is the *All-Blacks*.

In *Union* the field is a maximum of 144 metres by 70 metres (160 yards by 77 yards). The game lasts eighty minutes in two forty-minute halves, with fifteen players on a side. The object is to advance the ball to the opposite team's goal by running it and kicking it, and to ground it between the goal post for a *try*, which is worth five points. Then the team gets to kick the ball through the goal posts for a two-point conversion.

An interesting feature is the *scrum*, which is a way of restarting the game after a stop in play because of an accidental infringement. Eight players from each side line up across from each other in three rows, with the ball on the ground in the middle. The front rows of the opposing teams interlock heads and shoulders. The whole formation pushes against each other. The object is to force the opposing team backward enough to get your front row over the ball, which is then kicked behind to the rear of the formation, to be tossed to a *back* to get the game moving again. It's a demonstration of brute force over finesse, which characterizes the game.

Being such a rough game, you don't see a lot of people playing either form of rugby in the park. Aussies call it *cross country wrestling*. Rugby is known as a thug's game played by gentlemen, where soccer has been called a gentlemen's game played by thugs.

Soccer is a major sport, though not as big as footy, rugby, or cricket. The national competition is dubbed the A-League, which is gaining in popularity.

The Australian national team, the *Socceroos*, did well in the 2006 World Cup. It seemed the whole country stayed up all night to watch the games live from Germany. It's played recreationally, with teams at all levels across the country.

Basketball   There's a professional league called the National Basketball League, with eleven teams in nine cities. Several players are American. It's also played recreationally, but not to the degree of cricket or footy. For a time, it was Australia's third sport, which could be attributed to the worldwide appeal of Michael Jordan and his influence with the Aussie youth. Basketball's decline in OZ coincided with his retirement.

Netball is a court game similar to basketball, played on a basketball court with a hoop at either end. Like basketball, the object is for the players move the ball to the hoop and shoot goals. Unlike basketball, the only way to move the ball is by passing, as no dribbling or running with the ball is allowed.

There's no backboard behind the hoop, so to score you have to "swish" the shot. There are seven players on a side and three distinct areas on the court. Players are assigned positions and wear bibs with the initials of that position. They can't move out of their assigned area or they're *offside*. It's usually a girls-only sport, very popular in schools, in adult recreational leagues, and within British Commonwealth countries. National competitions are televised

Lawn bowling (bowls) is a very popular sport, with approximately 800,000 registered bowlers—which means one in twenty-five Australians bowl. Almost every town and suburb has a lawn bowling club. The clubs are well-established and are fixtures of the community. Some have *pokies* (poker or slot machines), licensed bars, and restaurants where you can eat and drink for cheap—and you can bowl, of course.

The greens are meticulously maintained by professionally trained greens keepers who go though a five-year apprenticeship. The ball is an asymmetric sphere about the size of a cantaloupe. The object of the game is to get your ball closest to the *jack* (a white ball placed at the far end of the *rink*). There are usually four players on a team, the game goes twenty-one *ends* (rounds). Devotees take the game very seriously.

Note: American style bowling is called Ten-Pin bowling; most large cities have indoor bowling *lanes*.

Skiing/snowboarding   Hotham, Thredbo, and Perisher are the largest and most popular, though Falls Creek will give you a more intimate experience. All are located in the mountains between Melbourne and Canberra. The slopes don't have pine trees; you ski through low eucalypts called *snow gums*. It isn't Utah, but it will get you moving down the hill on snow.

If you're looking for something more intense, hop a flight to Queenstown on the South Island of New Zealand. All skiing there is above the tree line, kind of like the top of Arapahoe Basin in Colorado.

Ski areas are set up and run similar to North America. *Lifted* means a slope with chairlifts. The bunny hill is called the *learner's area* or the *nursery slope*. A *magic carpet* is a conveyor belt that skiers stand on to get to the top of the *learner's area*.

Four-wheeling might not seem like a sport, but the outdoorsmanship required can involve skill, endurance, and physical ability. There are epic trips across the outback, like the Canning Stock Route, a three-week unsupported run down the old inland cattle trail in Western Australia.

There are also day runs in the bush or on the beach. Camping, fishing, and exploring are usually involved, with perhaps a couple of kayaks or a small aluminum skiff brought along on the roof for fun.

Swimming   Aussie swimmers are world-class and have collected hundreds of Olympic medals. Ian Thorpe, Grant Hackett, and Libby Lenton are some recent Olympic stars. The

Aussies continue to be dominant players in the worldwide sport.

The freestyle stroke was originally called the *Australian Crawl* because it was developed in Australia—a combination of an English trudgen and a South Pacific Islander flutter kick.

The beach is a sport in itself. With swimming, surfing, wind and kite sailing, snorkeling, scuba diving, jogging, beach volleyball, footy, and cricket.

The **surf life saving clubs** are government-sanctioned volunteer groups that provide safety patrols and lifeguards. There are few paid professional beach lifeguards in Australia, so volunteer groups fill the gap. The clubs are an Australian tradition that goes back a hundred years. The safest place to go for a dip in the ocean is in front of the local surf life saving club; swim between their flags.

The surf life saving clubs patrol sections of beach—marked with flags—in front of their clubhouses. They're an institution similar to bowling clubs with private restaurants, bars, weight rooms, etc. You usually join as a family. There are *little nippers* (youth) programs from age seven through late-teens that train kids to be strong, safe, confident ocean swimmers. Many move on to adult programs, which are built around patrolling the beach and competing in carnivals.

Throughout the summer, *surf carnivals* (competitions) are held between neighboring life saving clubs. There's a state championship and a national carnival. These are for both kids and adults and consist of beach sprints, ocean swimming, and rescue surf boat races. If you can, catch a competition. If you've never seen a dozen five-man surf-rowboats shooting through the breakers, catching air off the crests, you're in for a treat.

Fishing is too large a subject to cover in a short section in a book like this. For more info try **www.recfishoz.com.au**.

Misc. sports   Golf, tennis, swimming, surfing, fishing, motor racing, etc. are popular and work the same as in America. There are amateur baseball and American football (*gridiron*) leagues in most major capitals. Softball and T-ball are taught in the schools.

Scuba diving

Including all the islands and inlets, Australia has a 36,700km (22,800 mile) coastline. This provides an endless variety of dive sites. The northern half of the country has warm tropical waters with coral reefs. The southern half has cooler waters with sponges and kelp-like algae. All abound with colorful sea life.

The far north coast is dangerous because of marine crocodiles and box stinger jellyfish, especially near river mouths [see section on **wildlife**], and be aware of typhoon season, December to March: these are Australian hurricanes. The south coast can have *king waves* (large rogue waves) that occasionally sweep people off coastal rocks. These are generated by storms off Antarctica, an uninterrupted 2,500 miles directly south.

The **Great Barrier Reef** stretches along 1,500 miles of North Queensland on the east coast, in the Coral Sea of the South Pacific. The reef is twenty to one-hundred-fifty miles offshore and accessible only by boat, placing it well beyond the range of salty crocs and box stingers, which occur just off the beach near the mouths of rivers and creeks. Numerous day boats go out to anchored platforms on the reef, though they are very touristy. For the more serious diver, multi-day live-aboard dive boats go out farther to the outer reef, and into the Coral Sea to dive volcanic coral atolls like Osprey Reef. These are mostly based out of Cairns, Townsville, and Port Douglas. There are island resorts scattered along the reef, like Herron, Hamilton, and Lizard Islands.

The smaller **Ningaloo Reef** is on the northwest coast of Western Australia, in the Indian Ocean. It's closer inshore and can be dived and snorkeled from the beach, though dive boats are available, based out of Coral Bay and Exmouth. Box stingers and crocs aren't a problem on this part of the west coast because there are no rivers—but watch out for them in the wetter Kimberley, 1,000 km. north. In April, the whale sharks appear along the Ningaloo to feed on the coral spawn, and charter boats take divers out to swim with these gentle giants. Further north are Rowley Shoals, reachable by long-range live-aboard charter boats out of Broome, and Christmas

Island, accessible by air.

Along the middle of the west coast is Shark Bay, a world Heritage Site, where *dugongs* (Australian manatee), dolphin, and mantas can be found. The vast bay is quite shallow, but there are a few coral reefs if you know where to find them. The only dive shop is at Monkey Mia (famous for the daily wild dolphin feeding), but it's mostly a snorkelers' service. Also in Shark Bay, at Hamelin Pool, is one of the best stands of stromatolites in the world. They're the oldest living life form on Earth, a rock-like structure of primitive bacteria unchanged for billions of years.

Further south you come to the Houtman Abrolhos, off Geraldton (dive charters available). Then begins the shallow limestone reef structures one-to-five miles offshore, which line the coast past Perth to the southern tip of the continent, where the Indian Ocean meets the Southern Ocean at Cape Leeuwin.

Just north of Perth is the Marmion Marine Park, and just offshore is Rottnest Island, both of which have great diving in the limestone structures amidst cold and warm water species of sponges, corals, and fishes. This unique mix is attributable to the Leeuwin Current, which is the only current in the world on a western-facing coast that flows <u>away</u> from the equator. The Leeuwin wraps around the southern coast and sometimes flows east all the way to Tasmania. Charters are available from numerous dive shops in the area.

WA has some nice diving wrecks; the *HMAS Swan* off Dunsborough, and the *HMAS Perth* off Albany, both 1960s-era destroyers sunk for dive reefs. Charters are available from shops in those towns.

Along the south coast of the Australian mainland and the island state of Tasmania, the water is cooler, with abundant sponge life, sea fans, sea dragons, thick schools of fish, etc., and yes, there are sharks.

There are great dive sites out of Adelaide, Melbourne, Sydney, and Brisbane; check out local shop websites for details.

PADI is the most popular certification, though others are recognized. As a tourist at a resort, you'll be asked for your Certification-card (C-card), but if you're living in Australia and diving as a local, this will be a rare occurrence.

Dive gear   Tanks are also called *cylinders* or *air bottles*. Hookahs, or surface supplied compressed air systems, are commonly used, as there's a lot of diving at remote areas far from dive shops. Hookahs can be on floats or mounted on the deck of a boat.

Wetsuits: a full-length suit is a *steamer*, one with short sleeves and short legs is a *springie*, a *7mm* suit is equivalent to quarter-inch.

As a NAUI divemaster for the past twenty years, I'm in the habit of presenting my C-card whenever I bring tanks into a shop for a fill. In America, this is the norm, but when I do this in Australia, the salesperson usually looks at me like I'm from Mars. However, as much as they disregard your C-card, they'll scrupulously check the test markings on your tank. In the U.S., tanks are visually tested yearly and hydro-tested every five years. In Australia, they're hydro'd <u>every</u> year. If you're buying a tank, check the test date stamped into the metal and make sure it's current.

Tank valves are the same as in North America, so your regulator will fit. Most tanks are pumped to 3400 psi (232 bar). 100 cubic foot steel tanks are common, about the size of a steel 72, but pumped to 3400 psi. They remain at almost the same buoyancy throughout the dive. Aluminum 80s are available, but aluminum 95s are more common. Some, Catalina 95s, float like a cork when empty at the end of the dive, so you'll need to wear more weight. Luxfer aluminum tanks are more neutrally buoyant.

In Queensland, which is home to the Great Barrier Reef and therefore gets the most tourist divers, you'll be required to use an octopus regulator. Other states are looser. You can use American gauges and dive computers that measure in feet and psi, but pre-dive briefings will be in metres and *bar*.

Bar is the metric method of measuring pressure. Surface pressure at sea level is 14.7 pounds per square inch. The metric equivalent is one *bar*. To be precise, one bar is 14.51 psi, but it's too close to fuss about.

A reading of 3,000 psi is about 207 bar, and 3,400 psi is about 232 bar. Most divemasters will ask you to return to the boat with fifty bar in your tank—about 725 psi.

If you're used to working in feet, be careful guessing depth in metres. It's easy to estimate three feet to a metre, but it's really 3.3 feet per metre—so three metres is actually ten feet, not nine. You could easily guess your way into the next no-decompression group without knowing it.

Sixty-feet is about eighteen metres.

Diving for game   There are seasons for abalone and *crays* (lobster), and most states require licenses. In some states, it's legal to spear fish on scuba; in others, it isn't. Check locally. Some states require licenses to fish, others don't. Some, like Western Australia, require licenses for freshwater fishing and none for saltwater fishing, but restrictions on size and number of a species taken apply. WA requires you bring the whole fish to shore; you can't fillet them at sea. Fillet is pronounced *"fill-et"* with a hard "t".

In WA, you need a license for taking *crays* (lobster). You're allowed to use a snare tool, which is a loop of cable at the end of a long tube: you slip the noose around the cray's tail and pull the cable through, snaring it. Night diving for crays in WA is prohibited, though divers routinely take *prawns* (shrimp) and crabs while night diving in the Swan River, which flows through the center of Perth.

Abalone season in south-central Western Australia is worth mentioning for its novel approach. The season lasts one hour, from 7 to 8 a.m. on six concurrent Sundays each spring, early November to mid-December. You're allowed twenty roes abs sized over 60 mm (2 3/8") and five green lip or brown lip sized over 140 mm (5 1/2"). Fishing for abs is done by wading out during low tide, as scuba or hookah diving isn't allowed. In the north and south of the state, there's a traditional fishing season (October 1 to May 15) and the larger browns and green lips can be taken on scuba. A license, available from a post office, is required for taking abs in WA.

Misc.   A *shorie* is a beach dive. The inflatable rescue tube is called a *safety sausage*. An inflatable boat, like a Zodiac, is called a *rubber ducky*.

Underwater animal hazards [see the **wildlife** section]
Remember, the most dangerous thing in the ocean is you.

Boating

There are some basic differences in boating between America and Australia.

You need a *skipper's ticket* (a boat driver's license) to operate a boat in all states. To get one, you take both a *theory* (written) test and a driving test, where you run a boat and put it through a series of maneuvers. Some states (like New South Wales) require you to renew the license periodically, while other states (like WA and Queensland) issue the licence for life. New South Wales also requires a separate license to operate a PWC (personal watercraft, such as a Jet Ski). If you're visiting, you can show some sort of proficiency rating, like those required by international yacht charter services, to qualify.

In Australia, the navigational buoys are reversed. The old adage American boaters learned, "red right returning," is exactly opposite in Australia. Instead, the **green** buoy or light is on the right as you return to a harbor or channel. The navigational lights on the boats themselves are the same: port is red, starboard is green. Even though you keep to the left when driving a car in Australia, you keep to the right when piloting a boat, just like driving on an American road. The "burdened vessel" is called the *give way vessel*; you give way to the boat on your right. Sailboats have the right of way while under sail.

Tides are listed in metres. You take the number on the nautical chart and add the height of the tide to it. Tide changes can be quite extreme in the north and mild in the south.

You're required to carry: Type 1 lifejackets for everyone onboard, an anchor with line, and a bailer. Most states require children under ten to wear a life jacket at all times when underway. Some states require fire extinguishers only if you have an inboard engine, others require them on all boats. If travelling more than two nautical miles offshore you must carry an EPIRB (rescue beacon), and some states require radios.

VHF radios are used, and HF radios. In some states (Queensland, New South Wales, Western Australia, Tasmania), a glorified CB system using the 27 MHz band is also used and is more common amongst recreational boaters. On these radios channel 88 is the hailing frequency. No radio license is required for 27 MHz radios, but if you use VHF, it'll cost you about A$250 to pass the licensing test.

To use an American VHF radio in Australia, you'll have to put it into *International Mode*—see the radio's manual for instructions. As in the U.S., channel 16 is used for hailing.

Water skiing: an observer at least fourteen years of age besides the boat driver must be watching the skier at all times. A red flag is not raised when the skier goes down; instead the safety person may raise their hand—then again, they may not. This is convention and isn't required.

Boat construction Though fibreglass boats are popular, aluminum boats are the most common. This isn't surprising, since Australia has huge natural deposits of the metal.

Typical designs are: *dinghies* or *tinnies* (small aluminum boats with tiller-operated outboards), *centre consoles* (skiffs with a stand-up center control station, *runabouts* (a skiff with forward steering and a windscreen), *half-cabins* (a raised bow with an open area underneath), and *cabin cruisers* (a raised bow with a closable cabin). These can be made of aluminum or fiberglass.

The term *yacht* in Australia refers to any sailboat, but not a motorboat, no matter how large. A twenty-foot day sailor is a *yacht*, while a sixty-foot Bertram motor cruiser isn't. A large power boat is called a *launch*.

Boat sizes are usually measured in metres. Six metres is about twenty-feet.

Aluminum boats Aluminum pleasure craft tend to be lighter and less expensive than fiberglass. The light weight means they can be more easily beach launched, as large stretches of the coast are without ramps.

Aluminum's lighter weight also means you can go with a boat a few feet longer than a fibreglass boat and still be able to tow it and launch it with ease. This is crucial, since Aussie tow vehicles tend to be smaller than ones in North America. The downside to *ally* boats is that the ride is rougher. The plates are hard to form into the same graceful shapes achievable in molded fiberglass, and that—combined with the light weight—results in *ally* boats not riding as well in choppy seas. Engine vibration is transmitted throughout the hull, which sometimes makes an annoying buzz and after time takes a toll on the welds. If buying an older *ally* boat, beware of broken welds, some of which can be hidden under the floor. Newer designs and smoother engines make newer *ally* boats more comfortable.

Other things to beware of in an aluminum boat are the use of silicone sealers—some contain acids which will eventually eat through the metal. Another danger is dissimilar metals. If a non-aluminum metal part, like a steel nut or bolt, slid under the floorboards of an ally boat and into a puddle of saltwater, electrolysis would occur which could eat a hole in the bottom where the two metals touch.

There are two kinds of ally boats: ones that are pressed into shape, and ones made of welded plate.

Pressed boats are made by molding thin aluminum plates into the shape of half-hulls with longitudinal corrugations for strength—the corrugations allow usage of thinner materials. These are then welded together and strengthened with ribs. The bottoms are usually 3mm thick, the sides 2mm. These boats are usually smaller, lighter, cheaper, mass-produced skiffs and runabouts. This type of boat is called a *tinny*, which is Aussie slang for a beer can.

Tinnies are great for close-to-shore boating/fishing/diving, and are light enough to launch off the beach—don't forget to lower the tire pressure on your 4WD before launching or you'll be making new friends. Boaters also carry them on top of their cars and 4WDs, which allows them to get onto more secluded beaches. They're a very light craft, so beware of going too far offshore in one.

The other type of ally boat is called a *plate boat*. They're made from thicker aluminum plates (usually 4mm sides with 5mm bottoms), then curved and welded together. These tend to be custom made, larger, and heavier-duty vessels, and can range from fifteen-foot skiffs to sixty-foot commercial fishing boats.

The typical *plate boat* is about 18 feet long (5.5 metres), with a high, enclosed bow, a windscreen with sun canopy, high gunnels, and a swing-open gate through the transom onto a wide swim step that's actually the back two-feet of the boat. Most are powered by outboards, though inboard-outboards are also common on larger boats.

Australia leads the world in building big aluminum boats. The most notable manufacturer is Austal, based in Western Australia, with yards in Tasmania and the U.S. They make 300-foot hydrofoil-catamaran ferries that go fifty knots, a 185' fast naval patrol boat, and are building a prototype of the Littoral Combat Ship for the U.S. Navy.

Aluminum is spelled and pronounced aluminium in Australia.

Fiberglass boats Some of the better fibreglass trailer boats are: Haines Hunter, Haines Signature (two different companies), Kevalcat, Caribbean (Australian-built Bertram), Chivers, and Fraser. Aussie trailer boats tend to be skinnier than American ones, with the exception of the big, fast, stable twin-hull motorcats, like the Kevalcat, Noosacat, and Sharkcat.

Some American brands are imported: Boston Whaler, Sea Ray, Trophy, Bayliner, Polar, Magnum, and Mustang. Besides being quite pricey, they're generally larger than Australian boats and can be a problem to tow.

Fiberglass is spelled fibreglass in Australia.

Boat trailers The standard large American trailer boat has a beam of 8½ feet (2.6 metres), which is legal to tow in the U.S. but is just over the 2.5 metre maximum normal width allowed on the road in Australia. A load over 2.5 metres becomes a *wide load* that needs a special yearly permit and special *wide load* signs hung on the front of the tow car and the back of the boat when towed. A boat that is 2.7 metres (8.85 feet) wide can't be towed on any freeway, on highways at certain times, or at night.

Aussie boat trailers often have sets of rollers that go the length of the boat to make launching and retrieval easier. The downside is if the winch gave way on the road, the boat could roll off. With these systems, it's important to secure the boat to the trailer with a bow-eye safety chain and stern straps. It's amazing how many boats you see being towed on the highway with nothing but the winch cable securing them to the trailer.

Tinnies are so light that you hardly have to get the trailer wet to launch and retrieve. I backed my fifteen-footer in until the trailer license plate was just touching the water—the wheel hubs rarely got wet. I did all the work with the trailer winch.

Small tinny trailers don't have brakes. Mid-sized trailers use a non-hydraulic brake system. There's a sliding sprung hitch that pulls a cable, which actuates a lever on each wheel hub. The levers press a disc brake calliper on each wheel. They're easy to service and there's not much to go wrong. Bigger trailer boats use hydraulic and electric brake systems.

A neat modification I've seen in some beach areas where the water is shallow a long way out is a swing-down spare tire on a functional wheel hub. That way the spare acts as a full-sized tongue wheel. You can unhitch the trailer from the boat and roll the whole thing out to deeper water to launch. To retrieve, you set the brakes on the trailer and either winch the boat or drive it onto the trailer under its own power. Then you hook a long rope to your 4WD, pull the trailer to the edge of the sand, and reattach it to the tow car.

Boat prices   Good quality boats can be expensive in Australia. A new, bare fifteen-foot pressed aluminum *tinny* with a 40-horsepower outboard on a trailer will go for A$10,000. A new 20-foot pressed-hull aluminum cabin cruiser with a 150-horsepower outboard on a trailer with electronics can go for A$50,000. A comparably equipped aluminum plate boat will go for A$75,000, while a fibreglass version will top A$90,000.

Misc.   Built-in fuel tanks, especially in fiberglass boats, tend to be about half the size of those on American boats. Switches on the control panels flip down for "on"—the opposite of American switches.

Aussie trailer boaters do an interesting thing with their dock lines. Instead of having separate bow and stern lines, they have one long line tied in a big loop: one end to the bow and the other to the stern. That way, one person can easily control both ends of the boat with one line. When the boat is back on the trailer, they use the line to secure the stern to the trailer.

Nylon anchor-line isn't commonly used on small boats because (like so many things in Australia) it's expensive.

Instead people use *silver-line*, which is polyethylene and floats (nylon sinks). This isn't the best idea, because if the wind is slack and the line is floating on the surface, a passing boat could slice it. It also has no stretch like nylon and isn't as strong. Why do they use it? It's cheap. As a salesman in my local chandlery once told me, "Aussies would use shoestring to anchor if they thought they could get away with it."

The lower unit on an outboard or out-drive is called the *leg*. An inflatable boat, like a Zodiac or an Avon, is called a *rubber ducky*. The tube you tow your kids around in is called a *biscuit* or *bickie*. A slip is a *pen*. Fishermen are called *fishers*. The tongue wheel on a trailer is called a *jockey wheel*.

Beach launching   Just because you have a heavier trailer boat doesn't mean it can't be beach-launched. Boaters in remote areas often use old tractors, modified for beach use, to put 25' boats in the water. It's an impressive operation, especially on a day with a bit of surf.

If you do beach launch, watch the tides. You'll need at least a 4WD, and be sure to let down the air in your tires.

Big boats   There are large Australian-made power boats, like Fraser, Whittley, and the bigger Kevalcats and Noosacats; and American ones, like Bertram, Riviera, and Sea Ray.

The largest private aluminum luxury boat ever launched was Greg Norman's 228-foot motor cruiser, built by Austal boats near Perth. It's a full ocean liner-like luxury cruiser, set up for sports. It can equip thirty divers and has a decompression chamber. There's a 42' sportfisher on the back deck, ready for marlin.

Sailing   There are tens of thousands of sailboats, from small harbor racers to around-the world cruisers; mono-hulls, catamarans, and trimarans.

The Aussies took the America's Cup away from the Yanks for the first time ever in 1983. The Sydney to Hobart race is one of the top sailing races in the world. The youngest person to sail solo nonstop around the world was David Dicks of Fremantle, who circumnavigated at age seventeen.

Wildlife

The basic rule is: "If it doesn't have fur or feathers, assume it's fatal."

This is an overstatement, but it should keep you out of trouble—the only exception is the cassowary [more below].

Don't be intimidated; only a few people out of a population of 21 million die each year from wildlife, so the odds are in your favor.

Fear not. I've been visiting Australia since 1989, been living there since 2003, and haven't been bit by anything yet.

Snakes   Fact is, Australia has the most venomous snakes in the world. Not poisonous, venomous: poisonous means if you eat it you get sick or die, venomous means if it bites you, you get sick or die.

Stay away from snakes. Watch where you're going in the bush or even in a backyard shed or along the edge of the beach. If you get bit, stay calm, apply a pressure bandage; don't wash the wound—and get help. Anti-venom from a local emergency room is your best course of action.

Spiders can be nasty. The *redback* is a spider similar to the black widow, except the red hourglass shape is on the back not the belly—which makes it easier to spot. Like the black widow, they hide under shelves, in old tarps, cardboard boxes, corners of sheds, etc. The bite won't kill you, but it will make you sick. It hurts instantly and intensely, and after a while you'll start to feel ill. Stay calm and get yourself to medical help, preferably a hospital emergency room. You'll be given a few injections of anti-venom and should start to feel better in a few hours.

The white-tail spider is another nasty. Its bite isn't that significant at first, but it gets much worse over time, causing tissue to die. They're about 1½" long, with a dark red or grey body and red-and-brown banded legs.

There are lots of varieties of spiders, large and small, venomous and non-venomous. If you don't know which spiders are bad, stay away from all of them.

Scorpions are in the spider family. The ones in the north tend to be larger and more venomous. Shake out your shoes before you put them on. The sting is painful, but not dangerous; it's kind of like a bee sting. If you do get stung, catch the bastard and have it identified. Treat the bite by taking an antihistamine like Benadryl; it'll control the inflammation and the itch. Stingose is a good topical for pain.

Insects   There are large ants that will bite hard and hang on, so watch where you step. Wasps and bees will sting. *Mozzies* (mosquitoes) can carry Ross River Virus and Murray Valley Encephalitis, so use repellent. The large March fly lands on bare skin without making so much as a tickle, then bites down and takes a piece out of you. It hurts for the moment, but the little buggers are so intent on biting that they won't fly away and can easily be swatted.

Flies can occur in huge numbers at certain times of the year in the bush. The constant action of waving them from in front of your face is known as the *Aussie salute*. Some people have been known to wear hats with corks dangling on strings tied to the brim to repel the flies. This is effective only because the flies are too embarrassed to be seen near them.

Lizards are not venomous, though the bites can become infected.

There are some large lizards, like the *goanna*. Misnamed after iguanas, they're actually in the monitor family. Goannas will grow to six feet long, though most top out at about four feet—and half of that is tail. They can run fast, sometimes on their back legs. They aren't aggressive, but have a nasty, non-venomous bite. Reportedly, when frightened, they'll climb the tallest object around, and if that happens to be you, you could end up with one on your head.

Blue tongue and bobtail lizards look like the gila monsters of the American southwest, with a bobbed tail and a wide mouth. They measure about a foot long and when cornered, open their mouths and hiss, they look nasty but they're not venomous and are basically harmless. They're good to have in your garden, since they eat slugs, snails, and *slaters* (wood lice), but they'll also eat your strawberries.

Box jellyfish are a big problem along the northern tropical coasts. They occur in shallow tidal areas and near river mouths and breed in the *wet* (rainy season), December through April. They're pale blue with a bell-shaped body about 4" long, with fifteen, three-foot tentacles in each corner that have thousands of stinging cells. They can kill a human in less than a minute.

According to medical texts, once stung you have virtually no chance of surviving. You'll experience excruciating pain and go into shock and drown before you can get to shore. If you're found, you'll be in cardiac arrest and not breathing. CPR and heart massage may keep you alive until formal medical care can be established. Vinegar can neutralize the tentacles, which can then be removed. For some reason, the texts say never use mentholated spirits. First responders should not touch the tentacles. **Heed the warning signs posted at beaches and don't swim along the shore in those months.**

The Great Barrier Reef isn't affected. The reef starts 20 miles out to sea, and box jellyfish don't go into deep water or that far offshore.

Crocodiles take several Australians each year. Again, this is in the northern tropics, near river mouths or in rivers, where you have no business being (read the signs). The marine (or salty) crocodile is the big nasty, growing to twenty feet long and weighing 1,500 pounds. They can lie motionless for hours hidden in a foot of water, then spring up and grab their prey in a flash. **Stay out of their territory, away from the riverbanks, and heed the signs.**

Sharks   Yeah, they're out there, but you'll never see the one that gets you—or so they say—so don't sweat it. Seriously, they seem to like dawn and dusk and murky water. *White pointers* (great whites) occur along the southern coasts; tiger sharks are more tropical; bull sharks and bronze whalers can occur in temperate waters. It's nice to know that most sharks don't target humans; they just mistake us for something else they like to eat, like a seal or *dugong* (Australian manatee). There are a number of shark attacks each year. Some beaches have shark nets, others (like Perth) have an airplane patrolling the coast, watching for them. Check with the locals before you venture out. A few people are eaten every year.

The **blue-ringed octopus** is a cute little mollusc that lives all around the coasts of Australia, usually in shallow water and rocky pools. It has enough venom to kill ten people and there's no known antidote. Often you won't even know you've been bit until your vision goes blurry and you start to have trouble breathing. You can try rescue-breathing a victim and seeking immediate medical aid. Once in the hospital, breathing assistance will be applied and if the victim lives through the first twenty-four hours they'll probably make a complete recovery. When you're in the ocean, don't go poking around in holes bare-handed.

Stingrays   Since Steve Irwin met his tragic and untimely death, people are suddenly concerned about stingrays. They're basically harmless animals, unless you're a shellfish in shallow sand or a TV adventurer mugging for a close-up on top of one. You're more likely to be killed by a bolt of lighting during a blue moon in leap year than by a stingray. The most common danger is stepping on one, and that will result only in a sting that can be treated with hot water and meat tenderizer. Wear dive booties or sneakers when wading in sandy areas, and shuffle your feet. If you snorkel near one—it goes without saying—keep well out of reach of the tail.

Cone shells   Beware of these lowly, oblong-shaped, irresistibly pretty shell-fish.   Some are the size of an olive, some—like the Southern Bailer—are the size of a football. They have a stinger that can paralyse. If stung, have someone keep a close watch on your breathing and get medical aid.

Cassowaries are large (four to six feet tall) flightless birds with brilliant red-and-blue markings on their necks and a horn on their heads. They live in North Queensland and can become aggressive in self-defense. It's not the horn you have to worry about, it's the big middle toe—they try to eviscerate you. Don't run away or they'll chase you. Stand your ground, pick up a big stick, wave it, and yell at them. They're about as smart as a chicken.

Kangaroos and emus   Probably the most common wildlife danger in Australia is hitting a kangaroo or *emu* (ostrich-like flightless bird) with your car. Be careful driving in bush areas around dawn or dusk when they're most active.

A herd of kangaroos is called a *mob*.

Cute & cuddlies   Enough with the scary stuff—there are lots of cute and cuddlies out there: kangaroos, koalas, bandicoots, furry possums, and quokkas. Be careful; the koalas can bite and a big 'roo can stomp you. Anything with teeth is liable to bite if you try to pick it up.

Birds   Australia is a bird watcher's paradise. There's everything from tiny wrens and honeyeaters to large emus and cassowaries. There are hundreds of species of parrots, like the pink and grey galas, green and yellow twenty-eights, sulfur-crested and black cockatoos, corellas, rainbow lorikeets, Australian ringnecks, eclectus parrots and millions of *budgies* (parakeets). There are raven-like crows, magpies, giant wedgetail eagles, hawks, swans, herons, the biggest pelicans you've ever seen, ibis, bustards, etc.

If you love birds this is the place to be. Bring your binoculars and get a copy of "The Claremont Field Guide to the Birds of Australia", or "The Slater Field Guide to Australian Birds".

Ferals and exotics

Ferals are animals that were domesticated, but have since gone wild. Feral cats are a problem; they kill native birds, small marsupials, and lizards. Dingos are wild dogs that accompanied the Aboriginal migrations and have become wild. In some areas, packs of abandoned dogs attack sheep. Feral pigs and goats destroy flora, ripping out roots and eating native plants. Wild horses (*brumbies*) and wild camels (descended from those imported and used for transport in the 19th century) harm the native grasses in the inland deserts

Rabbits, which were imported as food, have taken over huge tracts of land. They destroy wheat and other crops. A series of rabbit-proof fences thousands of miles long was built in the late 19th century to keep them in the desert interior. In the late 20th century, various viruses were introduced to cull their numbers, but they've since evolved resistance to them and continue to be a pest.

Exotics are foreign wild animals that have become pests. Starlings are small swallow-like birds that were introduced to Australia, just as in North America. They raid vineyards and orchards in huge flocks and can strip one bare in a few hours.

Foxes were introduced for hunting and have thrived, assuming the role coyotes play in North America, but without any natural predators except for the occasional truck on the highway. The most effective way of culling them is through poison baiting, using a formula called *1080*, which is made from native plants so native animals aren't effected. Meat is used as bait, so beware the *1080 poison* signs when walking your dog.

The cane toad was introduced to North Queensland from South America in the 1930s to control the greyback cane beetle. Unfortunately, the beetle lives on the upper stalks of the sugar cane and the toads can't jump that high, so it was a failure. The toads have turned into a mega-pest. Not only do they out-compete native frogs for food, they eat them, too, along with anything else they can fit in their mouths. The toads exude a slimy poison though the skin on their backs, so almost nothing will eat them, and anything that does dies. Supposedly you can get high off this poison, and it's now illegal to lick a toad in Queensland. Big cane toads can measure ten inches across and weigh ten pounds. They've spread from Queensland through the Northern Territory and are encroaching into Western Australia. It's predicted they could occupy almost all of coastal Australia in a few years. Professional toad trappers have been engaged to stop them. There's also a small industry making leather goods from their hides, so you can surprise the folks back home with a cane toad wallet or key case. Just don't get caught licking your wallet in Queensland.

Pets

Pets in Australia are lucky beasts. In my experience, dogs seem to be better regarded and cared for than in the U.S. There are fewer problem dogs, and ones relegated to a life in the backyard are rare.

Dogs   A few peculiarities: the Rottweiler is pronounced *rot-weeler*. Dobermans rarely have their ears clipped and are much mellower as a result. Pit bulls are called *American pit bulls* and are banned from breeding due to their dangerous character.

Most of the same popular breeds are available, along with a few not widely seen in North America, such the Staffordshire terrier (or *Staffy*), which makes a great family pet.

Ironically, Australian shepherds don't exist in Australia, even though that breed has recently been formally recognized by the American Kennel Club. The Australian shepherd has nothing to do with Australia and was developed from working dogs in the U.S.

The Australian *blue heeler* breed has a similar bluish-brindle color as an American Australian shepherd, but with a much shorter coat, wider stance, and blustery personality. *Bluies* are bred to herd cattle, they are tough as guts, and can take a stomping from a *bullock* (steer), then get up and run the bastard through a fence.

Then there is the Kelpie, a slim, medium-sized reddish-brown dog with a tan mask. Kelpies are brilliant shepherds: one dog can gather an entire flock, drive it across meadows, through narrow gates, force them up a ramp and into a truck, often running over the backs of the sheep to urge them through bottlenecks. If you ever get a chance to go to a country sheepdog trial, do it; it's amazing.

Dogs are rarely given away as puppies. Mixed-breeds, as well as purebreds, are sold, and not cheaply. A purebred Kelpie can go for several thousand dollars. If you're moving to Australia and want to get a dog (but don't want to pay dearly), try an animal shelter or the RSPCA.

When a dog or cat is neutered or spayed, it's referred to having been *de-sexed*.

Cats can be problematic. Most are loved pets, but many go wild and prey upon the native birds and small marsupials, which have no natural defense. Politically correct cat etiquette is to keep them indoors. Feral cats are shot on sight in rural areas.

Horses are a lifestyle of their own, with breeders shows, pony clubs, rodeos, and casual riding. As with the American mustangs, some got loose and formed wild populations in the outback. They're called *brumbies*.

Birds Parakeets are natives of the north, and are called *budgies* (short for *budgerigar*), an Aboriginal name. Cockatiels are also called *weiros*. Budgies and weiros are also raised in captivity in simple backyard aviaries.

Some wild parrots have been domesticated, mostly corellas and galahs. These are really wild birds in cages, though some were rescued injured. Corellas and Major Mitchells can be good talkers, but also tend to be biters.

Many people, both in the suburbs and in rural areas, raise chickens for their eggs, and good layers are regarded as pets. Extra roosters are regarded as Sunday dinner—but they're kind of tough, so you have to cook them a while. They make a nice matzo ball soup. It's a bit unsettling at first eating your former pets, but at least you know they aren't full of hormones and antibiotics. A tip: don't let your kids name the ones destined for the freezer.

Sheep are raised commercially by the thousands, but many people living on a few acres will keep a pair to keep the grass trimmed down. I named ours Briggs and Stratton.

Alpacas   For folks with acreage who are bored with sheep, there are Alpacas, which have become a kind of Gucci sheep. They're similar to a llama, a bit smaller, but with big eyes and a delicate face that makes them all look like you want to cuddle them. Beware: they can spit, and I'm told they usually aim for your eyes. The trick is to raise your hand and hold it in front of you, away from you face—they'll spit at that instead.

The males aren't afraid to fight a fox, so some *pastoralists* (shepherds) put a few out to guard the new lambs.

Alpacas are quite valuable; a pregnant female can go for A$2,500 or more. To help defray the costs, you can sell the fleece, because unlike other textiles, demand outweighs supply. There are about 85,000 alpacas in Australia.

Migrating with a pet from North America has gotten a lot easier. The quarantine period for dogs and cats has been shortened substantially. For birds, it's another story. Some (like the African grey parrot) are banned entirely. For more info, check out the government website at **www.aqis.gov.au**.

The motion picture industry

Overview   While the Australian movie industry has hosted many runaway American productions (like "Matrix" and the last three "Star Wars" films), it also has its own distinguished history. Arguably, the first feature film produced anywhere in the world was Australian, the 1903 "Ned Kelly Gang". The Aussie industry was becoming a significant force in the 1920s, but an American theater chain bought it out and shut it down, preferring to import American product. This was easy to do, since movies were still silent and there was no accent issue. Don't laugh; the first version of "Mad Max" imported into the U.S. had Mel Gibson's Aussie accent overdubbed with an American one.

With a small population of 21 million, Australia can't support a major film industry. Statistics show that you need a population of at least 90 million to do so. With government subsidies, Australian producers manage to turn out about a dozen small-budget features and another dozen TV series each year, along with hundreds of top-quality documentaries, *music clips* (music videos), and lots of commercials.

There are major studio facilities in Sydney, Melbourne, and on the Gold Coast south of Brisbane. The perennial hit TV series "McLeod's Daughters", a modern-day western soap, is filmed out of Adelaide. Perth is known for quality children's dramatic programming.

Children's TV production is helped by a government mandate requiring each commercial network to air a quota of new, locally produced and themed kids shows each year. Australian-produced series air in New Zealand, South Africa, the UK, and Europe.

Dramatic production falls into two main categories: American and domestic.

American "runaway" productions generally come to Australia for one reason: to save money. They bring their own rules: long hours, larger crews, more elaborate equipment, and big budgets. Recent projects are the last three Star Wars films, "Superman Returns", "Stealth", "Charlotte's Web", and "Band of Brothers—Pacific".

Many great Australian filmmakers go to the U.S. and Europe to work on a scale unavailable in Australia. Some prominent directors are: Peter Weir ("Witness", "Dead Poets Society", "Master and Commander"), Phillip Noyce ("Patriot Games", "The Saint"), Mel Gibson ("Braveheart", "Passion Of The Christ", "Apocalypto"), Bruce Beresford ("Driving Miss Daisy", "The Black Robe"), and Baz Luhrmann ("Moulin Rouge", "Alexander").

Some great Australian cameramen are: John Seale ("The American President", "Cold Mountain", "The Perfect Storm"), Dean Semler ("Dances With Wolves", "We Were Soldiers", "Bruce Almighty"), Russell Boyd ("Master and Commander", "Tin Cup"), and Don McAlpine ("Mrs. Doubtfire", "Chronicles of Narnia").

Domestic Australian productions are generally on much smaller budgets. Dramas like "Lantana", "Jindabyne", "Gallipoli", and "Rabbit Proof Fence" deal with contemporary and historic Australian issues. Comedies like "Strictly Ballroom", "Priscilla, Queen of the Desert", and "Kenny" offer the unique Aussie sense of humor.

Domestic TV drama includes doctor shows ("All Saints"), cop shows ("Blue Heelers"), Adventure shows ("Sea Patrol"), romantic contemporary westerns ("McLeod's Daughters"), soaps ("Neighbours" and "Home and Away"). Kids' shows include "Parallax", "Ocean Girl", "Bananas in Pyjamas", and "The Wiggles".

Australian films have a rating system similar to the one in the U.S.: G, PG, M, MA, R, and X. The ratings and censorship board is The Office of Film and Literature Classification.

Funded films are small films funded by state film boards, which are of social or cultural relevance. There's a long process to get funding, with many steps of script approval and budget review along the way, but it's a way of nurturing an otherwise neglected part of the industry and of providing a springboard for new directors, writers, and cinematographers.

Government assistance for production   Australia's relatively small population means it can't support an unsubsidized film industry. Therefore, if Australia wants to have a film identity to represent its culture domestically as well as internationally, it needs to be subsidized. Each state has a film board that provides seed money to help productions get started.

The federal government formed the *Australian Film Commission* (*AFC*) to stimulate production, and the *Film Finance Commission* (*FFC*) to provide financial assistance. In July 2008, they're to be merged into the *Australian Screen Authority* (*ASA*), which will provide one-stop shopping for production and funding assistance.

Over the years, there have been various schemes devised to stimulate movie production, mostly tax-incentive plans to encourage private financing. In the 1980s the Labor government established double tax credits for film production, and the number of movies being produced increased substantially, but in typical Australian style, many *rorts* occurred. (A *rort* is an abuse of opportunity, i.e. fraud.) Producers made films just to get the tax credit; it didn't matter if they were good or made a profit. The double tax credits were then written off by investors against profits from other businesses. This might have produced some bad films, but it also stimulated the industry. In 1999, because of the *rorts*, the government tax commissioner announced that he was disallowing $800 million in film investment tax credits, and that scared off investors. Ironically, a few days later he rescinded that ruling, but investors never returned. Double tax credits have since been discontinued. Motion picture production has fallen off since then, leaving only low-budget semi-subsidized films, foreign productions using Australian locations, and runaway American films.

In the 2007–08 federal budget (under the newly formed Australian Screen Authority), a system of production rebates will be initiated. Producers will be asked to apply for the rebate after they've secured guaranteed financing, but before production commences. They'll then be eligible for a *refundable tax offset* rebate of 40 percent of a feature film budget and 20 percent of a TV production. New long-form television series will qualify for Australian government support for the first time.

Starting in July 2007, foreign productions coming to Australia to film will be eligible for a 12.5 to 15 percent rebate. Foreign companies doing post-production, digital, and visual effects will be eligible for a 15 percent rebate for their expenditures in Australia, with a minimum threshold of A$5 million.

Government assistance will continue for locally produced theatrical, cultural and documentary films, and children's programs.

Film festivals   There are numerous film festivals. Some are big, like the Melbourne International Festival and the Brisbane International Festival. Some are small and off-beat, like the Adelaide Fringe Festival and the Eye Scream Festival.

Tropfest, held each February, began small but is now huge. It's a nationwide short film competition culminating with the sixteen winning films screening simultaneously in outdoor theaters in all the capital cities. It draws large crowds.

Movie industry technical information

Production   The basic shooting day is ten hours long. If overtime is required, the assistant director will go around to the crew and ask if anybody objects. Overtime is usually less than half an hour. Lunch break is forty-five minutes long and usually six hours into the day. Crafts services are limited: hot water for tea or instant coffee, and a few *biscuits* (cookies). There will usually be a tea break for snacks around 4:00 p.m. If the day is behind schedule, this might be at wrap.

Crew   Despite different terms and more humane hours, movies are shot pretty much the same way as in North America. The crews are competent and professional, but not as well paid. Crews are much smaller; there are fewer trucks and people double-up duties. Hair and makeup are often done by the same person. There are no drivers per se; departments handle their own trucks.

Australian productions work on the English system. Crewing is slightly different and some jobs have different names:

The Director of Photography is called the *DOP*. He/she usually operates the camera. If a second camera is used, a camera operator will run it; otherwise, no camera operator is employed.

The first assistant cameraman is called the *focus puller* (**Important Note:** lens focus marks are in feet, not metres).

The second assistant cameraman is called the *clapper loader*.

The sound mixer is sometimes called the *soundo*.

The microphone boom person is called the *boom swinger*.

A trainee is called an *attachment*.

An insert car is called a *tracking vehicle*.

Grips work with the camera. All C-stands, cutters, nets, and diffusion in front of the lights, silks, and *fleckies* (reflectors) are handled by the gaffer and his electricians (sometimes called *sparkies*).

Hair and makeup are often done by the same person.

Lighting stand-ins are rarely used. Often the clapper loader or an AD will stand on the actor's mark if needed. If asked, the actors themselves will oblige.

There's usually a *safety officer* on each show who is responsible for safety on the set. They supervise work from a safety standpoint and coordinate traffic control when shooting on the street.

Police aren't normally present when shooting on the street. If necessary, an independent traffic management company will be hired to provide warning signs, *witches' hats* (safety cones) and *lollipop men* (flag men holding stop signs).

There are no teamsters; someone from each department will drive that department's truck(s).

Different terms

Music videos are called *video clips*.

TV commercials are called *TVCs*.

A TV season is called a *series*, as in "the second *series* of "Friends"," meaning all the shows in the second year it ran.

The slate is called the *clapper board*.

Video assist is called *video split*, or just the *split*.

A tree branch used to create a dappled shadow effect is called a *dingle*.

An umbrella is a *brolly*.

A *grovel mat* (or a *grovelly*) is a furniture pad or anything you throw on the ground for an actor or camera operator to sit, kneel, or lie down on to shoot a scene.

A *lazy leg* is an extendable leg on a light stand ("rocky mountain leg" in the U.S.).

Oysters means to shoot with available or natural light, as in *oysters natural*.

A bit on the piss" means a Dutch angle (tilted framing).

A *KD* is a pop-up canopy to provide shade and rain protection.

If you leave your mobile phone on and it rings during a take or do anything equally stupid on a set, you'll be *slabbed*. This means you'll have to buy a *slab* (case) of beer to share with the crew after wrap the next day.

Slates and scene numbers   The scene numbers, as on the slate (*clapper board*) and the camera report, are done differently than in North America. It's not based on the scene number, but on the *shot number*. Shot numbers go up sequentially from the first shot of the movie. A letter isn't added to the scene number for a different angle of coverage of the same scene as in America; you just go to the next shot number. A pick-up shot for a scene filmed days earlier would have a totally different shot number on the slate. Good camera reports are critical.

Shot number conventions: at shot 100, the director buys the beers; shot 111, the producer; shot 123, the sound crew; shot 216, electrical; shot 246, the grips.

Unions   There's no strong motion picture union. The Media Entertainment and Arts Alliance (also known as ATAEA) traces its history back to the early 1900s. Unlike the IATSE in North America, it has little clout. The contract and working conditions can been seen at: **www.alliance.org.au**. A lot of work is outside the Alliance, but the rates set by it are used as a starting point for negotiations when one is hired.

No residuals are paid to actors, directors, or writers, though if a series is rerun more than five times, they get additional payments.

Booking agents   Each capital city has booking agents. Call them to hire crew or to seek representation. Check the Yellow Pages, online, or with the government film board in that state.

Shipping equipment [see section on **postal matters, shipping**].

Conclusions?

Generalizations are generally too general, but if any can be drawn from our years of living in the country, it's simply that Australia is probably what the U.S. would be like if there had been no American Revolution.

If you remember your history, after the Revolutionary War and until well after the War of 1812, the U.S. intentionally distanced itself from Great Britain. The U.S. developed on its own, and by the turn of the 20th century had a well-established identity, along with a substantial population, and had become industrialized.

Australia, on the other hand, was a decentralized group of British colonies until 1901, and like Canada, had a small population and was dependant on the motherland for both manufactured imports and markets to export to. However, unlike Canada, which is next door to the U.S., the Australian identity had to evolve in near isolation on the far side of the world, and therefore developed its own cultural peculiarities and idiosyncrasies—in a fun kind of way.

Australia is basically a sunny version of provincial England, with some America-envy thrown in. But don't bring this up to an Aussie—they'll wonder what the heck you're talking about.

My personal conclusion? Take a lesson from the Aussies: don't take anything too seriously. Repeat after me: *No worries...she'll be right.*

Australian-American Dictionary

Just because Americans and Australians use a language based on English doesn't mean they speak the same language. To again paraphrase Winston Churchill, they are "two peoples separated by a common language." The big stuff is obvious; it's the subtle differences that get you. An American living in Australia finds him or herself having to repeat things and having to ask for things to be repeated. It's partly the accent and partly the terminology. The accent you'll have to pick up on; it's like learning to play music by ear. The terminology is absorbed over time. The next section is your cheat sheet.

The following contains 1,542 Australian words and phrases, their meanings and usages, which will be handy when travelling, doing business, or settling in Australia. Some words and terms are hard to evaluate grammatically, so the categorization is loose. My apologies to Merriam-Webster, Thorndike-Barnhart, and Funk & Wagnall's for having the audacity to call it a "dictionary". I kept the definitions as brief and specific as possible.

I hope you have as much fun using it as I had in putting it together.

Australian	American	Details—Usage
a bit rough (adj)	something sub-standard	"Your work is *a bit rough*."
A4 (n)	standard business-size letter (8.25" x 11.75")	
abattoir (n)	slaughterhouse	
ABN (n)	Australian Business Number	A tax number that qualifies you as a business.
a bit on the piss (adj)	tilted camera angle in the movies	same as "Dutch angle" in U.S.
Abo (n)	derogatory term for Aboriginal	
Aborigine (n)	indigenous Australians	Latin: "from the beginning"

abseil (v)	to rappel (rock climbing)	
ace (adj)	great	"That's *ace!*" Used in Melbourne.
ACT (n)	Australian Capital Territory	Australian equivalent of the District of Columbia
ADF (n)	Australian Defence Forces	Army, Navy, Air Force, SAS
adjustable spanner (n)	crescent wrench, monkey wrench	
aerial ping pong (n)	Australian Rules Football (Footy)	
aggro (adj)	Aggravated, aggressive	"He's acting kind of *aggro.*"
agistment (v) (adj)	horse boarding	
air bottles (n)	Scuba tanks	also "air cylinder"
airy fairy (adj)	wishful thinking, unrealistic	
all the fruit (adj)	all the accessories or goodies	"I ordered the new Ford with *all the fruit.*"
all the go (adj)	the latest thing, very popular	"The new Holden is *all the go.*"
ally (n)	aluminum	
aluminium (n) (note second letter "i" in the last syllable)	British/Australian pronunciation and spelling of aluminum	(see text section on **pronunciation differences**)
always in the shit (adj)	always in trouble	
amber fluid (n)	beer	
ambo (n)	ambulance driver	
anticlockwise (adj)	counterclockwise	
anti-social behavior (adj)	Hooliganism, disruptive actions (also known as *"hooning"*)	anything from hot-rodding to being drunk in public, painting graffiti, harassing oldies, etc.
ant's pants (adj)	real good, the best	
"Any joy there?"	Had any success?	

Apple Mac (n)	name for any Apple or Macintosh computer	
apples, she'll be (adj)	alright, it'll be OK	also *apps*
arc up (v)	to get mad	"Look out, or I'm going to *arc up*."
agry-bargy (adj)	argument	
arse (n) (pronounced *ass*)	ass	
arsey (adj)	lucky	
arvo (n) (pronounced *avo*)	afternoon	
as cross as a frog in a sock (adj)	angry	
as full as a goog (adj)	drunk	From English slang for egg: *googy*.
a sparrow's fart (n)	dawn	"I'll wake you at *a sparrow's fart*."
at the end of the day	when all is said and done	
at the mo (adj)	at the moment	
ATO (n)	Australian Tax Office	equivalent to the IRS
AUD, AUD$, A$ (n)	Australian dollar	
Aunty (n)	The ABC (Australian Broadcasting Corporation)	Australia's government-owned public broadcasting networks
AUSFTA (n)	Australia-United States Free Trade Agreement	
Aussie (n)	Australian	
Aussie salute (v) (n)	waving flies from in front of your face	
Autogas (n)	LPG, liquid propane gas	Used as a fuel in cars.
auto trimmer (n)	auto upholsterer	
autumn (n)	fall (The word "fall" is not used.)	Leaves don't seasonally fall off eucalyptus trees.
average (adj)	mediocre	"The meal was pretty *average*."
avos (n)	avocados	

awning over the toy shop (adj)	a man's beer belly	
award rates (n)	minimum standard pay and conditions (pay scale)	
B & S (n)	Bachelor and Spinsters Ball	A drinking and dancing party for single people, usually in rural areas.
BAC (n)	blood alcohol concentration	used to determine drunk driving
back bencher (n)	Member of Parliament not holding a ministerial position	
back foot, on the (adj)	being defensive, under attack	"The accused politician was *on the back foot*."
back hander (n)	a bribe	
back of Bourke (adj)	far away	From the remote town of Bourke in western New South Wales.
back-to-front (adj)	opposite	
backy (n)	tobacco	"Got any *backy*?"
backyard job (n)	improper or illegal job	
bad trot (adj)	a period of bad luck	"I've had a *bad trot* this week."
bagging (v)	giving someone a hard time	
bags (v)	claim (kid's term)	"I *bags* the front seat."
bail up (v)	a hold up, to corner someone	
bailiff (n)	private process server, marshal of the court	
bale (n)	The top piece on a cricket wicket.	
ball and chain (n)	wife	
ball huggers (n)	Speedos (also see budgie smugglers)	

Bali belly (adj)	diarrhea	Bali is a popular vacation spot in nearby Indonesia.
balls-up (adj)	screw-up, mistake	
ball-tearer (adj)	something really special	
balustrade (n) (pronounced *bah-liz-trahd*)	Railing, hand rail, banister	
banana bender (n)	person from Queensland	
bandicoot (n)	a small marsupial about the size of a rabbit	
bangle (n)	bracelet	
Banksia (n)	a flowering tree indigenous to Australia	
barbed wire (n)	Four X beer	XXXX looks like barbed wire
barbie (n)	barbecue	
barbie pack (n)	sausages, steak, and chops to cook on a barbecue	"I went to the shops and bought a *barbie pack*."
bar heater (n)	electric heater, radiator	
Barmy army (n)	English cricket fans	
barney (n)	a fight	
barrack (v)	to cheer for	
barramundi, barra (n)	a tasty, brackish water fish from the northern coast of Australia, often served in restaurants or as fish and chips	can be wild or raised in mariculture
barrister (n)	lawyer who appears in court	usually suggested by your solicitor
BAS (n) (pronounced *baaz*)	Business Activity Statement	Tax form for figuring your GST payment.
bash (v)	to try something	"I'll give it a *bash*."
bashed (v)	hit, battered, assaulted	"The man was *bashed* in the robbery."

bathers (n)	swimsuit	"He put on his *bathers*."
battle axe, battle axe block (adj)	(real estate) rear lot, flag lot	A land-locked lot that has a narrow section to connect with a road.
battler (n)	someone working hard but barely making it	
bean curd (n)	tofu	
beanie (n)	knit cap	
beaut, beauty (adj)	great, real good	"That car's a real *beaut*!" "You little *beauty*!"
beavering (v)	working hard	
bed-sit (n)	an efficiency or studio apartment	
beer buddy (adj)	drinking buddy	
bee's dick, a (adj)	a small amount	"Move it a *bee's dick* to the left"
beet root (n)	beets	
behind (n)	a one-point score in footy	
bell (v)	to call someone	"I'll give you a *bell* later."
bench top (n)	kitchen counter	
bend the elbow (v)	drink too much	"He's been known to *bend the elbow*."
berko (adj)	angry	
berley (n)	chum, bait (fishing)	"*Berley* is spread behind the boat to lure in the fish."
beyond the black stump (adj)	far away, referring to giving bad directions.	"We live just *beyond the black stump*." (The outback is littered with burned-black stumps.)
bickie (n) also spelled: bikkie	cookie (from *biscuit*)	"We baked *bickies*."
bickie (n)	dollar	
biffo, biff (v) (adj)	a fight	"I gave him the *biff*." "We had a bit of a *biffo*."

big note, to (v)	to boast or brag	"Sean was *big noting* himself again."
bikies (n)	motorcyclists	Usually referring to members of bad-guy motorcycle gangs.
billabong (n)	pool in a streambed or waterhole.	
billy (n)	A pot used on an open fire to boil water for tea or cooking.	
billy cart (n)	homemade wooden cart, soapbox racer	
biltong (n)	jerky	South African term
bin (n)	trash can (green top for rubbish, yellow top for recyclables)	"Put out the rubbish *bin*."
bindies (n)	little stickers that grow on grass	
bingle (n)	minor car accident	"He was in a *bingle*."
bird (n)	girl, gal	From British slang.
biro (n) (pronounced *bye-ro*)	ballpoint pen	Laszlo Biro invented the ballpoint pen. Biro is a brand name, and *biro* is used generically for any ballpoint pen.
biscuit (n)	cookie	
bit of a train smash (adj)	a disaster, something that doesn't work well, a mistake	"The job was a *bit of a train smash*."
bities (n)	biting bugs	"The *bities* are out tonight."
bits (n) (adj)	pieces	"Pick up all the *bits*."
bits and bobs (adj)	miscellaneous things	
bitumen (n)	asphalt, pavement	
bitzer (n)	mongrel dog, something pieced together from various parts	bits of this and that
bizzo (n)	business	"Mind your own *bizzo*."

black spot (n)	trouble spot in a roadway targeted for improvement or policing	
block, block of land (n)	lot (real estate)	"We bought a *block* in Subiaco."
bloke (n)	man, guy, fellow	"He's a good bloke."
bloodnut (adj)(n)	person with red hair	
bloody (adj)	very, also an expletive	"That *bloody* fool!"
"Bloody oath!"	"Very true!"	
bloomers (n)	shorts worn over undies and under a skirt	
blower (n)	telephone	"Get on the *blower* and call him."
blowie (v) (n)	windy weather, a blowfly	
blow in (adj)	someone unexpected and uninvited	
blow in the bag (v)	taking a breathalyser test	
bludge, bludger (n)	person who dodges work	
blue (n)	a fight	
blue heeler (n)	a cop	
blue metal (n)	granite gravel	
blue tongue (n)	a bobtailed lizard, common in WA	
blue, make a (adj)	make a mistake	
bluestone (n)	granite	"They walked over a *bluestone* bridge.
bluey (n)	multiple meanings: a backpack, equipment, traffic ticket, a type of cattle dog, $10 bill, a jacket worn by miners, bluebottle jellyfish, a person with red hair	
Blundies (n)	Blundstone work boots	
Blu-Tack (n)	an adhesive putty that is used to hang posters on walls, etc.	

board shorts, boardies (n)	surfer's baggie swim trunks, knee-length or longer	
bob-a-job (n)	An odd-job performed by a kid for a neighbor, usually for a small amount.	A *bob* is slang for a pound, the Aussie denomination of money before switching to the dollar in 1966.
Bob's your uncle	and there you have it, a done deal	
bodgy (adj)	bad quality, worthless	
bog in (v)	to start eating	
bog standard (adj)	ordinary, basic, unadorned	"His Holden was *bog standard*."
bog, the (n)	toilet	"I gotta go to the *bog*."
bogan (n)	a low-life person	
bogey (n)	fifth wheel-hitch on a semi-truck (also called a booger)	
bogged (adj)	stuck, vehicle stuck in sand or mud	"We got *bogged* on the beach."
boilermaker, boilie (n)	person qualified to cut and fabricate metal, a welder	
bolshie (n) (adj)	revolutionary, agitator, rebel	From *Bolshevik.*
bonk (v)	to have sex	
bonnet (n)	car hood	
bonzer (adj) (pronounced *bon-za*)	great	
boofhead (n) (adj)	idiot	
boofy (adj)	fluffy, usually referring to hair	
booking (v)	reservation for a restaurant, hotel, hire car	"I made a *booking* for dinner."
booking out (adj)	booked up, no vacancy	

boom swinger (n)	person who holds the mike boom on a movie crew	
boomer (n)	large male kangaroo	
boomerang (adj)	loaned item that hasn't been returned	
boondy (n)	(Western Australian term) dirt clod	"I chucked a *boondy* and hit him in the eye."
boot (n)	car trunk	
booze bus (n)	police van used in road blocks to catch drink drivers	
boozer (n)	pub or tavern, a drinker	
booze-up (n)	drinking spree	
bore (n)	well (water)	
bossy boots (adj)	pushy person	
bottle shop, bottle-o (n)	liquor store	
bottler (adj)	something excellent	
bounce (adj)	bully	
bourse (n)	stock exchange	
bowled me over (adj)	surprised	"You could have *bowled me over*."
bowler (n)	the pitcher in cricket	
bowser (n)	gas pump	"He got petrol from the *bowser*."
box and dice (adj)	everything	From "the whole box of dice."
box of beer (n)	case of beer	also *slab* or *carton*
Boxing Day (n)	the day after Christmas	
brackets (n)	parenthesis (punctuation)	
brass, brass razoo (adj)	money	"He hasn't got a *brass razoo*."
brassiere (n)	bar, inexpensive restaurant and bar	
breaker (n)	person who breaks horses for riding	
brekky, brekkie (n)	breakfast	

brickie (n)	brick layer	
brickie's cleavage (adj)	crack of a man's ass, visible when his pants slide too low	
bring a plate (v)	pot luck, bring your own meat (barbecue)	
Brizzie (n)	Brisbane	
brolly (n)	umbrella	
brown-eyed mullet (n)	turd	
Brownie Guides (n)	Brownies (first level of Girl Guides)	
brumby (n)	mustang, wild horse	
bub (n)	baby	
Buckley's, Buckley's chance (adj)	no chance at all	"He hasn't got *Buckley's* chance of winning the Lotto."
bucks night (adj)	bachelor party	
budgie smugglers (n)	Speedos (tight swimsuit, like competitive swimmers wear)	
budgie, budgerigar (n)	parakeet	Aboriginal word
bug (n)	delicious crab-like crustacean (Queensland)	
bugger (v) (adj)	unpleasant person, affectionate term for someone, an exclamation of amazement	"*Bugger* them all!" "He's a *bugger*." "I'll be *buggered*."
"Bugger off!"	"Go away!"	
bulk billing (n) (v)	Medical billing where physician directly bills the government and accepts whatever the government pays as full payment.	

bull bars (n)	Big brush bar on the front of a vehicle for protection from hitting kangaroos or emus in outback and shopping trolleys in supermarket car parks.	also *'roo bars*
bull dust (n)	deep dust on a dirt road	
bull twang (adj)	lies	
bum (n)	butt, ass, derrière	
bum bag (n)	waist pack	"*Fanny*" is a word not used in polite company.
bumf, bumph (adj)	official documents, forms, toilet paper	
Bundy (n)	Bundaberg rum, made in Bundaberg, Queensland	
bunfight (n)	argument, dispute, brouhaha	
bunger (n)	firecracker (usually large and illegal), cigarette	
bunged, bunky (adj)	broken	"Bring that *bunky* regulator over here."
bung hole (n)	mouth	"Put that in your *bunghole!*"
bung (v)	to put an object on something	"*Bung* that tyre on my ute."
bunny (adj)	victim in a swindle	
Bunyip (n)	legendary swamp monster, Aussie bogeyman	
burl (v)	to try	"Give it a *burl*."
bush (n)	anyplace outside a town	
bush bash	a race through the bush	
bush oyster (n)	spit-out nasal mucus, a "loogy"	
bush ranger (n)	outlaw	
bush telegraph (n)	spreading rumors or gossip, the grapevine	

bush tellie (n)	campfire	A *tellie* is a television.
bush tucker (n)	native food foraged or hunted	
bushfire	brushfire	
bushie (n) (adj)	person who lives in the bush	"He's a bit *bushie*."
busker (n)	street performer, usually paid by tips	
bust-up	fight, brawl	
busy as a cat burying shit (adj)	being busy	
busy bee (n)	volunteer work party	
butcher (n)	half-pint glass of beer (South Australia)	
butter up (v)	To fix a mistake you've made.	
BYO (adj)	restaurant where you can bring your own alcohol	
cack (v)	to laugh	
cack-a-dacks (v)	to drop trousers, to moon someone.	
cactus (adj)	dead	"That car is *cactus*."
Caesars (n)	Caesarean section	"Too posh to push."
cake hole (n)	mouth	
call Ralph (v)	to vomit	
CALM (n)	Western Australian Department of Conservation and Land Management	In 2007, changed to DEC, Department of Environment and Conservation.
camp (adj)	one who acts very gay	
Canadian canoe (n)	canoe	Differentiates from simply *canoe*, which can also mean a kayak.
cane it (v)	drive fast	

cane toad (n) (adj)	Amphibian originally imported to control beetles that has become an exotic pest. Also a nickname for a person from Queensland.	
canteen (n)	school cafeteria	
capsicum (n)	bell pepper	
Captain Cook (v)	a look (rhyming slang)	"Go take a *Captain Cook*."
car bays (n)	parking places	
car park (n)	parking lot	
caravan (n)	travel trailer	
carer (n)	caregiver	
cark, carked, carked it (v)	to die	"He *carked* it."
carn (v)	short for "come on"	used as encouragement
carriageway (n)	roadway	
carry on like a cat burying shit (adj)	very busy	
carry on like a pork chop (v) (adj)	throw a fit about nothing	
carton (n)	case of beer, also *box* or *slab* of beer	
caster sugar (n)	fine grain sugar used for icing	
cat flap (n)	doggie door	
cat's piss, mean as (adj)	cheap, stingy	
cattle duffer (n)	rustler	
CBD (n)	Central Business District, downtown area of a city	"I've got to go into the *CBD*."
celebrant (n)	A person who performs a non-religious wedding or funeral.	
cellar door (n)	wine tasting room	

chalk and cheese (adj)	no comparison	"The difference between Budweiser and Crown Lager is *chalk and cheese*."
chalkie (n)	teacher	
chase him up (v)	look for him	"I'll *chase him up*."
chasie (n)	tag (game of)	
chat (n)	shit	
chat show (n)	talk show	
chat up (n)	flirting talk	"He was *chatting* her *up*."
Chateau Cardboard (adj)	cheap wine that comes in a cardboard box	
cheek, cheeky (adj)	impudence, to show gall	"The *cheeky* bastard stole my girl!"
cheerio	goodbye	
cheers	thanks, good bye, also a drinking salute.	
chemist (n)	pharmacy, pharmacist	"I'll drop by the *chemist's* and have a chat with the *chemist*.
chewie (n)	chewing gum	
Chiko Roll (n)	a sausage wrapped in pastry	
China (n)	old friend	rhyming slang: China plate = mate
chin wag (n) (v)	a chat	
chippy (n)	carpenter	
chips (n)	French fries	
chock a spaz (v)	throw a fit	
chock-a-block (adj)	full	"The theatre was *chock-a-block*."
chockers (adj) (pronounced *chokkas*)	full (from *chock full*)	"After that meal, I'm *chockers*!"
chocolate sauce (n)	chocolate syrup	
choke a darkie (v)	defecate	
chokkie (n)	chocolate	
choof-off (v)	to go away quickly	
chook (n)	chicken	

chook raffle (n)	money raiser selling chicken	Can also be used generically for any raffle.
Chrissy (n)	Christmas	
Christmas on a stick (adj)	Sarcastic comment about someone who thinks he or she is special.	"What do you think you are, *Christmas on a stick?*"
Christmas tree (n)	Western Australian native tree (nuytsia floribunda) that blooms orange around Christmastime.	A member of the mistletoe family, Aboriginal people peeled and ate the suckers, which are sweet and taste like candy.
chuck a brown eye (v)	to hang a BA, to "moon" someone	
chuck a sad (adj)	to be depressed	
chuck a sickie (v)	To take a sick day from work, often when you're not sick.	
chuck a wobbly (v)	throw a tantrum	
chuffed (adj)	pleased and excited	"He was *chuffed* about his promotion."
chukas	good luck	
chunder (v)	throw up (from "watch under")	"He got seasick and *chundered.*"
CJs (cock jocks) (n)	Speedos (also *budgie smugglers*, *ball huggers*)	
clacker (n)	anus	From "cloaca;", platypus or bird anal pore.
cladding (n)	siding (building materials)	"The house has aluminium *cladding.*"
clanger (n)	a lie, accidental insult, faux pas, embarrassing mistake	
clawback (v) (adj)	the recovery of funds already disbursed	"The plan would *clawback* benefits."

Clayton's (adj)	fake, substitute	Comes from a non-alcohol whiskey-like beverage called *Clayton's*.
cleanskin (n)	bottle of wine with no label; something that hasn't been used; an unbranded cow	cleanskin wines can be bought cheap, or custom-relabelled
clobber (n)	clothes, belongings	
clothes peg (n)	clothespin	
cloud cuckoo land (adj)	fantasy	
clucky (adj)	feeling motherly	A hen goes *clucky* when she begins to sit on her eggs.
coach (n)	tour bus	
Coat Hanger, the (n)	Sydney Harbour Bridge	
cobber (n)	friend, mate	old term, rarely used
cockatoo (n)	type of Australian parrot	
cockie (n)	a cockatoo, a farmer, a cockroach	
cockie gate (n)	a homemade farm gate	
cockroach (n)	person from New South Wales	
codswallop	load of shit	"Sounds like *codswallop* to me."
cohort (adj)	a group at the same level	commonly used for students
coldie (n)	a cold beer	
college (n)	a high school	
come a gutser (adj)	made a bad mistake, had an accident	
come on like a raw prawn (adj)	being disagreeable	
compo (n)	worker's compensation	
concession, concessionaire (n)	student or senior (for discounts)	"Entrance is $5; *concessionaires* $3."

conchy (adj)	From "conscientious,", person who would rather study or work than play.	
"Cooee!" (exclamation)	"Hey, where are you? I'm over here!"	A way of calling out to someone in the bush.
cooee (adj)	nearby, within ear shot	"It's not within *cooee* of here."
cooker (n)	oven	
cool drinks (n)	sodas	
Coolgardie safe (n)	a cabinet for storing perishable foods, used before refrigeration	Named after the town of Coolgardie, where it was invented. It was a box covered in wet hessian (burlap) that kept the contents cool through evaporation.
cordial (n)	flavoured sweet drink like Kool-Aid	comes in liquid concentrate, you add a little to a glass of water
corflute (n)	waxed cardboard used in making signs	
corker (adj)	really good	"This band is a *corker*!"
coronial (n)	having to do with a coroner	"The *coronial* inquest proved he was murdered."
corroboree (n)	Aboriginal traditional celebration with song and dance	"We danced and sang at the *corroboree*."
cos (n) (pronounced *koss*)	romaine lettuce	
cot (n)	baby crib	
cotton (n)	generic term for any type of thread	
cotton wool (n)	cotton balls	

counter meal (n)	A meal served by ordering at a counter.	Counter meals are common, from fast food to mid-priced restaurants and pubs
country cousin (adj)	a dozen (rhyming slang)	
course (n)	a series of doses (prescription drugs)	"I took a *course* of Imodium to get rid of traveller's tummy."
cozzie, cossie (n)	swimsuit	From *swimming costume.*
crack a fat (v)	to get an erection	
crack onto (v)	hit on someone romantically	
cracked a spack (v)	throw a fit, go crazy, get very angry	
cray (n)	lobster	From *crayfish*
crazier than a cut snake (adj)	crazy, in a friendly sort of way	
creche (n) (pronounced "*kresh*"	day care centre, baby's room	
"Crikey!"	"Wow!"	
crim (adj)	criminal	
crisps (n)	potato chips	Not to be confused with *chips*, which are French fries.
crook (adj)	sick or ill, can also mean "thief"	"I feel *crook*. I think I'll take a sickie."
cross country wrestling (adj)	The game of rugby.	
crotchet (n) (pronounced "*crotch-et*")	quarter note (music)	
crow eater	person from South Australia	
crust (adj)	wage money	
CSIRO (n)	Commonwealth Scientific and Industrial Research Organisation	Official scientific arm of the government.

CUB (adj)	acronym for *Cashed-Up Bogan*	A *bogan* (low-life) who's come into money and is indulging questionable tastes.
cubby (n)	kids playhouse, tree house	
cuppa (n)	cup of tea or coffee	"Hey mate, ya wanna *cuppa*?"
curly (adj)	nickname for a bald man	
cut lunch (n)	sandwiches	
cylinder (n)	Scuba tank	also *air bottle*
dab hand at (adj)	one who's good at something	
Dad & Dave (v)	to shave	rhyming slang
dag (n)	a funny character; a nerd; a goof-off; a bit of dung stuck to a sheep's behind	
daggy (adj)	outdated	"His clothes were *daggy*."
daks, dacks (n)	trousers	
damper (n)	simple unleavened scone-like bread	A traditional campfire bread cooked in the outback, now available in supermarkets.
date (adj)	ass, asshole	"Get off your *date*!"
dead horse (n)	tomato sauce	rhyming slang
deadly treadly (n)	bicycle	
dear, dearer (adj)	expensive	"That BMW is a bit *dear*."
debutante (adj)	anyone making their debut (pronounced *de-boo*), most commonly used in sports	
dekko (v)	to look	"Have a *dekko* at this."
demister (n)	car windshield defogger	

demob (v)	leave the armed forces	From *demobilize*.
demountable (n)	modular or temporary building, as at a school, mine site, etc.	
deputy principal (n)	vice principal	
der (adj)	phoney look of stupidity	
dero (n)	derelict, homeless person, vagrant	
de-sexed (adv)	neutered or spayed (dogs and cats)	
despo (adj)	desperate	
details (n)	personal information, (name, address, phone number, ID numbers, etc.)	"Write down your *details*, mate."
devon (n)	bologna (baloney), regional term used in Melbourne	
Devonshire tea (n)	A small meal of scones, whipped cream, and tea	Served in better tea rooms.
diary (n)	appointment book or calendar, Day Runner	
dicky (adj)	defective	"His heart was *dicky* since birth."
did a runner (v)	to leave unexpectedly, to abscond	"He owed me money and *did a runner*."
diddled (v)	to trick someone out of something	
didgeridoo, didge (n)	Indigenous Australian wind instrument made from a tree branch hollowed by termites.	Makes a droning sound; native name *yirdaki*.

dieback (n)	scientific name: *phytophera cinnomomii*, a disease that attacks the roots of some native trees. Imported in fruit trees, it's a fungus that spreads through wet soil.	Predominantly in WA, it's killing off the native jarrah, banksia, and grass tree forests. Can be treated short-term with sprays or injections of weak solution of phosphorus acid. (Outlook: grim.)
digger (n)	Australian soldier	
dill (n)	an idiot	"He's a *dill*."
dim sums (n)	testicles	
dinger (n)	condom	
dingle (n) (v)	cuckoloris or go-bo (movie industry)	A device hung in front of a light source to create a shadow effect.
dingo (n)	indigenous, coyote-like wild dog introduced by Aboriginal migrants 10,000 years ago.; a small stand-up earth-moving tractor	
dingo's breakfast (adj)	"A yawn, a piss and a look around."	What you do in the bush after getting out of your *swag*.
dinkum (adj)	real, true	
dinky, dink (v)	giving someone a ride on your bicycle, usually on the handlebars	"Give us a *dink*."
dinky di (adj) (pronounced *dinky-die*)	real, genuine.	"He's a *dinki-di* Aussie."
dipstick (adj)	an idiot, loser	
display home (n)	model home (real estate)	
display village (n)	model homes (real estate)	
divvy van (n)	police paddy wagon	From *division van*.

DIY (adj)	do-it-yourself	Part of the Aussie tradition of self-reliance.
do not take (v)	do not take internally (prescription)	From warning label on pharmaceutical crèmes, ointments, etc.
do up (v)	to fasten	"*Do up* your seat belt."
do your nut (v)	throw a tantrum	
dob (v)	to tell on someone	"He *dobbed* on me."
docket (n)	receipt, ticket	
doco (n)	documentary (film, video, or radio)	
dodgy (adj)	not good, suspicious	"His work is a bit *dodgy*."
dog's breakfast (adj)	a mess	"You look like a *dog's breakfast*."
dog's eye (n)	meat pie	rhyming slang
dole (n)	welfare	"He's on the *dole*."
dole bludger (adj)	welfare cheat	
don't come the raw prawn (v)	"Don't try to play me for a fool."	
done my dash (v)	"I'm finished; I already did it."	"I've *done my dash* with marriage."
donga (n)	pre-fabricated cabin with few creature comforts	Common accommodation on mine sites and trailer parks
donger (n)	penis	
donk (n)	engine	
donkey vote (adj)	In preferential voting, just going down the list and numbering in order, not really voting.	
donkey's years (adj)	a long time	
donnybrook (n)	a fight	
doodle (n)	penis	
doona (n)	comforter, quilted bed cover	

Dorothy Dixer (adj)	an obvious or easily answered question	Named after Dorothy Dix, an early 20th century American advice columnist.
dosh (n)	money	"Bring the *dosh*."
double G (n)	a very nasty type of thorn	
down the gurgler (adj)	failure, down the tubes	
down the track (adj)	somewhere far from here	
Down Under (n)	Australia and New Zealand	
draught (n)	Aussie spelling for "draft", wind or beer.	"I feel a *draught*." "I'll take a *draught* beer."
dreaded lurgy (n)	infectious cold or flu	
dreamtime (n)	Aboriginal mythology	
drink driver (n)	drunk driver	
drink with the flies (v) (adj)	drink alone	
drive-away (adj)	out-the-door price (car dealership)	Price of the car, GST, stamp duty, license, and third party insurance included.
drongo (adj)	idiot, dimwit	
drop (n)	wine, drink	"The Cab-Merlot is a good *drop*."
drop off the perch (v)	to die	"Old Bob *dropped off the perch* last week."
drop your guts, drop lunch (v)	to fart	
dropkick (n)	an idiot, someone no-one wants to hang around with	
drug driver (n)	driver under the influence of drugs	
drum (n) (v)	a tip-off, inside information	"Give me the *drum*."
dry as a dead dingo's donger (adj)	dry, thirsty	

dry as a nun's nasty (adj)	very dry	
dry as a pommy's towel (adj)	very dry	From the old myth that the English rarely bathe.
dry hire (adj)	equipment rented without the operator	
dual carriageway (n)	road with two lanes in each direction and a center divider down the middle	
duchess (n)	sideboard (furniture)	
duck's dinner (adj)	drinking on an empty stomach	
duco (n)	car paint	
duff, up the (adj)	pregnant	
duffing (v)	cattle rustling	
dummy (n)	baby pacifier	
dunny (n)	toilet usually, but not always, outdoor	
dunny roll (n)	toilet paper	
durry (n)	cigarette, tobacco	
Dutch oven (v)	To fart under the blankets.	
dux (adj)	top in the class, valedictorian (school)	"He's the *dux*."
earbash (v)	too much talk, non-stop chatter, nagging	"She was *earbashing* me."
ears flapping (adj)	to listen intensely	
earth (n)	electrical ground	"The negative wire was connected to *earth*."
earth closet (n)	19th century self-composting dry toilet	
earth leak circuit breaker (ELCB) (n)	ground fault interrupter	Automatically shuts off the current if there's a short.
easy on (v)	calm down	
easy peasy (adj)	easy job or task	

EFTPOS (n)	debit card, *Electronic Funds Transfer At Point Of Sale*	Can access check or savings accounts by credit or bank card through a terminal in a shop or bank.
egg soldier (n)	strip of toast dipped in egg yolk	
Ekka (n)	the annual Brisbane Exhibition	First held in 1876, now the Royal Queensland Exposition.
elastic bands (n)	rubber bands	Also called *lackies*.
ensuite (adj)	toilet/bathroom attached to room	in hotel room or accommodation
entree (n)	on a menu, appetiser, salad, soup course	
esky (n)	ice chest	From *Eskimo cooler*.
euro (n)	a small type of kangaroo, wallaby	
evo (n)	evening	
excess (n)	deductible (insurance)	"My car insurance has a $200 *excess* on theft."
excursion (n)	a school field trip	
expression of interest (n)	a real estate term meaning one is asked to bid on a property	
exy (adj)	expensive	
face fungus (n)	a beard	
fag (n)	cigarette	
fair dinkum (adj)	the truth, genuine in an Aussie sense	
fair go (adj)	to give a good chance	"Give it a *fair go*."
"Fair suck of the sav!"	"Give me a chance!"	
fairy floss (n)	cotton candy	
fairy lights (n)	small white Christmas lights	
fancy dress (n) (adj)	costumes: <u>not</u> a formal dress or tuxedo (you rent a tux at a *suit hire*)	"They went to a *fancy dress* ball."

fang it (v) (adj)	to drive fast	"The hoons were *fanging it* on the road."
fanny (n)	slang for vagina, not used in nice company	Call a fanny pack a *bum bag*.
fault (n)	problem	"We found the *fault* in the motor."
fell off the back of the truck (adj)	something stolen	
feral (n)	hippie; wild person; a wild-looking loud car with lights, bars, and stickers; wild kids	
fete (n)	small event	
fibro (n)	asbestos board used in construction of old houses	
figs (n)	balls, male genitalia	
figjam (adj)	acronym for: *F**k, I'm Good, Just Ask Me*, an egotist	
file (n)	binder, notebook for punched paper	
filter lane (n)	the transition road on the left or right side of the roadway	
filter light (n)	turn arrow	
fine (adj)	(weather) clear and sunny, used instead of "fair"	"Tomorrow's weather will be *fine*."
fining (v)	clearing weather	"It's *fining* up for the weekend."
FIRB (n)	Federal Investment Review Board	
fire brigade (n)	fire department	
firies (n)	firemen	"Quick, call the *firies*."
first in, best dressed (adj)	first come, first served	
first past the post (adj)	The one with the most votes wins, majority not needed.	election term

fisher (n)	fisherman	
fisho (n)	fish seller, fisherman	
fitted (v)	installed, mounted, put on	"We had new tyres *fitted* to the ute."
fitter (n)	one who assembles mechanical equipment, mechanic	
fixings (n)	screws, nuts & bolts, nails	
fixture (n)	game schedule (sport)	
fizzy drinks (n)	sodas	
FJ (n)	The most famous model of Holden automobile.	"My favourite car is a 1953 *FJ* Holden."
flake (n)	fillet of shark (in fish & chips)	
flannel (n)	a washcloth or hand towel	
flare (n)	a tiki torch, a boat signalling device	
flash (adj)	fancy, stylish	"His new clothes were *flash*."
flash as a rat with a gold tooth (adj)	a sleazy charmer	
flash for cash (n)	traffic or speed camera	
flat (n)	apartment	
flat chat (v)	very busy, very fast	
flat out like a lizard drinking (adj)	very busy	
flat spot (adj)	an opening in the schedule	"Do you have a *flat spot* tomorrow?"
flat stick (adj)	full speed	
flatmate (n)	roommate	
fleckie (n)	reflector used to bounce light onto the subject in camera work.	
flick (v)	to get rid of someone, usually a date	"She gave me the *flick*."
flick it on (v)	quick resale	
float (n)	a horse trailer	

flog (v)	to sell something	"I'm going to *flog* off my old Ford Falcon."
fluoro (n)	fluorescent light	
flutter (n)	a bet	
Flying Doctor Service (n)	Air rescue service for remote areas	
flywire, flyscreen (n)	window screen	
flywire door (n)	screen door	
fob off (v)	to treat someone rudely	
follow on customer (adj)	repeat customer	
football (n)	soccer (Europe)	
footpath (n)	sidewalk	
Footy (n)	Australian Rules Football	
form, form room (n)	high school home room	
fossick (v)	to search, prospect	"I was *fossicking* in the op shops."
four-be-two (n)	Jew	Rhyming slang. A two-by-four piece of wood is what Australians call a four-by two, which rhymes with Jew.
fraka (v) (adj)	fracas	
franger (n)	condom	
franking credits (n)	Tax credits for investors on dividends from company profits that have already had taxes paid on them.	Eliminates double taxation: first on company's profits, second on dividends from those profits. A standard stock benefit.
freckle (n)	anus	
Fremantle Doctor (n)	afternoon sea breeze off Perth	
Freo	Fremantle, the port of Perth	
freshie (adj)	freshwater crocodile, fresh cow pile	"Don't step in that *freshie,* mate."

fried eggs (adj)	flat breasts	
fringe (n)	bangs (hair)	"She trimmed her *fringe*."
from go to whoa (adj)	from start to finish	
front bencher (n) (adj)	member of Parliament who holds a ministerial position	"He's a *front bencher*."
front foot, on the (adj)	on the offensive, pushing ahead	"The new manager is *on the front foot*."
Frosties (n)	Name used for Frosted Flakes cereal.	
fruit machine (n)	slot machine	
full, full as a boot (adj)	drunk	"He's a bit *full*."
full milk, full crème milk (n)	regular milk	
full stop (n)	a period (.) (punctuation)	
function (n)	banquet	
function centre (n)	banquet hall	
funfair (n)	a small carnival	
funny bunny (n)	a gay man	
furphy (n)	unreliable rumor, tall tale, scuttlebutt	Named after the Furphy water cart used in WWI; soldiers got the gossip while filling their water jugs.
Gabba, the (n)	Woolloongabba, the Brisbane cricket ground	
galah (adj)	noisy idiot, also a pink-and-grey parrot	named after the noisy parrot
gaol (n)	jail	(pronounced the same)
gap year (n) (adj)	A period of time taken off school, usually between high school and university, to travel and work.	

gap (n)	The difference in what Medicare pays for a medical service and what the healthcare provider charges.	The patient has to make up the difference.
garbo (n)	garbage truck driver	
gas (n)	propane, LPG	
gasper (n)	cigarette	
gazetted (v)	to be made official in government publications	"The company was *gazetted* last week."
gazumped (v)	outbid	"He was *gazumped* on that property."
g'day	good day	standard Australian greeting
get nicked (v)	go away	
get the arse (adj)	to get fired	
getting up, getting the shits up (v)	to verbally abuse someone	"I'm *getting up* him for the rent."
gin (n)	offensive name for an Aboriginal woman	
ging (n)	slingshot	
Ginger (n)	nickname for a person with red hair	
Girl Guides (n)	similar to Girl Scouts	
give a gobful (v)	to verbally abuse	
give 'em some stick (v)	verbally abusing someone	
give it a burl (v)	try it out	
give it a miss (v)	to avoid something	
give them curry (v)	give them trouble	
give up (n) (v)	the equivalent of a punt in Australian Rules Football (Footy)	
glandular fever (n)	mononucleosis	
globe (n)	lightbulb	
go for a burn (v)	to test drive a car, to drive fast	
go like clappers, go like a shower of shit (v)	to go very fast	

goanna (n)	monitor lizard	Early arrivals mistook them for iguanas, hence the name.
gob-smacked (adj)	very surprised, "mouth agape"	"He was *gob-smacked* when he saw the bill."
"God bless his cotton socks."	He's completely wrong, but we still love him.	
gold coin (n)	$1 or $2 Australian coins (gold-colored)	"Admission to the charity fete by *gold coin* donation."
gone troppo (adj)	tropical madness, having too a good time	
good nick (adj)	good condition	"The old ute's in *good nick*."
good oil (adj)	good information, useful idea	
good on ya	well done, good job	Often just *onya* is used.
Good Sammy's (n)	the Good Samaritan charity	sometimes just "Sammy's"
googie (n)	egg	"I'll have a *googie sanger*."
good value (adj)	worthwhile	"That ute is *good value*."
goss (n) (v)	gossip	"What's the *goss*?"
grazier (n)	large scale sheep or cattle farmer	
greenie (n)	environmentalist, member of the Greens Party	
gridiron (n)	American football	Football is soccer, Footy is Australian Rules Football, *gridiron* is American football.
grinning like a shot fox (adj)	happy, smug	If you ever shot a fox, you'd know why.
grizzle (v)	to complain	
grog (n)	beer, liquor	

grommet (n)	young surfer	
grouse (adj)	good, cool	
grundies (n)	underwear	
GST	Goods and Services Tax	ten percent nationwide
guernsey (n)	jersey, shirt	
gum sucker (n)	resident of Victoria	
gum, gum tree (n)	eucalyptus tree	
gunya (n)	temporary shelter	Aboriginal: *ganya*
gurgler (n)	the drain	"When the wife and kiddies left, my life went down the *gurgler*."
gutful of piss (adj)	drunk	
gutzer, come a (v)	to have an accident; something that didn't work out	
gyno (n)	gynecologist	
gypboard (n)	Sheetrock, gyprock	wallboard made of gypsum
hair lackies (n)	elastic hair bands	
handle (n)	glass of beer (Northern Territory), pitcher of beer (Western Australia)	
Hansard (n)	Printed transcript of State and Federal Parliament sessions, with minor corrections and explanations added.	Like the U.S. Congressional record
happy as Larry (adj)	very happy	
hard word (adj)	a stern talking to	"I gave him the *hard word* about that mistake."
hard yakka (n)	hard work	
Hardie Board	asbestos board used in construction of old homes	

Hardie Fence (n)	corrugated pressed fiber and cement boards used for fencing	
hash key (n)	The pound sign on a telephone.	"Dial the number then press the *hash key*."
hasn't got a brass razzoo (adj)	one who has nothing	"I haven't got a *brass razzo*."
have a burl (v)	give it a try	
have a fang (v)	to eat	
have a go (v)	to try	
have a lend of (v)	take advantage of someone's gullibility	
have a naughty (v)	to have sex	
heaps (adj)	many, lots of	"I have *heaps* of good ideas."
HECS (n)	Higher Education Contribution Scheme	a university loan
hens night (n)	bachelorette party	
he's past it (adj)	over the hill	
High Court (n)	Equivalent of the U.S. Supreme Court	
high dependency unit (n)	intensive care ward in a hospital	
Hills Hoist (n)	Australian designed variable height rotary clothes line	
hire (n) (v)	rental, to rent	"I dropped off the *hire* car."
his blood's worth bottling (adj)	a great guy	
hissy fit (v)	to lose one's temper	"He's just having a *hissy fit.*
hit and giggle (v)	women's tennis game	
hob (n)	stovetop, gas or electric	
Holden (n)	General Motors Australia auto manufacturing subsidiary	See section on **Australian cars**.
holiday (n)	vacation	"She's on *holiday*."
holus-bolus (v)	everything, all at once	

home and hosed (adj)	finished, fixed, all done in a positive way	
home open (n) (adj)	open house (real estate)	Very short, less than an hour long.
hook turn (v)	Method of turning right in traffic around trams in Melbourne.	See section on **driving**
"Hooly-dooly!"	"My goodness!"	
hoon (n)	hooligan	Usually a 16–35-year-old male displaying anti-social behavior, often in an automobile.
hooroo	goodbye	
hoover (v)	to vacuum	From the Hoover vacuum cleaner.
horses for courses (adj)	A way of pointing out obvious differences.	From "different horses for different courses."
hotchpotch (adj)	Aussie for "hodge podge", an odd collection	
hotel (n)	a pub with a bottle shop, can also be a place that rents rooms	
hottie (n)	hot water bottle	"On cold nights, I sleep with a *hottie*."
hotting up (adj)	heating up	"The real estate market is *hotting up*.
"How'd ya pull up?"	"How did you do?"	
"How ya goin?"	standard greeting, American equivalent: "How ya doing?"	
how's your father (adj)	to have sex (British slang)	"We were indulging in a spot of *how's your father*."
humpy (n)	temporary shelter	Aboriginal: *yumpi*
hungi (n)	a charcoal-filled hole in the ground you cook in	
hurl (v)	to vomit	

I'll pay that (v)	I admit, you outsmarted me.	
ice block (n)	Popsicle, sometimes used for ice cube.	
ice cream spider (n)	soda float	Usually coke with ice cream on top, since root beer isn't generally available.
icy pole (n)	Popsicle	
identity (adj)	person of note, celebrity	"Prominent Perth *identity* Joe Blow was arrested."
"I'll be stuffed!"	expression of surprise	
impact sprinkler (n)	rainbird sprinkler	
impost (n)	customs duty; tax penalty; race horse handicap weight	
imputation (adj)	way of avoiding double taxation on dividends	See section on *franking credits*.
I'm stuffed (adj)	I'm tired.	
incursion (n)	An exhibition that travels to a school	
interval (n)	intermission, as in a play or concert	"The band will return after the *interval*."
inverted commas (n)	quotation marks	
irrits (v)	to irritate someone	
it's a goer (adj)	it will work	
it's a take (adj)	it's a fraud	
it's gone missing (adj)	it's disappeared	
I-tie (n)	Italian	
it's gone walkabout (adj)	it's missing	
it's yum (adj)	it's yummy	
jab (n)	an injection by hypodermic needle	
Jack Dancer	cancer	rhyming slang
jackeroo (n)	cowboy	

jacket potato (n)	baked potato with the skin on	
jacking-up (v)	hassling someone	
jaffle (n)	toasted sandwich	
jam (n)	jelly	
jamball donut (n)	jelly donut	
jarrah (n)	A type of eucalyptus tree found in SW Western Australia, it produces a very hard, heavy wood used in furniture	Also known as *Swan River Mahogany*, it was heavily logged and exported. At one point, the streets of London were paved with it.
jelly (n)	Jell-O	
jillaroo (n)	cowgirl	
jimjams (n)	pajamas (spelled *pyjamas*)	
Joe Blake (n)	snake	rhyming slang
joey (n)	baby kangaroo	
joule (n)	metric measurement of energy equivalent to the calorie, short hand: *J*	approx. 4.2 Joules per calorie
journo (n)	journalist	
jug (n)	kettle, pitcher of beer	
jumbuck (n)	sheep	
jumped-up (adj)	one full of self-importance, arrogant	
jumper (n)	sweatshirt, sweater, jersey	"It's cold today, wear a *jumper*."
jumper punch (n) (v)	A technique in footy where one player grabs another's jumper (jersey) and punches him in the chest, making it look like they're grappling.	Illegal, but hard to enforce.
just across the road (adj)	someplace nearby	
k's (n)	kilometres	"It's a hundred *k's* from here."

kangaroos loose in the top paddock (adj)	describing a crazy person	
kebab (n) (pronounced *kee-bab*)	wrap with meat, cheese, salad, sauce	not on a skewer, not a shish-kebab
keen (adj)	eager	"He's *keen* about that property."
keen as mustard (adj)	enthusiastic	
Kelpie (n)	a breed of Aussie sheepdog	
kerb (n)	Aussie spelling of *curb*	
kero (n)	kerosene	
kettle of fish (adj)	problem	"That's a different *kettle of fish*"
Khyber Pass (n)	ass	rhyming slang
kindy (n) (pronounced *kin-dee*)	kindergarten	U.S. equivalent to preschool. *Pre-primary* is the U.S. equivalent of kindergarten.
king hit (v)	sucker punch, to "cold cock" someone	"The hoon *king hit* him."
kiosk (n)	snack bar at a theater	
kip (n)	flat piece of wood used to toss the pennies in the game of Two Up	
kip (v)	to nap	
kit (n) (adj)	equipment	"I bought all the latest *kit*."
kitchen bench (n)	kitchen countertop	
Kiwi (n)	New Zealander	From the kiwi fruit that grows there.
knackered (adj.)	exhausted	
knickers in a knot, don't get your (v)	to get upset	
knickies (n)	underwear	
knob head (adj)	dick head	

knobble (v)	interference causing someone to fail, also to stop a horse from whinnying	
knock (v)	to criticise	
knock back (v)	rejected, turned down	"The proposal was *knocked back*."
knock shop (n)	brothel	
knuckle dusters (n)	brass knuckles	
Kombi (n)	VW bus	
kW	kilowatt	Measurement of electricity (1,000 watts); also the power of an engine, 1 kW= .746 horsepower
lackies (n)	rubber bands	From "elastic bands".
Lady Muck (adj)	arrogant woman who puts on airs	
lair, lairy (adj)	flashily dressed, brash, vulgar man, to dress someone or something in bad taste	
lair it up (adj)	act brashly or vulgarly	
Lamington (n)	sponge cake covered in chocolate and coconut	
land bank (adj)	to hold onto land for later release	
laneway (n)	alley	"Put the rubbish bin in the *laneway*."
larking around (v)	goofing off	
larrikin (n)	harmless prankster, loud goof-off	
lash (v)	to leave	
laughin' , we're (adj)	we got it made	"We sell that house and *we're laughin'*."
launch (n)	large power boat	
lay by (adj)	lay away, to put a deposit on something and gradually pay it off	
leadlight (n)	stained glass windows	
leave it with me (v)	I'll do it.	

leavers (n)	recent school graduate	"The school *leavers* gave the cops strife."
lecturer (n)	instructor at a university or TAFE	
leg (boating) (n)	outboard motor or out-drive lower unit	"The *leg* broke and stranded them on the reef."
leg spin bowler, spin bowler (adj)	Bowler in cricket who flips the ball off his wrist as he releases it.	"Shane Warne was the best *leg spin bowler*."
lemonade (n)	Seven-Up, Sprite, or any clear lemon soda	not fresh-squeezed American style lemonade.
let off (v)	to be laid off from a job	
letter box (n)	mailbox (home)	You put your mail into a *post box* and receive it in your *letter box*.
letter drop (n) (v)	bulk mail	
let your hair open (v)	let your hair down, relax	
licensed restaurant (n)	restaurant that can serve liquor	
lifestyle (adj)	leisure, quality of life, enjoying oneself	
lift (n)	elevator	"Take the *lift* to the top floor."
lift your game (adj)	improve	
like a shag on a rock (adj)	something that sticks out like a sore thumb.	
like a two-bob watch (adj)	something unreliable	
like buggery (adj)	with lots of energy	"Run *like buggery*!"
like the clappers (adj)	fast	
lippy (n)	lipstick	
liquid laugh (v)	vomit	
little boy (n)	small red sausage	
littlies (v)	small children	

little vegemites (adj)	children	
lob, lob in (v)	drop in for a visit, often unannounced	
loggerwood (n)	a person going nowhere, deadwood	
lollies (n)	candy	
lollypop man (n)	Person with the "stop" and "slow" signs, directing traffic at a road construction site.	The signs are round and on a stick, like a large lollypop.
London to a brick (adj)	absolute certainty	
long paddock (n)	side of the road where livestock graze during droughts	When the fields are bare, farmers let the cattle graze the grass alongside the road.
long service leave (n)	a sabbatical	
long weekend (n)	a three-day holiday weekend	
longneck (n)	large bottle of beer in South Australia	
loo (n)	toilet	
loo tickets (n)	toilet paper	
lorry (n)	truck	
lost the plot (adj)	went crazy	"He *lost the plot* and trashed the office."
lot (adj)	a daily dosage of medicine (pharmaceuticals)	
lot, the (adj)	everything	"I'll have a hamburger with *the lot*."
lounge, lounge room (n)	living room	
lubra (n)	Aboriginal woman (from *lubara*, Aboriginal word from Tasmania)	Not a popular word to use; American equivalent would be squaw.

lunch bar (n)	independent fast food shop serving sandwiches, rolls, pies, etc.	
lurk (adj)	illegal activity or endeavor	
lurks (adj)	benefits of a situation outside legal or ethical guidelines.	
lurks and perks (adj)	benefits: illegal (lurks) and legal (perks)	"They're the *lurks and perks* of elected office."
Macca's (n) (pronounced *Macker's*)	McDonald's	
mad as a cut snake (adj)	very angry	
mail (n)	gossip	"I've got the latest *mail* on her."
main, mains (n) (adj)	main course in a restaurant	
make a quid (v)	earn a living	A *quid* is slang for a pound (unit of money in Aus. until 1966).
mall (n)	street with shops closed to car traffic	A large enclosed building full of shops is called a shopping centre.
mallee bull, as fit as a (adj)	strong and fit	The Mallee is tough cattle country in the dry southeast.
malley root (n)	prostitute	rhyming slang
manchester (n)	household linen, sheets, etc.	
mandarin (n)	tangerine	
mappa Tassie (adj)	woman's pubic area	From *map of Tasmania,* which is triangular-shaped.
Margherita pizza (n)	Cheese and tomato pizza with spices	
mark (n)	clean catch in footy (Aussie rules football)	sets up a free kick

marri (n)	a type of eucalyptus tree in Western Australia (also known as *red gum*)	
marriage celebrant (n)	non-religious person licensed to conduct weddings and funerals	
marron (n)	large freshwater crawfish	a delicacy, farm raised in WA
mate (n)	friend, buddy	
mates rates (n)	special deal for friends	
maths (n)	math, mathematics	For some reason, the "s" is left on.
matilda (n)	mattress, sleeping roll	Story goes, the lonely sheepmen danced with their mattresses, hence *Waltzing Matilda*.
MCG	Melbourne Cricket Ground	The cricket stadium in Melbourne.
mean (adj)	stingy	
mean as cat's piss (adj)	mean, stingy, tight-fisted	
meat pie (n)	A round of pastry rolled over a meat or vegetable filling.	Individual serving size, can be eaten like a sandwich.
Medicare (n)	Universal healthcare for all Australian residents and citizens.	It's pretty good, it isn't ideal, but at least everybody's covered.
Melbourne Cup (n)	most famous horse race in Australia, held in Melbourne the first Tuesday in November	The whole country celebrates, goes to parties; women wear fancy hats.
Merc (n) (pronounced *Merk*)	Short for Mercedes Benz	Not a Mercury; Mercurys aren't sold in Australia.
methylated spirits, metho (n)	methylated spirits, used as a solvent and cleaner	They add the methylated part so people won't be tempted to drink it.

Mexican (n)	person from the south of Queensland along the New South Wales border; also *snowbirds* who travel to Queensland from southeast Australia to avoid the cold winter	
mickey mouse (adj)	really good, but can have the opposite meaning in some regions	
middy (n)	half-pint glass of beer	
milk bar (n)	corner shop that sells take-away food	
milk shake (n)	flavored milk, usually not thick like in the U.S.	
milko (n)	milkman	
mince (n)	ground meat: beef, lamb, chicken, turkey	Aussies don't call hamburger ground meat; hamburger is pre-formed patties of ground meat.
minim (n)	half note (music)	
mixed grill (n)	sausages, steak, and chops, cooked on a BBQ	
mo (n)	moustache	
mob (n)	any group of people (not necessarily harmful); a herd of kangaroos	
mobile (n) (pronounced *moe-byle*)	cellular phone	
mod cons	modern conveniences	"My new apartment has all the *mod cons*."
moggie (n)	house cat of indeterminate breed	
moke (adj)	bad horse	originally meant *donkey*

money for old jam (adj)	an unexpected gift	
money for old rope (adj)	an unexpected gift	
mongrel (adj)	bad person or thing	
moot (n)	jamboree for older Boy Scouts (Rovers)	
mooted (v)	suggested	
motza (n) (alternate spelling: *motser*)	large amount of money, usually a gambling win	From Yiddish
mozzie (n)	mosquito	
much of a muchness (adj)	much the same	
mud map (n)	map or diagram drawn in the dirt, any hand drawn map	"I'll draw you a *mud map* of how to get there."
muddy (n)	mud crab	
muesli (n)	rolled oats and grain cold cereal	
mug (adj)	friendly insult	
mulga (n)	a type of tree, also name for the *bush* (rough country)	
mull (n)	marijuana	
mull up (v)	roll a joint and smoke it	
mullet (n)	haircut favored by *bogans*: short on the top and the sides, long in the back	
Multanova (n)	portable speeding camera	Brand name of the Swiss-made device.
munted (adj)	messed up	
mushy peas (n)	over cooked peas served mushy	
muso (n) (pronounced *muse-oh*)	musician	
mystery bag (n)	sausage	

naff (adj)	something trendy, but can have opposite meaning.	
nappies (n)	diapers	
narked, narky (adj)	annoyed, short-tempered	
narniebar (n)	banana	
narrowcast (n) (v)	limited radio station	
Nasho (n)	National Service (the draft)	
Nashos (n)	Soldier's association for those who were drafted under the National Service Act 1951-1972	
naught (n)	zero	
naughts and crosses (n)	tic tac toe	
neck yourself (v)	to commit suicide	
neddies (n)	race horses	
needle (n)	hypodermic injection, shot	also *jab*
Never-Never, the (n)	the interior desert of Australia	
new chum (adj)	immigrant, new arrival	
New Holland	original name for Australia	
newsreader (n)	anchorperson on TV or radio	
nibblies (n)	finger foods, hors d'oeuvres	"You bring the wine, I'll bring the *nibblies*."
nick (v)	to steal	"He *nicked* those sunnies at Woolie's."
nick off	go away, get lost	used as an order or request
nick over (v)	go there	"I'll *nick over* to the bottle shop for a slab of stubbies."
niggle, niggling (adj)	minor complaint, pain, inconvenience	
nil (n)	zero	also *naught*

nipper (n)	young surf lifesaver, little kid	
Nm	Newton Meter	Measurement of torque, U.S. equivalent of foot-pounds (1Nm=.738 ft/lbs.)
nobble (v)	to tamper with or damage	
no drama (adj)	one level up from *no worries*	
no great shakes (adj)	not outstanding	
no-hoper (n)	a loser	
nong (adj)	slow-witted person	
no object (adj)	no problem	
no room to swing a cat (adj)	a small or cramped place	
no shortage of oscar (adj)	having lots of money	
no standing (n)	a no parking zone	"No parking" signs say this.
not a patch on (adj)	not as good as	
not fussed (adj)	not worried	
not in a pink fit (adv)	not until hell freezes over	
not much chop (adj)	not very good	
not on (adj)	not right, not happening, won't work	
not on your nellie (adj)	no way	
not the full quid (adj)	a way of describing an imbecile	
not to be taken (adj)	do not take internally	Directions printed on poisons, ointments, etc.
not within cooee (adj)	beyond hearing distance	An Aussie might yell "*cooee*" to locate someone in the bush.
no worries (adj)	OK, no problem	

NSW (n)	New South Wales	
NT (n)	Northern Territory	
nuddy, in the (adj)	naked	
nudge the bottle (v)	to drink too much alcohol	
Nullarbor Plain (n)	The treeless desert between South Australia and Western Australia	Nullarbor is Latin for "no trees."
nursery slope (n)	bunny hill (skiing)	
NZ (pronounced: "en-zed) (n)	abbreviation for New Zealand	"We're going to *en-zed* on holiday."
ocker (n)	an unsophisticated person, a laid-back character, uncouth Aussie male	
ockie strap (n)	bungee cord	From "octopus."
off one's face (adj)	describing one who is drunk	
off with the fairies (adj)	describing one who is a bit loony	
offsider (n)	sidekick, assistant, helper	
"Oi!"	"Hey!"	
oil (adj)	information	"Give the *oil* on that project."
old fella (n)	penis	
oldies, olds (n)	adults, parents, seniors	"Let's ask the *olds* if they know."
omelette (n) (Chinese restaurant)	egg foo yung	
on a good lurk (adj)	on a good job	
ono (adj)	abbreviation in classified ad for *or near offer*	Used the same as "obo" ("or best offer") in U.S.
on the back foot (adj)	on the defensive	
on the bones of his bum (adj)	destitute, broke	
on the mend (adj)	getting better	

on the nose (adj)	bad-smelling, stinky	"Your dog's a bit *on the nose*."
on the turps (adj)	drunk	
on your bike (v) (pronounced *onyerbike*)	get out of here, go away, get going	
onya	short for "*good on you*," i.e., "well done"	commonly used as a congratulation
op shop (n)	thrift store	opportunity shop
open slather (adj)	A situation where there are no limits or constraints on behavior.	"Liberalizing liquor store hours would give *open slather* to public drunkenness."
oregon, oregon pine (n)	light American pine wood used in furniture, panelling	technically referring to Douglas Fir, grown as a crop in Australia
O.S. (adj)	overseas	"Les is *O.S.*"
outback (n)	distant Australian bushland	
outcome (n) (adj)	results	
outgoings (adj)	expenditures	
oval (n)	athletic field or stadium	
over east (adj)	the east coast of Australia	
overtime loadings (n)	overtime pay	
oysters (motion pictures)	to shoot in available (or natural) light	From "oysters natural"
Oz (n)	Australia	
packing polenta (adj)	scared	
paddlepop (n)	Popsicle	*Paddlepop* is a brand name, but it's used generically for any Popsicle.
paddock (n)	fenced pasture	
panel beater (n)	auto body repairman	
para, paralytic (adj)	very drunk	
paroo uppercut (adj)	to hit someone in the jaw with a 2 x 4	

partner (n)	spouse, married or not, of either sex	
pash, pashing (n) (v)	making out, a long, passionate kiss	
pasty (n)	A round of pastry rolled over a meat or vegetable filling, a meat pie.	
pastoralist (adj)	large scale cattle or sheep farmer	
Pat Malone (adj)	on my own, alone (rhyming slang)	"I went with *Pat Malone.*"
Pat the Rat (adj)	meddling neighbor (from a character in Aussie TV show "Sons and Daughters")	
patch (n)	area, business	"Tend your own *patch.*" (Mind your own business.)
pavement pizza (n)	vomit	
pavers (n)	exterior brick flooring	
Pavlova, Pav (n)	a light and dreamy meringue dessert	Whipped egg whites, vanilla, and sugar, created in Perth in 1935 for the visiting Russian ballerina, Anna Pavlova.
pawpaw (n)	papaya	
pay rise (n)	pay raise	
PAYG (n)	payroll withholding tax	*Pay As You Go*
PBS (n)	Prescription Benefit Scheme	Medicare's subsidized drug system
PCYC (n)	Police & Citizens Youth Club	like the YMCA
peak hour (adj)	rush hour (traffic)	
peanut paste (n)	peanut butter	
pearler (adj)	of excellence	"The batsman hit a *pearler.*"
pear-shaped (adj)	a situation that's gone bad	"When things go bad, they go *pear-shaped.*"

peckish (adj)	hunger-induced crabbiness	"I'm feeling *peckish*."
pelican crossing (n)	crosswalk where pedestrians activate red crossing lights.	short for **PE**destrian **LI**ght **CON**trolled crossing: *PELICON*
pelmet (n)	valance	"The curtains hung behind the *pelmet*."
pen (n)	slip (boating)	"Tie up the boat in the *pen*."
penalty rates (n)	rates of pay higher than normal rates, for work performed outside normal working hours	
pension day (n)	the day government pension *cheques* arrive	
pensioner (adj)	retiree	
periodical tenancy (adj)	month-to-month rental (real estate)	
person of interest (n)	suspect (police work)	"He was declared a *person of interest* by the police."
Perspex (n)	clear plastic panel: Lucite, acrylic, Plexiglas	actual chemical name: polymethyl methacrylate
perve (n) (v)	a pervert, to lust	
petrol (n)	gasoline	
physio (n)	physical therapist	
pickled (adj)	drunk	
pie (n)	an individual sized meat pie, with meat and/or vegetable filling, can be eaten like a burger	
piece of piss (adj)	something easy	"That job's a *piece of piss*."
pig's arse (adj) (pronounced *ass*)	I disagree	"In a *pig's arse*!"
pig's bum (adj)	something that's not true	

pikelet (n)	small pancake served cold	
piker (adj)	willing outcast	
pinch (v)	to steal	"You *pinched* the last bickie."
pint (n)	large glass of beer	
pipped (adj)	marginally beaten for price, stolen, taken illegally	
pips (n)	seeds in fruit or vegetables	
piss (n)	beer	
piss off (v)	go away	
piss tank (adj)	big drinker	
pitch (n)	cricket field	
plagon (adj)	gallon bottle of cheap wine	
plant the foot (v)	to drive fast	
play funny buggers (adj)	to cheat, act stupidly	
play over (n)	play date (kids)	
plonk (n)	cheap wine	
P & C (n)	Parents and Citizens Association	equivalent to U.S. PTA
pokies (n)	slot machines, poker machines, gambling machines	
pollie, pols (n)	politician	
polony (n)	bologna, baloney (lunch meat)	
poly, poly pipe (n)	polyethylene pipe used in irrigation	
Pom, Pommy, Pommy bastard (n)	Anyone from England. There are numerous explanations.	"Prisoner of His Majesty," "Port of Melbourne," "Permit of Migration," also rhyming slang: pomegranate (immigrant)
pommy shower (adj)	to use deodorant instead of bathing	
pong (adj)	bad smell	

poo (n) (v)	feces, from any species	
poo tickets (n)	toilet paper	
poof, poofter (n) (pronounced *poof-tah*)	gay man	
poor fist (adj)	a bad effort	
pop (v)	to go	"I'm going to *pop* over to the shops."
porky (adj)	a lie (rhyming slang: pork pie)	"He told another *porky*."
porridge (n)	any hot cereal	
port (n)	suitcase	From *portmanteau*.
posh (adj)	fancy, elegant	
post (n)(v)	mail	
post box (n)	mailbox (corner)	"You send your mail in a *post box;* you receive your mail in a letter box."
postie (n)	postman	
pot (beer) (n)	half pint glass of beer (Queensland, Victoria)	
pot plants (n)	potted plants (not marijuana)	
power point (n)	plug outlet	usually individually switched at outlet, 240 volt
pozzy, possie (adj)	position	"What's your *pozzy* on that issue?"
P-parking	on a sign indicating a paid parking zone	The maximum time allowed follows the "P." A ticket can be purchased at a nearby *kerb*-side vending machine.
PPS (n)	Prescribed Payments System	Tax collection system for business with a high cash income.
pracs, practicals (n)	science experiment	
prairie dog (n)	gay man	
pram (n)	stroller, baby buggy	
prang (n) (v)	car accident	

prawn (n)	shrimp	"It's 'put another *prawn* on the barbie,' ya ignorant seppo."
preggers (adj)	pregnant	
Premier (n)	elected head of an Australian state	equivalent to U.S. state governor
premiership (n)	championship	"The Eagles won the footy *premiership* in 2006."
pre-primary (n)	Equivalent to U.S. kindergarten	Kindergarten, or *kindy,* is preschool.
preselect (v)	nominations in the Australian political process	Done by a closed party committee, not by popular vote.
presenter (n)	announcer, DJ **(radio, TV)**	
prezzy (n)	gift, present	
primary school (n)	elementary school	
prime mover (n)	tractor-truck that pulls a semi-trailer	
prolly (adv)	probably	
pub-crawl (n) (v)	drinking tour of the local taverns	
puffed (adj)	tired	"I was *puffed* after work."
puffer (n)	inhaler (pharmaceutical)	
pull your head in (v)	get real,	
pull your socks up	get it together, improve	
puncy (adj)	effeminate, weak	
punnet (n) (adj)	basket of berries, about 250 grams	"I bought a *punnet* of strawberries."
punt (v)	to gamble	In Australian Rules Football, a *punt* is a kick at the goal.
punter (n)	paying customer, tourist, also a gambler	"The *punters* rode the coach to the museum."
purler (adj)	something great	
purple patch (adj)	things are going well, in a good place	"I'm in a *purple patch.*"

push bike, pushie (n)	bicycle	"I'll ride my *pushie* to school."
push chair (n)	wheelchair	
pusher (n)	child's stroller	
put on the wobbly boot (v)	to get drunk	
put the wind up (v)	to urge someone on	"I *put the wind up* him."
put some ginger into it	try harder	
p/w	per week, referring to rentals	Apartments, furniture and appliances are rented by the week.
Qantas (n)	Australian airline	"Queensland and Northern Territories Aerial Service"
Qnsld. (n)	abbreviation for Queensland	
quango (n)	Quasi Autonomous Non-Governmental Organization	A semi-official regulatory board with actual power.
quaver (n)	eighth note (music)	
Queens Council, Q.C. (n)	senior barrister (courtroom lawyer)	
Question Time (n)	public session in Parliament where members question each other	This is where it all comes out in government: the good, the bad, and the ugly.
queue (n) (v)	the line to enter something, to line up	"We got in the *queue* for the movie."
quid (n)	slang for a pound (Aussie currency up to the 1960s)	"I made a good *quid* off that game."
quids	something you feel strongly about	"I wouldn't move for *quids*!"
quokka (n)	small marsupial the size of a soccer ball, indigenous to an island off Perth	
rack off (v)	go away, get lost	

radiogram (n)	older multi-band radio set	
Rafferty's Rules (adj)	no rules	
rage (n) (v)	a party, to party	
raisins (n)	large dried grapes, larger than American raisins	American-type raisins are called *sultanas*.
ranga (n) (adj)	red-haired person (derogatory)	From "orangutan" (an ape with reddish hair).
rapt (adj)	overjoyed	"I'm *rapt* about it."
ratbag (adj)	mild insult, untrustworthy person	"You old *ratbag!*"
ratepayer (n)	taxpayer, landowner	
rates (n)	property taxes	
rationalisation (v)	To eliminate equipment or staff to make a business more efficient.	
rattle your dags (v)	to ride your bike	
raw prawn (v)	To bullshit someone, to be disagreeable, to act ignorant	"Don't come the *raw prawn* with me!"
ready as a drover's dog (adj)	horny	
reception (n)	registration desk in a hotel, front counter in a restaurant	"I'll pay the bill at *reception*."
red ned (adj)	cheap red wine	
redundant (v) (adj)	laid off from work	"I was made *redundant*."
reffo (n)	refugee	
registrar (n)	doctor who is a specialist	
rego (n)	car registration	
relief teacher (n)	substitute teacher	
rellie, rellies, relo (n)	relative(s)	
removals, removalists (n)	movers, moving company	"When they shifted to Cairns, they called the *removalists*."

rendered (adj)	plastered, as in house wall finishes	
renos (v)	renovations	
repayments (v)	mortgage payments	
ressies (n)	reservations, a booking	
results (adj)	final outcome	
resume (v)	how the government takes back land for public use	"The state *resumed* our paddock to build the highway."
reticulation (n)	sprinklers, irrigation	
retrospective (adj)	retroactive	"The law takes effect *retrospectively*."
return (adj)	round trip	"The flight is $750 *return*."
rev up (v)	to get mad	
Rice Bubbles (n)	Rice Krispies	
Richard Cranium (adj)	dickhead	
ridgy-didge (adj)	something that's true, genuine	
ring (n)	asshole	
ring (v)	to call on a telephone	"I'll *ring* you later."
ripper (adj)	something outstanding	
road train (n)	truck pulling two or three trailers	
Rock Eisteddfod (n)	dance competition between schools	
rock melon (n)	cantaloupe	
rocket (n)	arugula lettuce	
rock-up (v)	to arrive	
roll (n)	type of sandwich served on a roll, also a sausage wrapped in dough	
rollback (v)	backwash	"You can have a sip of my Coke, but don't *rollback*."
rollie (n)	a "roll your own" cigarette	
roo (n)	kangaroo	

roo bar (n)	Brush bar on the front of a vehicle for protection when colliding with a kangaroo.	Also good for protecting your paint from shopping trolleys at the mall.
roofie (n)	roofer	
root (n) (v)	crude slang for having sex	
root rat (adj)	one who only thinks about sex	
rooted (adj)	exhausted, ruined	"I'm *rooted*."
rooting around (adj)	screwing around	
ropable (adj)	very angry	
rort (v)	to steal, illegally taking advantage of the system (an Aussie tradition)	"The *pollies* travelling first class on the *ratepayers* is a *rort*."
rotten (adj)	drunk	
rough as guts (adj)	bad, poorly made	"That truck rides *rough as guts*."
rounds of the kitchen (v)	to tell someone off	
Rovers (n)	designation for older Boy Scouts	
RSL (n)	Returned Service League	Australia's primary veteran's association
rubber (n)	eraser	
rubbery (adj)	unprovable, non-rigorous	
rubbish, to (v)	to criticise	
rug up (v)	to cover up for the cold	
Rugby League (n)	Gentlemen's game played by thugs.	
Rugby Union (n)	Thug's game played by gentlemen.	
running around like a blue ass fly (adj)	running around like a chicken without a head	
SA (n)	abbreviation for South Australia	

sack, to (v)	to fire someone	"The boss *sacked* him for taking too many *sickies*."
salad (n)	sandwich topping: lettuce, tomato, shredded carrot, etc.	
saltie (n)	saltwater crocodile	
Salvos, Sally Ann (n)	Salvation Army	
sandgroper (n)	Western Australian	
Sandman (n)	Holden panel van, a favorite car of surfers in the 1980s	
sandwich (n)	small finger sandwiches, big ones are called *rolls*	
sanga, sanger, sarnie, sammos (n)	sandwich	
sarvo (n)	this afternoon	contraction of *this arvo*
sausage sizzle (n)	weenie roast, cooking hot dogs on a BBQ	
scab duty (n)	picking up rubbish at school for punishment	
scheme (n)	plan (no negative connotation)	"We're on *scheme* water."
schmick (adj)	something that's real good	"That's *schmick!*"
schnitzel (n)	breaded fried meat	
school leaver (n)	high school graduate	
schoolie (n)	high school student in final month of final year	
schoolies week (n)	spring break for *school leavers*	
schooner (n)	pint of beer (Queensland, Victoria), half-pint (South Australia)	
scoob (n)	marijuana cigarette	
scorching (adj)	fast	

Scotty (adj)	's got no friends and never will	
Scouts (n)	co-ed scouting in Australia, no Boy Scouts or Girl Scouts	
scratchies (n)	instant lottery ticket	
screamer (n)	party lover, easy drunk	
sealed road (adj)	paved road	
SEATS (n)	Stock Exchange Automated Trading System	replaced the "cry-out" trading on the *share* (stock) exchange floor.
see your last gum tree (v)	to die	
semibrieve (n)	whole note (music)	
semiquaver (n)	sixteenth note (music)	
seppo (n)	an American (rhyming slang)	*Yank* rhymes with septic tank, *seppo* is short for septic, hence *seppo*.
series (n)	Used to describe each season of a TV show.	"The second *series* of "Friends" start tonight."
serve (adj)	a serving	"I'd like a *serve* of rice."
serve (v)	to tell one off	"I *served* them up."
serviette (n)	napkin	
servo (n)	service station	
set down (v)	to seat	"The jury was *set down* last week."
settlement (n)	escrow (real estate)	"The property is in *settlement*."
sex-worker (n)	prostitute	
shadow government (n)	the minority party *shadow ministers* in Parliament	a *shadow minister* is appointed for every actual minister
shag (v)	to have sex	
shaggin' wagon (adj)	panel van	
shaping up a beaut (adj)	turning out nicely	

shares (n)	stocks (stock market)	also known as: *share market*
shark biscuit (n)	novice surfer	
sheety (n)	sheet metal worker	
sheila (n)	young woman	From Gaelic *shaler.*
she'll be right (adj)	it'll be OK	
shickered (adj)	drunk	From Yiddish.
shift (v)	to move something, also to move house	"They *shifted* from Perth to Sydney."
shifter (n)	wrench (tool)	
shiraz (n) pronounced: *sheer-ahz*	sirah (wine)	
shirt lifter (n)	gay man	
shirty (v)	to get upset	"Don't get *shirty*."
shit house (n) (adj)	poor quality, toilet	
shocker (adj)	a surprise	"His appearance was a bit of a *shocker*."
shockies (n)	shock absorbers	
shonky (adj)	dodgy, cheap, not right, unreliable	
shot though (v)	to leave quickly	"He was late for the plane, so he *shot through* the meeting."
shopping centre (n)	equivalent of an American mall	In Australia, a mall is a shopping street, closed to car traffic.
shopping town (n)	shopping center	
shops (n)	stores	"I'm going to the *shops*."
shorie (adj)	shore or beach dive (Scuba diving)	
short and curlies (adj)	pubic hairs	"She got him by the *short and curlies*."
short listed (adj)	finalist	"She was *short listed* for the Booker Prize."
short of numbers in the Upper House (adj)	stupid, low I.Q.	
short soup (n)	wonton soup (Chinese restaurant)	

shout (v)	to buy a round of drinks, to pick up the tab	"It's my *shout*."
show pony (n)	show-off	"He's a *show pony*."
sick (adj)	good	"Hey, mate, that's *sick*!"
sickie (n)	sick day	"He's taking a *sickie* to go surfing."
side (n)	team (sport)	"The Australian *side* won the game."
Silk (n)	court lawyer, Queens Council or Q.C. (from the silk robes worn in court)	"He and his fellow *Silks* attended court"
silly season (adj)	The time from just before Christmas through Australia Day (Jan. 26), when everyone is on holiday and little gets done business-wise.	
silverside (n)	corned beef	"We're having *silverside* for tea."
sin bin (n)	penalty box in Rugby League	
singlet (n)	tank top (clothing)	"He wore a *singlet* to the beach."
sink a few (v)	to drink a few beers	
sister (n)	nurse (not necessarily of a religious order)	
sit (v)	to take an exam	"I'm to *sit* the exam."
sixty-sixes and ninety-nines (n)	quotation marks	also called *inverted commas*
skim the discs (v)	to turn the brake rotors (automotive)	
skint (adj)	broke, out of money	
skite (v)	to brag	
skittled (v)	physically knocked over	"He got *skittled* by the car."
skiver (n)	person who dodges work	

skivvy (n)	long sleeve crew neck shirt	
skull (v) (pronounced *skol*)	to chug a beer	
sky show (n)	fireworks show	
slab (n)	case of beer	also *carton, box*
slabbed (v)	Being penalized for a mistake by having to buy beer for everyone (a *slab* is a case of beer).	"The director *slabbed* the cameraman when his mobile rang in the middle of a take."
slash (v)	to urinate	"Hold my beer while I take a *slash*."
slate (v)	to criticize	"She *slated* me for being late."
slater (n)	sow bug, wood lice	
sledge (v)	to make a derogatory remark, often amongst sports competitors, heckling	
sleep out (n)	sleeping porch	
slip, slap, slop	*slip* on a shirt, *slap* on some sunscreen, *slop* on a hat.	Slogan from advertising campaign to counter the intense effects of the Southern Hemisphere sun. Australia is the skin cancer capital of the world.
sloppy joe (n)	sweatshirt	
SLSC (n)	Surf Life Saving Club	local volunteer beach lifesaving service
smack (v)	to spank someone	
smash (n)	car accident	
smash repairs (n)	auto body repair shop	also *panel beaters*
smoko (n)	a work-break: cigarette, coffee, tea, etc.	"I'm going for a *smoko*."
snag, snagga (n)	sausage	The Aussie hot dog: grilled, not boiled.
snog (v)	to kiss	
soapies (n)	soap operas on TV	

Socceroos (n)	Australia's national soccer team.	
soft-roader (n) (adj)	light duty 4WD	"The RAV4 is comfy, but it's really just a *soft-roader*."
soft toy (n)	stuffed toy	
solicitor (n)	a lower-level lawyer who specializes in contract law and may appear in lower courts	gives legal advice and draws up legal papers, appoints a barrister for court cases
sook (n)	wimp	
sorted (v)	to arrange, fix, or solve something	"Did you get your taxes *sorted*?"
spaghetti bolognaise, spag bol (n)	spaghetti in meat sauce	
spanner (n)	wrench (tool)	
spares (n)	parts (machinery)	
sparky (n)	electrician	
spat it (v)	was very surprised	From *spat the dummy*. A *dummy* is a baby pacifier.
speckie, speccy (n)	spectacular	"The sky show was *speckie*!"
speech marks (n)	quotation marks, also *inverted commas*	
spew (v)	to throw up	
spewing (adj)	very angry	
spider (n)	soda with ice cream on top, like a float	originally brandy and lemonade
spinner (n)	the pitcher in the game of cricket	
S-pipe (n)	elbow pipe (plumbing)	
spirit of salts (n)	hydrochloric acid	
spit the dummy	to get upset	A *dummy* is a baby pacifier.
spivs (adj)	assholes	
splash the boots (v)	urinate	
splashed out on (adj)	overspent	"I really *splashed out* on her present."
spoof (adj)	semen stains	

sport	sports	no "s," one of those Aussie plural things
spotties (n)	driving lights, spotlights	
spotto (adj)	spotless	"I want the house *spotto* by the time I get back."
spread (n)	plasterer	
spring onion (n)	scallion, green onion	
springy (n)	short wetsuit (shortie)	
spruik, spruiker (n)	to promote; a huckster, pitchman, super salesman	
sprung (v)	caught doing something wrong	
squatter (adj)	large landowner from early times	government tenant
squiz (v)	to look	"Take a *squizz* at that *hoon*."
stall (n)	row of seats in a theater	
standover man (n)	thug, strong-arm man, enforcer	
stands out like a shag on a rock (adj)	it's obvious	
stands out like dogs' balls (adj)	it's obvious	
starkers (adj)	naked	
station (n)	large grazing property	Bigger than a ranch; we're talking tens of thousands of acres.
steady on	get real	
Steak and Kidney (n)	Sydney (rhyming slang)	
steamer (n)	full-length one-piece wetsuit	"The water is cold; I'm going to wear my *steamer*."
stickybeak (n) (v)	nosey person, busy body, looky-loo	"He's a *stickybeak*." "I'll have a *stickybeak* at that display home."

stock take (n) (v)	inventory	"Myer are having a huge end of year *stock take* sale."
stockman (adj)	station hand, cattle herder	
Stolen Generation (n)	Referring to the generation of Aboriginal children of mixed-blood who were forcibly taken from their families and raised as domestic servants.	Most never saw their families again. This is blamed for the breakdown of the Aboriginal family. It is considered by most Australians as a national tragedy and disgrace.
"Stone the crows!"	"I'll be darned!" "Wow!"	
stonkered (adj)	drunk	"I'm *stonkered*."
stood down (v)	laid off, forced to resign	"They were *stood down* without pay."
stores (n)	supplies	"The *stores* were delivered to the clinic."
stoush (n)	a fight	
strap on the nosebag (v)	to eat (a nosebag is used to feed a horse when it's hooked to a wagon)	"The executives had a long meeting, then proceeded to *strap on the nosebag*."
strata, strata-titled (n)	condominium style ownership	"He sold his *strata* home at the beach development."
stretcher (n)	cot	"The toddler slept well on the *stretcher*."
"Strewth!"	it's the truth, from "God's truth!"	"*Strewth*, I'm dry!"
strides (n)	trousers	
strife (adj)	trouble	"That old car gave him *strife*."
"Strike a light!"	expression of amazement	

Strine (n)	The word *Australian*, spoken with a thick accent.	"That bloke speaks fair dinkum *Strine*."
stripey (adj)	striped	"He wore *stripey* trousers."
stroppy (adj)	in a bad mood	
stubby, stubbies (n)	bottle of beer, also short-short pants	
stubby holder (n)	can cooler	
stuffed (adj)	tired, also something that's broken	"I'm *stuffed*." "That car is *stuffed*."
stuffed up, I'll be (adj)	expression of surprise	
stumps (n)	The upright sticks in a cricket wicket, the posts that hold up a building	
suit hire (n)	tuxedo rental	
sultanas (n)	seedless raisins	In Australia, raisins are larger dried grapes with seeds.
summonsed (v)	to receive a legal summons	strange suffix
sunnies (n)	sunglasses	
superannuation, super (n)	retirement fund	
supply bill (adj)	budget or appropriation bill in Parliament	
Supreme Court (n)	state superior court	where serious crimes are tried
surfies (n)	surfers	
surf lifesaver (n)	beach lifeguard (see SLSC)	
surf ski (n)	small, sit-on-top ocean kayak	
surgery (n)	doctor's clinic/office	
suss (v)	suspicious	
suss out (v)	find out information	
swag (adj)	a lot of something, plenty	"The new Ford has a *swag* of extras."

swag (n)	traditional Aussie sleeping roll used in the bush; a Matilda, as in "Waltzing…"	bedding and padding inside a heavy canvas sack
swagman, swaggie (n)	tramp, hobo	
Sweet Fanny Adams	nothing, (actually *f**k all*, *FA*, or *Fanny Adams*)	
sweets (n)	dessert	
swimming costume, swimmers (n)	bathing suit	"She put on her *swimmers*."
swings and roundabouts (adj)	checks and balances	
swish (adj)	good, in fashion (no gay connotation)	"You look *swish*."
switched on (adj)	tuned in	"He was *switched on* about the issues."
ta (interjection)	thank you	imitation of baby talk
TAB (n)	Totalizator Agency Board,	neighborhood legal betting shop
tailor made (adj)	ready made cigarette	not hand-rolled
take away (n) (v)	take-out (food)	
taken the mick out of (v)	to make fun of someone	
taking the piss (out of) (v)	to mock someone, to bring someone back to level	
tall poppies (adj)	successful people	
tall poppy syndrome (n)	Aussie habit of resenting and putting down successful people	
tallie (n)	big bottle of beer	
TAS	abbreviation for Tasmania	
Tassie (n)	Tasmania	
Taswegian (n)	person from Tasmania (derogatory)	
tat (n)	tattoo	
tea (n)	dinner, evening meal	

tea towel (n)	dish towel	
Technicolor yawn (v)	to vomit	
teddy (n)	any stuffed toy	not exclusively a teddy bear
TEE (n)	Tertiary Entrance Exams (Western Australia)	Extensive testing on high school *leavers*. The primary criteria for admittance to university.
tee-up (v)	to set up an appointment	We'll *tee-up* a meeting
telly (n)	television	
Telstra (n)	the partly-government owned phone monopoly	It was once wholly government-owned and is currently being privatized.
ten-pin bowling (n)	American style bowling, as opposed to lawn bowling.	
test (n)	a cricket game	
texta (n)	felt-tip marking pen	Texta is a brand, but is used generically for any felt-tip colored pen.
TFN (n)	Tax File Number	equivalent to Social Security Number
"Thank your mother for the lunch money."	"You've been taken advantage of."	
the lot (n)	everything	"In the divorce, she took *the lot*."
the lot (n) (as on a hamburger)	everything on it	Usually lettuce, tomato, shredded carrots, a slice of beet, a slab of bacon, and a fried egg; for some reason, cheese isn't included.
the order of the boot (adj)	to get fired	

the whole box of dice (adj)	everything	
thingo, thingy (n)	a thing, gizmo, watchamacallit	
thisiv (n)	this afternoon	For those too lazy to say *sarvo*.
tight arse (adj)	stingy person	
throw a tanty (v)	throw a tantrum	
throw a wobbly (v)	throw a tantrum	
throw-down (n)	small bottle of beer	
tickets (v)	bragging	"You've got *tickets* on yourself."
tickety-boo (adj)	good, OK	
timber (n)	wood for construction	"The house was built of *timber* and iron."
timber getter (n)	logger	
tin-arsed (adj) (pronounced *assed*)	lucky	
tinkle (v)	to call someone on the telephone	"Give me a *tinkle* tomorrow."
tinny (adj)	lucky	"You *tinny* bastard!"
tinny (n)	aluminum can of beer; small aluminum skiff	
tip (n)	garbage dump	"I took that load of rubbish to the *tip*."
tip truck (n)	garbage truck	
tipping (v)	sports betting, predicting the winner of a game or series	Tipping competitions are common and legal.
tired and emotional (adj)	drunk	
toast soldier (n)	strip of toast dipped in egg yolk	
toey (adj)	edgy, horny, nervous	
toff (n)	upper class or richly-dressed person	British slang
togs (n)	sports clothes, swim suit	
toilet (n)	restroom, bathroom	
tomato sauce (n)	ketchup	
tonne (adj)	metric ton, 1,000 kilos, 2,200 lbs.	

toolies (n)	older male sexual predator	
Top End (n)	far north of Australia	
top-dress (n) (v)	to surface a playing field	
torch (n)	flashlight	
towing A-frame (n)	tow bar for pulling one car with another	
town bike (adj)	slut	
track (n)	trail	"They hiked along the *track*."
trackies, tracky-dacks (n)	track suit, sweatpants	
tracking vehicle (n)	insert car (movie production)	
tradie (n)	tradesman (carpenter, bricklayer, etc.)	
trannie (n)	transistor radio	
trapezium (n)	trapezoid (geometric shape)	
trolley (n)	shopping cart, hand truck	
trouble and strife (n)	wife	rhyming slang
truckie (n)	truck driver	
true blue (adj)	patriotic Aussie	
tuck shop (n)	school cafeteria	
tucker (n)	food	
turfed (v)	thrown out	"He got *turfed* out of the pub."
turnover (v)	Order used instead of "roll camera" on an Aussie movie set.	
turps (n)	turpentine, also any hard liquor	"He's on the *turps*."
twenty-eight bird (n)	Australian ringneck parrot	Their cry sounds like, "Twenty-eight!"
twenty to the dozen (adj)	to do something very fast	

Two Up (n)	gambling game, tossing two coins into the air to see how they land	Played in the bush and casinos.
two-pot screamer (adj)	one who gets drunk easily, often sloppily	
typhoon (n)	Southern Hemisphere hurricane	
tyre (n)	tire	
Ugg boots (n) (also spelled *Ugh*)	slip-on casual boot made of fleecy sheepskin	
Uluru (n)	Ayers Rock	Aboriginal name for the huge red rock in the center of the country.
Uncle Chester (adj)	child molester	
unco (adj)	uncoordinated	
undercroft (n) (adj)	split-level home: garage below, living areas above	area under main floor of a building, with it's own entrance
undercroft parking (adj)	parking on ground level with living, working areas above	
underdaks (n)	underwear	
uni (n)	university	
up himself (adj)	inflated ego, also "head up his ass"	"He's *up himself*."
up the duff (adj)	pregnant	
ute (n)	flatbed pickup truck	Short for *utility*.
vague out (v)	not paying attention	
van (n)	enclosed truck, ute, also short for *caravan* (travel trailer)	
VB (n)	Victoria Bitter beer	
veg, veggies (n)	vegetables	"I bought fruit and *veg* today."
Vegemite (n)	a salty black yeast spread eaten on toast	
veggo, vejjo (n)	vegetarian	
verandah (n)	balcony, patio, etc.	

verge (n)	roadside parkway between sidewalk and street	"He parked on the *verge*."
VET (n)	Vocation Education Training	
VIC (n)	abbreviation for the state of Victoria	
video library (n)	video rental store	
vigneron (n)	winemaker	From the French.
village bike (adj)	promiscuous woman	
Vinnie's (n)	St. Vincent De Paul's charity	
voucher (n)	coupon, certificate, receipt	
WA (n)	Western Australia	
WACA (n) (pronounced *wack-a*)	West Australian Cricket Association, the Perth Cricket Oval	
wack (v)	a try at something	"I'll take a *wack* at it."
WAFL (n) (pronounced *waffle*)	West Australian Football League	
wag (adj)	amusing person	
wag, wagging school (v)	playing hooky, ditching school	
waist pack (n)	fanny pack ("fanny" in Australia means female genitalia, so it isn't normally used)	also *bum bag*
walkabout (n)	Aboriginal walk in the Outback, of indeterminate length, a rite of passage. Can refer to anybody who's left unexpectedly.	"He's gone *walkabout*."
Wallabies (n)	name of Australia's National Rugby team	
wallaby (n)	small kangaroo-type marsupial	

wanker (adj)	common usage: arrogant, stupid person who thinks he's great	actual meaning: one who masturbates
war paint (n)	woman's makeup	
warrigal (n)	dingo (wild dog)	
watch house (n)	police station	
way gone (adj)	very drunk	
weatherboard (n)	a sheet or board made of fiber and cement or wood, used in home construction	
weepie (n) (adj)	sad story, movie, or TV show	
weir (n)	dam	"The Mundaring *Weir* created the C.Y. O'Connor Reservoir."
weiro (n)	cockatiel	a small parrot
well turned out (adj)	well dressed	
we're laughing (adj)	something that turns out well	"Fix this car and *we're laughing*."
wet (adj)	the rainy season in the tropics	
wettie (n)	wetsuit	
whacker (n)	an idiot you have no patience for	
wharfie (n)	dock worker	
What's the John Dory?	What's the story?	rhyming slang
wheelie bin (n)	the main trash can for the house, with wheels on the bottom.	"Take the *wheelie bin* out to the street so the garbos can empty it."
whilst (adj)	while	
winding up (v)	to pull someone's leg	"You're *winding* me *up*."
whinge (v)	to complain	
whip hand (adj)	top position, really good at something	"He's the *whip hand* on the farm."
whipper-snipper (n)	motor-powered weed-wacker or brush cutter	
white ant (v)	to undermine, sabotage	

white ants (n)	termites	
white pointers (n)	great white sharks; topless sunbathers	
"Who opened their lunch?" (v)	"Who farted?"	
"Who's your daddy?"	an insult	
whole meal (adj)	whole wheat bread	
woof pigeon (adj)	kookaburra	
whoop-whoop (n)	the boondocks, someplace far away, a small unimportant town	"He lives way out *whoop-whoop*."
whopped (v)	to play hooky from school	
wicket (n)	The three posts and top piece (bale) in the game of cricket.	
willy willy (n)	mini-tornado, dust devil	
willy woofter (adj) (pronounced *woof-tah*)	gay man	
wind cheater (n)	windbreaker, light jacket	
windy (v)	to fart	
witch's hat (n)	orange plastic safety cone used on roadways	
witchetty grub (n)	a large insect larvae eaten as bush tucker; it's tasty (?)	
wobbly (n) (v)	to lose one's temper	"He threw a *wobbly*."
wog (n)	immigrants from Southern Europe; flu or cold; insects.	not considered a racist term as in the UK
wombat (adj)	Play on words: describing one who eats, roots (has sex), and leaves.	Wombats are animals that eat vegetative material such as roots and leaves.
won't be a minute	please wait	
won't be a moment	please wait	
won't be a sec	please wait	

won't be a tick	please wait	
woofy (adj)	something that isn't good	
Woolie's (n)	short for Woolworth's, half the Aussie grocery store duopoly, Coles being the other half.	
working bee (adj)	volunteer work party	
wring its neck (adj)	to drive a vehicle hard	
wurst (n)	baloney or bologna, regional term used in South Australia	
wuss (adj)	coward	
yabber (adj)	lots of talk	
yabby (n)	freshwater crawdad	
yakka (adj)	work	"It's hard *yakka*."
Yank (n)	An American from anywhere in the U.S.	
yankee shout (adj)	round of drinks where everyone pays for themselves	
yardie (n)	A yard-long glass for drinking beer, holds almost a half gallon.	Former Prime Minister Bob Hawke once held the world speed record for drinking one.
yobbo, yob (n)	uncouth male	
yodel (v)	vomit	
yonnie (n)	stone of useable size for building	
yonks (adj)	a long time	"It's been *yonks* since I've seen you."
"You der!"	"You idiot!"	
you got told (v)	you got in trouble	school kid talk
"You little ripper!"	exclamation upon hearing good news	
youse	plural of "you"	
Yowie (n)	mythical Australian monster, like Bigfoot	
zack (n)	sixpence (five cents)	"He isn't worth a *zack*."

zed (n)	pronunciation of the letter "z"	
Zimmer frame (n)	walker (medical equipment)	device used by people for whom a cane isn't enough
zine (n)	small magazine	

INDEX

About the Author

Rusty Geller was born and raised in suburban Los Angeles. After graduating from the University of Southern California, he spent several years travelling around Europe and North America. Looking for something interesting to do, he went to film school and embarked on a twenty-five-year career as a cameraman in the motion picture industry, specializing in Steadicam. His movie credits are at **www.rustygeller.com.**

In his spare time, he writes and photographs travel-adventure stories, which have appeared in magazines like *Skin Diver, Aloha, Treasure Diver, Mountain Biking*, and *American Cinematographer.*

In 2003—in what would either be the smartest or dumbest move in his life—he stepped out of the rat race and migrated with his family to Western Australia, hoping to find something that was no longer available in Southern California: a wide-open, uncrowded land with a slower-paced lifestyle. He now lives with his wife and two daughters in the hills above Perth, amongst kangaroos and kookaburras in a big stone house in a eucalyptus forest under a brilliant blue sky. It could be worse.

9 781602 640740